Born in Cork in 1927, Patrick Galvin is the author of seven collections of poetry, including *Folk Tales for the General* (Raven Arts, 1989), which was a Poetry Ireland Choice. His plays, including *The Last Burning*, have been regularly staged in Ireland and abroad, and he is a frequent broadcaster of his own work on RTÉ and BBC. A member of Aosdána, awards received for his work include the Irish–American Cultural Institute Award for Poetry. *Song for a Raggy Boy* has been made into a major motion picture, starring Aidan Quinn, and is due for release in 2003.

Other publications by Patrick Galvin
Heart of Grace
Christ in London
Man on the Porch: Selected Poems
The Woodburners
Folk Tales for the General
Death of Art O'Leary
New and Selected Poems

THE
RAGGY BOY
TRILOGY

Song for a Poor Boy
Song for a Raggy Boy
Song for a Fly Boy

Patrick Galvin

**NEW
ISLAND**

THE RAGGY BOY TRILOGY
First published November 2002
by New Island Books
2 Brookside
Dundrum Road
Dublin 14

Song for a Poor Boy, first published 1990 by Raven Arts Press,
copyright © 1990, 2002 Patrick Galvin
Song for a Raggy Boy, first published 1990 by Raven Arts Press,
copyright © 1991, 2002 Patrick Galvin
Song for a Fly Boy, first published 2002 by New Island,
copyright © 2002 Patrick Galvin

The moral rights of the author have been asserted.

ISBN 1 904301 08 8

British Library Cataloguing in Publication Data.
A CIP catalogue record for this book is available
from the British Library.

Cover design and typesetting by New Island
Printed in the UK by Cox & Wyman, Reading, Berks.

New Island receives financial assistance from The Arts Council,
(An Chomhairle Ealaíon), Dublin, Ireland.

5 4 3

CONTENTS

To María

SONG FOR A POOR BOY
A Cork Childhood

To my parents

Song For A Poor Boy

When he was young he had no sense
And souls were sold for eighteen pence
While he ran mad in streets of gold
And people said he must be old
And hard as nails.

When hunger tore the windows out
And all the rooms were steeped in sin
He prayed to witches in his bed
And painted all the doorknobs red
And danced and sang.

But sticks and stones came tumbling down
When he put on his royal gown
And overright the convent wall
We dressed him in his mother's shawl
And broke his back.

And strong men went to take his soul
When he refused his begging bowl
But he was made to stretch his wings
And lead a company of kings
And touch the stars.

And silver ghosts leapt from his hand
When famine raged across the land
We locked him in a padded cell
And said he'd surely go to hell
And twist and burn.

But in the dark he learned to creep
When all the guards were fast asleep
And in his house of spinning pearls
He hopped about in loops and whirls
And rang the bell.

We chained him to the madhouse floor
And heard his long night-goblin's roar
He split the chain and smashed the lock
And stopped the white wall-ticking clock
And climbed the stair.

We held him down inside his tomb
We robbed his heart and fired his room
He watched us from his bony place
And all the seas ran down his face
And drained the world.

But when the lamps were going down
He made himself a one-eyed clown
He saw the sun fall through the skies
And knew that all we knew was lies —
And grinned and grinned.

One

The house we lived in had a grey-brick face. A large tenement close to the Lee. Come spring tides, the river overflowed its banks, water rose in the streets and in our bare feet we paddled out our lives. Good lives. Spring-awakening lives – splashing wildly through cobbled streets and saving pennies for Bull's Eyes, Frog's Eyes and Annie's Gudge – a pudding-like cake sold by the slab and guaranteed to contain only the finest ingredients grown specially in foreign climes.

My friend Connors hated Gudge. He said it had been trampled on by natives. But he shared mine and when we'd finished eating we sat down and listened to the wireless.

For, sure enough, we had a wireless. A crystal-set with cat's whiskers. And if you listened carefully through both earphones you could hear music and laughter till the battery ran out.

Then you had to charge it. Top it up with burning acid or pure still water – or whatever it was that the man did down in the bicycle shop and charged twopence. He sold bicycles too, but he was known as The Battery Man and you could taste his genius. A man who could bring music out of the air and laughter into the living-room. The music was magic and the laughter was funny – though we seldom managed to see the joke. Maybe it was foreign.

But then, everything was foreign that existed beyond the North Gate Bridge – and we lived on the South Side. The old Cork. The real Cork and none of your blow-ins.

11

My grandparents, on my mother's side, were born there and their grandparents before them. And you could trace them back to when Cork was only a marsh and maybe even before that. My grandmother said so. She lived to be eighty-nine and never once crossed the North Gate Bridge.

"'Tis unknown the kind of people who'd be living over there. Bogmen and Shite-hawks who came in from beyond the lamps years ago with nothing to their feet but cow dung. Keep well away from them."

And so I did. Though my father said that my grandmother had a screw loose and 'twas no wonder her husband ran away from her and ended up dead in America.

My grandfather did end up dead in America, but my grandmother said it couldn't have happened to a better man. My grandmother didn't like men. She said they should be preserved in bottles.

When she was sixteen years of age, my grandmother married Mick O'Leary. He was a fisherman who never fished beyond the limits of Evergreen Street. And when he married my grandmother and was persuaded to move to Barrack Street, he was convinced that he'd settled abroad. He was happy enough, but he would have preferred to remain at home.

I never met Mick O'Leary, but his photograph stood upon the mantelpiece in my grandmother's house in Barrack Street. It was covered in dust, and the eyes peered through a mist and followed you everywhere. On Sundays, when I went to visit my grandmother, I would ask her about Mick, but she was reluctant to talk about him. And when I suggested that it might be a good idea to wipe the dust off the photograph she said, "The dust suits him." The remainder of the house was free of dust. She cleaned it meticulously.

When Mick married my grandmother, he was proud to give her his name. My grandmother told him to keep it.

Moll Delaney was her name and no scrap of paper was going to deprive her of her true identity. Moll was proud of her identity, proud of herself, and had little respect for marriage. Why she married Mick O'Leary is unknown, and when I was once bold enough to ask her, she said I was "astray in the head". I could never imagine my grandmother being astray in the head. She knew what she was doing and her mind was as sharp as a butcher's blade.

Two years after their marriage, my grandmother gave birth to my mother. She was their only child and my grandmother insisted that she be baptised in both their names. My mother was in no position to argue the matter at the time, but when it came to her turn to marry my father, she called herself Bridget O'Brien – which confused everybody, including herself.

My grandmother smiled. She never liked the Galvins anyway, and when I went to visit her for the first time in my youth she said that I wasn't a Galvin at all and that my proper name was Sweeney. I called myself Sweeney for a time, but gave it up when I discovered that Sweeney was a mad poet who lived in a tree and had nothing to eat for breakfast but pine nuts and tree bark.

Sometimes, my grandmother could be less confusing. One day, she looked at me and said "Chicago". I had never heard of Chicago. "It's in America," she said. And I waited.

"That's where he went. Mick. Went raving mad one day in the middle of Barrack Street and said he was going to Chicago. 'Go to hell,' I said. And off he went."

"I thought you said that he never ventured beyond the bottom of Barrack Street?"

"He didn't. I told you. He went mad suddenly. Left me and your mother and jumped on to the boat. Give him his due, he did ask me to go with him, but I wouldn't leave Cork."

"Why not, Grandma?"

"Don't ask stupid questions, Child. And don't call me Grandma. People who call me Grandma end up in a madhouse where they get tortured by Sister Mary. You know Sister Mary, don't you?"

"No."

"Well, you soon will do if you don't watch yourself. I used to tell Mick to watch himself. But he took no notice – and look what happened to him. Shot dead in Chicago. Bootlegging."

"What's bootlegging?"

"Ask that thing you call your father. He's probably an expert. Mick was just wanting. They sent me a telegram when he died, but I threw it on the fire."

The eyes peered from the photograph on the mantelpiece and my grandmother lapsed into silence. I wondered why Mick had gone mad suddenly and run off to Chicago. She refused to explain. She was like that. Nothing to explain. Her life was her own. She worked hard and gave thanks to no one.

"I took in washing. I plucked chickens. I had a black shawl and the feathers covered it."

I remembered the black shawl and I remembered the feathers. They clung to the soft black wool like snowflakes that would never melt. She tried to wash the shawl. She spent hours picking off the feathers with her fingers and her teeth, but they held fast – a constant reminder of hard work and eternal fortitude.

She was eighty-nine when she died. The room tidied. Everything in its place. The fire set in the grate. Only the photograph on the mantelpiece remained covered with dust. And Mick O'Leary's eyes followed her into death.

Two

When I was seven years of age my mother held my hand and walked me to school for the first time.

"I want you to be educated," she said.

I had no intention of being educated. The schoolroom stifled me. The educating air was filled with chalk and the heavy slate blackboard screeched whenever Brother Reynolds wrote on it.

Brother Reynolds was a big man – light on his feet and, sometimes, light in the head. He taught English to Irishmen. And every day he would read aloud from *The Ballad of Reading Gaol*. He never mentioned the author.

I remember the line: "For each man kills the thing he loves." Brother Reynolds must have loved me to distraction. He kept hitting me over the head with a ruler. He was dying to educate me and said it would be a miracle if he succeeded.

I was a great believer in miracles, but I did not believe they could be found in a classroom. And Brother Reynolds was not like my father or my mother – or my grandmother or my mad Aunt Bridget. They were miracles.

When my father was unemployed and my mother scrubbed floors for a living – that was a miracle. Her strength held us. Her gentle hands cradled us in miracles.

When my father played music – that was a miracle. The music flowed from the dream in his head and you could see it dancing on the tips of his fingers as he touched the holes in that shimmering instrument.

We dined on miracles. We found them at home and in

15

the streets and we found them on the east roof of Saint Finbarre's cathedral. A golden angel stood there waiting to proclaim the ending of the world. Cork would be favoured. Seven years before the last trumpet-sound the angel would turn green. We kept our eyes on the angel. And through summer days and summer nights he watched over us.

When autumn came and the leaves fell from the trees along the Mardyke, we sat as lovers in Fitzgerald's Park and kissed and kissed and promised never to tell a single soul or her father would kill her stone dead and bury her in a bottle. On our way home we stared hard at the angel – searching anxiously for signs of green. There were none. Our golden angel still shone and glittered over the city.

You could see its reflection on the waters of the Lee. You could feel its presence in the South Presentation Convent where Brother Reynolds struggled to educate us. And here was the final miracle – we survived his efforts and exploded through the oak doors every afternoon when school was over for another day.

There was freedom in the streets. Freedom to wander through the English and Irish markets where everything was sold – from rare spices to second-hand clothes. You could smell the spices, feel the texture of Chinese silk and dream of ships that sailed the seas in search of treasures for the people of Cork. On stormy nights we knelt at home and prayed hard for poor sailors at sea.

When winter came my father lit the oil lamp, raised the fire in the hearth and took down his tin whistle from its place above the mantelpiece. He played 'The Croppy Boy' and 'Erin's Lovely Lee' and my mother sang 'The Rookery'.

The neighbours came in. They climbed the stairs to our tenement flat and sat on the floor and sang and told stories. Mr Cotter played the flute and Salty Cleary said that at one time Ireland was ruled entirely by women and he could prove it. Didn't his father tell him one time of a woman who was washed up by the sea near Roche's Point and she was fifty feet tall from her shoulders to her feet and her chest was seven feet across and her head was cut off and it was in this way she was cast up by the sea? Oh yes, it was true enough and no one could deny it.

My mother smiled – and even my grandmother smiled. For she believed it and said it was a great pity that things had changed for the worst. My father, as usual, said little. He spoke through his music.

In a corner of the room with a cat named Tone I sat and listened. My father didn't like Tone and sometimes called him Wolfe, but said it was nothing political. He just didn't like cats.

In later years my father became an ardent Free Stater. My mother was a staunch Republican. But that was a long way off and I was young and dreamed of growing up. I didn't know then what growing up was all about. The music filled the memories of my room and I slept innocently.

Three

I remember the beginning. The pink and amber of my mother's womb and then the dark and dying of the light. The room was grey. And my first words, on being evicted into this world were – "I shall return!"

When my father was informed of this rather unexpected outburst from a child still attached to the umbilical cord, he said "That boy will be a poet". What my father did not know was that I already was.

Sitting there in the comfort of my mother's womb, I had already written some of the finest poems in the English language – to say nothing of Greek and the odd spot of Latin. My mother was not aware of all this activity going on inside her. Had she been so, she would not have been in such a hurry to evict me. My mother respected poets. She knew that they required warmth, tenderness and compassion – and she knew that such things would be in short supply in Margaret Street.

I emerged roaring. My mother lay on the double bed and my father stood over her and stared at what she'd brought forth.

"He looks odd," he said.

"What do you mean – odd? He's a poet, isn't he? You said that yourself."

"I did. And may the tongue be struck out of me. The country is full of poets. And here's you adding another one to our woes."

"You'll be proud of him yet," said my mother. But my

father was not convinced. He loved poetry, but he couldn't stand poets.

"I never met one who wasn't a pauper," he said. "A prey to bailiffs, lawyers and priests. Take my advice and send him back."

But my mother never sent anything back. I was her loving child and she held me close to her breast and smiled.

I was happy there. I felt soulful and poetic. I regretted the loss of my mother's womb and of all the poems I had written inside her. But everything happened so quickly that I had no time to collect the manuscripts – and there they remain in three languages, protected with love.

When my grandmother arrived to view the new arrival she said I didn't look like a poet. And when my mother asked her what I did look like, she said she'd prefer not to say. I ignored my grandmother. There was a mad drop in her somewhere and she had no sense of the occasion.

I looked at my father and held fast to my mother. Her breath was warm. Her mouth was gentle – and in spite of my regrets I felt there'd be some compensation. I would be breast-fed for one thing and that could last for years. Poets do well on breast-feeding. Our literature owes much to it.

I moved in closer. I could see myself writing poems about breast-feeding and dedicating them to mothers everywhere. I bit hard and was promptly slapped on the bottom. That slap on the bottom gave me amnesia. I forgot I was a poet and it took me twenty-three years to rediscover my true vocation.

Four

Being normal in some respects, I did have a paternal grandmother. Her name was Lizzie Baron. She was not born in Cork and neither was my grandfather. He was a Kinsale man. But sometime during the latter half of the nineteenth century he decided that he'd had enough of small seaside towns and set off for the Continent in search of a war. What my grandfather knew about the Continent of Europe wouldn't cover the back of a postage stamp, but the little he did know was enough to convince him that there must be a war going on out there somewhere.

Whether he found his war or not is one of the great mysteries of our time, but five years later he returned to Cork bearing what he described as a Greek wife – whom he claimed to have rescued from a band of marauding Turks.

My paternal grandmother – for that's who she turned out to be – didn't look like a Greek, or a Turk for that matter, but my grandfather said she was. And since he stood seven-feet-high in his stocking feet and had a fist on him like a sledgehammer, there seemed little point in arguing the matter. Greek she was – and in due course she managed to produce six children, including my father. She also, incidentally, gave birth to my Aunt Bridget. But Bridget went mad at the age of forty. So no one mentioned her, if they could possibly avoid it.

Lizzie, on the other hand, never went mad. Maybe because she was small and dark and quite unlike my grandfather. Or maybe because her English was bad and sounded like a tin can scraping on a wall. Either way, she remained remarkably sane, sat quietly in a corner, and smiled only when my grandfather smiled.

Sometimes, of course, she moved out of the corner and went shopping in the English market. My grandfather gave her eight shillings a week from his old age pension and when she returned from her shopping she still retained the eight shillings. My grandfather said she was the greatest house-keeper in Ireland and I was duly impressed. But my mother said she hadn't paid for a thing and was known far and wide as the "South Side Bandit".

Be that as it may, my grandfather seemed totally unaware of her reputed exploits and I doubt whether anyone had the courage to tell him. Had they done so he would have anointed them. For he was convinced that my grandmother was a saint and went to his grave offering up novenas for her eventual canonisation. Alas, however, for the vagaries of Rome. For the Pope either forgot to canonise Lizzie or he was bigoted against the Greeks. Either way, we are still waiting.

One morning, Lizzie rose from her bed and made my grandfather his usual breakfast of thick porridge and strong black tea. "It's the way he likes it," she said. "Strong enough to trot a mouse on." Having completed her task, she called to my grandfather, but there was no response.

She approached the bed and stared down at him. My grandfather was dead. He had died in his sleep. And though Lizzie had lain beside him all night, she was unaware of his passing. She touched his face. The body was still warm, but the light had gone out of it.

She moved away and sat close to the fire. She heard the clock ticking on the mantelpiece and the kettle boiling for a second time on the hob. She ignored the sound and sat there for a long time before informing the neighbours.

When the neighbours arrived, the women stripped my grandfather of his nightshirt and cap and then washed his body from head to toe. Mr Cotter shaved him. And when he was cleaned and stretched, the women dressed him again. But this time in a long brown habit that he would wear unto eternity.

Outside the room, my father and I sat on the stairs and my father wept. It was the first time I had seen him cry and he would never cry outwardly again. He would retreat into his music.

But now he bled. His shoulders sagged and his body trembled. He buried his face in the palms of his hands and he became an old man.

I would like to have spoken with my father then. I would like to have asked him to explain my grandfather's death – as he had explained so many other things that had frightened and confused me. But it was not the time and the tears in his eyes told me so.

He had said at one time, when a neighbour died after a long illness, that death was nothing to be afraid of. It was there from the moment of our birth and remained beside us all the days of our lives. It was not dark. It was bright. And when we died we became part of it – a moving into the light. A friendly call from the Creator of all things. But it did not seem like that now and I wondered if he still believed it.

"We should be going in now," he said. "It's time we paid our respects to your grandfather."

We entered the room. The neighbours stood at the foot of the bed and Lizzie sat beside it. She had covered the mattress with a clean white sheet and my grandfather lay stretched upon it with his hands clasped in front of him and the grey Connemara marble rosary beads entwined between his fingers.

My father raised me up.

"Kiss your grandfather goodbye," he said, and lowered me down towards my grandfather's lips. I kissed the corpse. I was eight years old. And I knew that death was not friendly. Nor a moving into the light. It was a freezing of the soul. A nightmare of ice that followed me down the years.

Five

A year after my grandfather's death I met Mannie Goldman. Mannie lived in The Marsh, the poorest part of the city, and earned his living writing letters for people who couldn't write themselves. Halfpenny a page, envelopes free, bring your own stamp. I knocked on Mannie's door.

"Go away!"

I opened the door and fell headlong over a pile of books.

"Stupid Boy! Do you realise what you've done? The entire history of the Roman Empire lies hidden in there."

"I'm sorry, Mr Goldman. But there's no light."

"That's your bad luck. At my age I don't need a light. Sit down."

"Where, Mr Goldman?"

"There! Beside you. Jane Austen. Sit on her."

I sat on Jane Austen. My first contact with creative literature. Mr Goldman lit a candle.

"Can you see now?"

"I think so, Mr Goldman."

Mr Goldman lived in two rooms and they were both filled, from floor to ceiling, with books. They lined the walls, blocked out the windows, covered the floor and lay scattered over the bed. Apart from the bed, the only furniture Mr Goldman possessed was a chair and a table which he never used except to lay books on.

When Mr Goldman wanted to sit, he sat on the *Oxford Dictionary*, all twenty-seven volumes of it, arranged to look like a throne. And when Mr Goldman wanted something to rest his arm on, he chose his *Collected Proust*.

"It's perfectly flat," he said, "one of the best editions available. I strongly recommend it."

Any money that Mr Goldman received from the letter-writing business, he spent on books. And when his cousin in America sent him five pounds every Christmas, he spent that on books. I never saw Mr Goldman eat. He fed on books.

"My wife left me. Do you know that? Couldn't stand the books. That woman was obsessed with furniture. She wanted sideboards in here. Mahogany wardrobes. Chairs, if you don't mind! Do you realise that furniture is a myth? It exists when you're there, but the moment you leave the room the furniture disappears. My wife couldn't understand that. Do you?"

"No, Mr Goldman."

"I'm surrounded by peasants. What do you want?"

"I came to ask you about Nano Nagle, Mr Goldman."

"Nano Nagle? You mean that female who built the South Presentation Convent? What about her? She's dead, isn't she?"

"I know that, Mr Goldman. But last night, I saw her walking up and down Margaret Street. And when I asked my father about that, he said she was in Heaven."

"So?"

"Well, if she's in Heaven – how come she's still walking up and down Margaret Street?"

"Split personality," said Mr Goldman. "Have you read Freud?"

"Was he a Catholic, Mr Goldman?"

Mr Goldman almost had a stroke. "No – he was not a flaming Catholic. But one of these days that Pope of yours is going to canonise him. Ask me why? Go on – ask me why!"

"Why, Mr Goldman?"

"That's a damned good question. I'm glad you asked me. Well, before Freud came along, the Catholic Church was just about getting ready to abandon the concept of Original Sin. Then along comes Freud and hands the whole thing back to them in the form of a guilt complex. Do you understand what I mean?"

I didn't. And Mr Goldman knew that I didn't. He shook his head.

"How old are you?"

"Nine."

"Are you going to school?"

"Yes."

"So much for education. When I was nine I was reading Dostoevsky. When I was ten I was reading Karl Marx. I understood him better then than I do now, but that's progress. Can you read?"

"A bit."

"What does that mean – comics?"

"There's big books in school, Mr Goldman."

"How big? Is there anything in them?"

"I don't know, Mr Goldman."

"Of course you don't. Who sent you to talk to me?"

"My father."

"Oh. I remember him. I wrote a letter for him one time. He was looking for a job. Did he get it?"

"I don't think so, Mr Goldman. He's still on the dole."

Mr Goldman paused. "A pity," he said. "Maybe next time he'll have more luck. You can go now. I've answered your question."

"Split personality."

"That's right. It's quite common among people with religion. Was there something else?"

"No, Mr Goldman."

"Then off you go."

He turned away, picked up a book and began to read. I moved towards the door and turned the handle.

"Just a minute," he said – and lowered the book he was holding. "I don't know why I'm doing this. I hate children. But if you want to borrow any of these books, you're welcome to do so. But ask your father first. I don't want those lunatics from the Purity League howling for my blood."

I had never heard of the Purity League and I would ask my father. For the books fascinated me. And Mr Goldman fascinated me as he sat there on the *Oxford Dictionary*, looking like a garden gnome.

"What's going to happen to all those books when you die, Mr Goldman?"

Mr Goldman laughed. "Die? Don't be ridiculous! But, if you must know – I've willed them all to my wife. And my one regret is that I won't be around to see her face when the delivery man dumps half-a-million books on her doorstep."

He laughed again and I forgot about Nano Nagle and why she was walking up and down Margaret Street when she should have been in Heaven. Maybe she didn't like Heaven, or maybe she did have a split personality as Mr Goldman had said.

I went to visit Mr Goldman every day after school and sometimes at night. He taught me to read and he taught me to write. And during the long winter evenings, when the rain danced upon those invisible windows in Mr Goldman's rooms, I sat at his feet while he read aloud from a myriad of books.

Tolstoy and Dostoevsky, Gorky and Emile Zola, Voltaire and Spinoza, Marlowe and Blake – Berkeley and Berkeley again – and for good measure the ballad history of my native city. He knew it well. His heart made room for it and it would always be there, as he was whenever I needed him.

27

I remember the room. The sound of his voice. The movement of his hands as he turned the pages. He read until he was tired and slept where he sat – perched high on the *Oxford Dictionary*.

Six

When the Spanish Civil War broke out, Mr Goldman stood at the corner of Washington Street and protested against the Fascists. My mother supported him, and in the evenings she painted slogans on our tenement wall, urging the natives of Cork to aid the Republicans and join the International Brigades.

My father thought differently. He said that the Republicans were burning the churches in Spain and he didn't want to see anything like that happening in Cork. But he refused to join the Blueshirts, who were marching through the city wearing holy medals and appealing to the people to join them in their Great Crusade against the Bolsheviks.

At a huge rally in the city, Monsignor Sexton said that twenty-four Sisters of the Poor had been crucified in Barcelona, and when two men asked him for proof, they were thrown into the River Lee and had to be rescued by the Salvation Army.

The Salvation Army said that it was their Christian duty to rescue people from the River Lee and offered to make tea for everybody, if only they'd be sensible and go home. But the crowd didn't go home. They knelt in the streets and prayed for General Franco.

At the corner of Washington Street, Mr Goldman still stood and protested loudly. My mother brought him a bowl of soup from the Penny Dinner house in Hanover Street, but he refused to eat it. He said he was starving for Spain. She offered to mend a hole in his jacket, too – but he said he was quite capable of doing that himself – though he never did.

He looked weary and old, as if he'd seen it all before and there was little he could do now to prevent it happening again. I wondered where he'd grown up and about his family background. He never mentioned it.

In the evenings, I sat at his feet and listened to him read. And during the day I attended school and listened to Brother Reynolds talking about Spain. Brother Reynolds knew everything about Spain. He'd read it in the newspapers. He said that Spain was a Catholic country and the Communists were out to destroy it. He said the Communists were everywhere. But if they were, so was General Franco.

Franco's photograph appeared in every newspaper. His eyes peered at you out of every shop window. And his spirit haunted the classroom where Brother Reynolds was telling us that what was happening in Spain today could be happening in Ireland tomorrow.

Atrocities were being committed out there. Children were being burned alive by the Reds, and their ashes scattered on pig farms in Galicia. Priests were being hanged. Bishops were being shot through the eyes. Nuns were being raped. And when my friend Connors asked him what rape meant, he split him over the head with a metal ruler and told him to wash his mouth out with salt and then drench himself in holy water. He asked us to pray.

We should pray for General Franco. We should pray for the Moors who were fighting now to save Christianity. We should pray for the Blueshirts and join them today and be remembered forever in the Great Book of Names that was now being prepared in Heaven by Blessed Michael and his angels.

My friend Connors threw up – and others joined the

Blueshirts. They danced and they marched and they wore uniforms and looked like Boy Scouts. But when Brother Reynolds saw them, he said they were like little angels who would one day grow up to be big angels and they then could fly off to Spain and help General Franco to kill the Reds.

He appealed for money to buy guns. He placed a collection box at the school gate and said that anyone who failed to contribute would burn in Hell for all Eternity. They would be tortured by demons.

When I told my mother about Brother Reynolds, she said he was a born eegit. But Mr Goldman said he was only one of many. The country was full of them. My father said nothing, but when he saw the collection box at the school gate, on his way to Mass, he kept his hand in his pocket.

One evening as I sat with Mr Goldman, listening to him read, someone threw a brick through the window. The shattered glass cascaded across the room and Mr Goldman flung his coat over my head. We sat in the dark and waited for a second brick. But there was only one – and it was followed by a man's voice shouting, "Dirty Jew. You murdered Christ!"

The following day, Mr Goldman returned to the corner of Washington Street. He continued to protest.

Seven

In our tenement flat in Margaret Street, my father sat at the window and played the tin whistle. There was a knock at the door and my mother went to answer it. The landlady stood there. You could tell it was Monday.

Mrs Denton always called on a Monday. She charged three shillings and sixpence a week for two rooms in the attic, and she took a personal interest in collecting the rent.

She entered the room. She carried a black Gladstone bag. She wore a feather in her hat. She had large white teeth and her mouth was full of them.

When Mrs Denton smiled, you could see the graveyards of Cork. And when she nodded her head, you could hear bells tolling for all those who had died clutching her rent books. She smiled now and demanded an extra sixpence off the arrears. My mother paid her four shillings and Mrs Denton thanked her. She was like that. Always polite when receiving money.

When my father told her that there were rats in the house, Mrs Denton showed her teeth. She said there were no rats in the house. My father said there were and showed her two dead ones he'd managed to trap in a cage.

Mrs Denton shook her head. The rats were foreign. They'd come in off the boats on the quays and she could not be held responsible for that. If the rats had been Irish, that would have been a different matter. But they weren't. They came from Japan or China, or some other outlandish place, and what else could you expect? Personally, she was against the whole business of trading with lesser nations and suggested that my father write to the Department of Foreign Affairs about it. My father said he'd never learned to write and Mrs Denton said it was a pity, but he was probably better off. Education was a curse and did nothing but give illusions of grandeur to the poor. You couldn't win with Mrs Denton.

When she was ill, she said that those who were in arrears with their rent had laid a curse on her. And when she recovered, she said God was on her side and no one could harm her. She said the poor were the salt of the earth – provided they paid their rent and remembered who they were. My mother threw a chair at her – and missed. Mrs Denton smiled and carried her teeth with her as she descended the stairs.

On the floor below lived the Murphy sisters and their brother, Pat. They were never in arrears because Pat was a a member of the Third Order of Saint Frances and believed it was a mortal sin to owe money. He was the only one in the house who didn't owe money and he wore his habit every night to keep the ghosts away.

But the ghosts came anyway. They hovered over his bed, waited for him in dark corners, and leapt at him from behind stone walls when he'd had too much to drink, or too little, or none at all. His two sisters said he was massive – their favourite word – meaning beautiful. When they saw me in my First Communion suit, they said I looked massive. I did. I always look massive when I'm expecting money.

My cousin Martin was always expecting money. He lived on the second floor back and had a notice in his window saying – "Still expecting. What the hell's keeping ye?" He had a pet dog and the dog followed him everywhere. When the expected money failed to arrive, Martin painted the dog green and tried to sell him in the Coal Quay Market.

"Green Dog for Sale. Going Cheap. Just Arrived from Ethiopia." There were no offers. The dog relieved himself on the pavement – and Martin spent a month trying to get the paint off with paraffin oil.

On the second floor front lived the Egan family, all mad from eating porridge. Mr Egan was a docker and an ardent supporter of General Franco. He said my mother was a disgrace and spent most of his time washing off the slogans she'd painted on the wall supporting the Republicans and the International Brigades. My mother replaced the slogans and added "Up Franco – with a bomb!" Mr Egan got confused. He thought my mother was about to change sides. "God moves in mysterious ways," he said. And, for once, my mother was speechless.

When Mr Egan wasn't busy washing slogans off our tenement wall, he was out collecting jam-jars in Galley's Dump. Mr Egan liked jam-jars and hated cups. He refused to let any of his family drink from one of them. He preferred jam-jars. And the entire flat creaked under the weight of them. All bound with steel bands to prevent them from exploding when Mrs Egan poured boiling hot tea into them.

On Sundays, Mr Egan called the family to order. He paraded them up and down Margaret Street and they all sang 'Faith of Our Fathers' in honour of General Franco. Then they marched to Galley's Dump to collect more jam-jars. Mr Egan said they were classic, but Mrs Egan wasn't too sure. She said art and that kind of thing was beyond her.

The ground floor flat was occupied by the Sweeneys – the largest family in the street – nine children and two linnets in cages. The eldest daughter was eleven and the only one of the family who could read. I was feeling wild at the time and fell madly in love with her. She had a bound volume of Grimm's fairy tales and every day we sat on the stairs and read 'The Singing Bone' and 'The Youth Who Could Not Shiver and Shake'. I could do both. And for Maisie Sweeney I could do more. I kissed her cheek. I combed my hair properly and covered it with bay rum. And then I tried to seduce her. I asked her if she'd take off all her clothes for a penny. She said she would if I turned my back. I gave her the penny, turned my back, and she screamed for her mother. The mother belted me across the head with the sweeping brush and then reported me to my father. He was upset. But my mother understood perfectly.

"It's natural enough," she said.

"At his age?" cried my father.

"Well, better late than never," my mother said. And that was that.

Two years later I fell in love with Mrs Cotter. She lived in Mary Street, was forty years old, and the mother of six children. Her husband was a boxer. But my father said he couldn't box eggs, so I ignored him.

When Mrs Cotter came to visit my mother, which she did as often as she could for a chat and a cigarette, she'd sit on a chair by the fire and cross her legs. Mrs Cotter was always crossing her legs and I couldn't keep my eyes off them. If I'd told Mr Goldman about that, he'd have said it was nothing more than a mother fixation. It was nothing of the kind. It was lust. And when I told Father Donovan in the confession box, he agreed it was lust and said I ought to be locked up.

I was praying to be locked up. I was down on my knees seven days a week praying to be locked up with Mrs Cotter. But there was no response. I gave up praying after that. The whole thing is a cod.

Eight

Jewtown was a long row of redbrick Corporation houses situated close to the gasworks. The houses had lain derelict for years, but were now occupied by the Jews. When I asked my father about that, he said that the Jews there had come from Limerick and, before that, Romania – or some other such place. They were first persecuted there and then in Limerick their graveyard had been desecrated by vandals. Now they had settled in Cork.

"The Lord help them," he said.

Jewtown was bleak. But on summer days the women sat on the pavement outside their doors, knitting scarves and pullovers which they later sold around the houses in Evergreen Street and Turner's Cross. The men remained inside. And if you looked through the windows you could see them making leather belts, wallets and handbags – all decorated with twisted pieces of coloured string and beads.

My father said the Jews were poor, but Mr Egan said they were all rich. My father said he was thick.

"If they're rich, what the hell are they doing living in Jewtown?" he shouted. "I wouldn't keep a dog in a place like that."

Mr Egan said that was camouflage. "You couldn't be up to the Jews; they'd have the eyes out of your head if you weren't looking."

My father turned his back on Mr Egan and refused to talk to him anymore.

"I've been listening to that kind of nonsense from as far

back as I can remember. If you're out of work, blame the Jews. If you haven't got enough to eat, blame the Jews. If the water doesn't taste right, the Jews have probably poisoned it. And if it's not the Jews, it's the bloody witches, or both. It's like living in a madhouse."

My mother made tea. My father sat by the fire. My mother handed him a cup.

"I don't know why you take notice of an eegit like that. You know what he's like."

"I had to take notice. The boy was listening."

"He's listening now," said my mother. "Why don't you explain?"

My father looked at me. He didn't want to explain. The subject angered him, but he felt he had to say something.

"Have you been to Jewtown?" he asked.

"Yes."

"And you've seen those people down there?"

"I have."

"Are they any different from us?"

"I don't know."

"Well, I'll tell you. They're not. And some of them are a damned sight worse off. They're the most persecuted people on the face of the earth, and I have to listen to rubbish like that from Egan! Is it any wonder the country is in the state that it is?"

"Drink your tea," said my mother, "before you have a stroke."

My father drank his tea and almost choked swallowing it. "I told you to be careful," my mother scolded – and patted him on the back.

"Mr Goldman is a Jew," I said. "Why doesn't he live in Jewtown?"

"He used to," my mother answered. "It was his cousin in America who found those rooms in the Marsh. And when he left, Mannie Goldman moved in. I think the cousin still pays the rent."

"He sends him five pounds every Christmas too."

"The Jews try to help each other," said my mother. "They have to. Nobody else will look after them."

"Did they murder Christ?" I asked.

My parents looked at me. "Divine Jesus!" exclaimed my father. "Who told you that?"

I remembered the night I had sat in Mr Goldman's room when someone threw a brick through the window. I told him what happened. He turned to my mother.

"Did you know about this?"

"No. But it doesn't surprise me."

My father paused. "It doesn't surprise me either," he said. And lapsed into silence. Presently, he spoke.

"I can't read," he said. "And I can't write – but I know how Mannie Goldman must have felt. So would your grandmother. You should ask her sometime."

"You're his father," said my mother. "You tell him. Trying to get a word out of Lizzie Baron is like pulling teeth."

I sing through my father.

Nine

When my grandfather arrived in the city with Lizzie Baron, it was plain to see that she was foreign. Her long black hair. The sun-brown colour of her skin. The dark glow of her eyes. My grandfather took pride in these things. And when Lizzie lay close by his side, he held her to his heart like a flower.

In the North Side of the city, they managed to find a small house to rent. One room on the ground floor and a loft upstairs where they slept. My father was born there and so was his sister, my Aunt Bridget.

"There was no lavatory," said my father – "just an old shed at the back. But we were happy enough. Bridget and I played in the lanes off Shandon Street and, sometimes, when the circus came to Blackpool, we sat in a tent and watched that."

Those were the good old days. The horses pranced round the sawdust ring and the lions roared at the man with the whip and the monkeys laughed when the penguins danced and the audience gasped when the lady who flew on the flying-trapeze fell down – and was saved – by the man with the net. Those were the good old days.

"That's what they say," my father said. "But I don't remember them like that anymore. I remember one day playing in the street and a boy of about my own age saying to me, 'Is your mother a witch?' I didn't know what to make of it at the time, but that was the beginning. My mother was different. She wasn't like other people. And she always wore black. That's a bad sign.

"After a while, other children started asking the same question. They wanted to know whether she could put curses on people and whether she stuffed children into the oven like the witch in 'Hänsel and Gretel'. They followed her in the streets, and when she told them to go away, they laughed because her English was bad and she couldn't pronounce the words properly. She screamed – and that made it even worse because witches always scream and they look at you with a witch's eye and you could catch a disease or maybe go blind or something.

> "*Lizzie Baron is a witch,*
> *She casts spells that make you itch.*
> *Toads and goblins in her bed,*
> *If she reads you, you are dead.*
> *Beat her with a holy stick,*
> *Send her down to join Old Nick.*
> *If she screeches, don't be slow,*
> *Give the witch another blow.*

"And they did. My father complained to the parents and threatened to beat the hell out of the next person who even looked sideways at her. He tried to persuade her to ignore the children and go on about her business. But she couldn't. She closed the door, refused to go out, and sat in the corner in silence.

"People said she was odd. They stood in pubs and at street corners and said she was strange all right and you could hardly blame the children for being frightened of her. Maybe she did cast spells? There was certainly a curse on this place and some people haven't had a day's work in years. People were dying all over the place with TB and God knows what else. And it's all very well saying these things are God's will – but there are other things, you know.

"Spells and curses,
Hidden rooms,
Witches riding on their brooms.
Jews and dead men on the prowl,
Cross yourself and make them howl.
When you see
The headless coach,
Or blood upon the waning moon,
Bolt your doors and paint them red,
Or in the morning you'll be dead.

"We didn't know then how much worse things could get. When my mother moved from the corner and sat by the fire, children climbed on to the roof and dropped stones down the chimney. Black smoke clouded the room and the hot ash lay scattered across the living-room floor. My father chased the children down the street, but it made no difference. They came back later with more stones.

"One day, when my father was out looking for work down the quays and Bridget and I were sitting on the floor playing cards, we thought we could smell smoke coming from the loft. My mother was resting up there, and when we rushed up the stairs, we found the curtains were on fire. Someone had thrown a lighted roll of paper through the open window and it was still burning close to the bed.

"My mother was fast asleep, but we finally managed to wake her up, and she helped us put the fire out with a bucket of cold water. When I looked out of the window to see if the children were still there, I saw two men standing at the corner. And one of them shouted – 'We thought you'd like a bit of heat in there. 'Tis desperate weather!'

"After that, my father decided we should move. We went to Kinsale first and stayed in my father's old place overlooking the harbour. But she couldn't settle and, finally, we returned to Cork and found a place on this side of the city.

"We had no trouble here and, gradually, your grandmother started going out again to do her shopping in the English Market. But she hasn't forgotten. I know that, though she seldom speaks now and hasn't been out at all since my father died. But she might talk to you. She likes children. She always has."

Those were the good old days. My father had spoken to me for the first time about his youth. Now he turned away. He reached up to the mantelpiece and removed his tin whistle from its place behind the clock. He played music. The sun shone through the open window and my mother sang 'The Culin'.

Ten

I almost drowned once. I fell into the horse's trough below in the South Mall and lay face down in two feet of water. My whole life refused to appear in front of me. It was the beginning of disillusion. My friend Connors hauled me out and said I was only trying to draw attention to myself.

Connors was a cynic. He was two years older than me, but we sat in the same class at school because Brother Reynolds said he had only half a brain and was unsuited to a higher grade. Connors was delighted to have only half a brain. It made him feel special.

I was special, too. I had a grandmother who sat in a corner all day and I had Greek blood in my veins. Connors didn't believe I had Greek blood and wanted to know what colour it was. When I said "pink", he stuck a pin in my arm and waited to see how I would bleed. Sometimes I hated Connors.

When he was short of money one time, he tried to sell me in an auction. An American liner had arrived in Cork and Connors hung a placard round my neck saying: "This boy is an orphan; Going now to the highest bidder. Any offers?" There were none. If there had been, I might now be President of America and Connors a millionaire from telling tourists about my humble beginnings.

Connors never had a beginning. He was born in a vacuum. And when his father died from lack of drink, his mother tried to hide Connors under the floorboards and pretend she was childless. When that failed, she sent him to school and asked Brother Reynolds to keep an eye on him. Brother Reynolds kept both eyes on him and when in doubt locked him in the coal cellar. There were rats in there, but Connors stared them out and emerged hours later, blinking but unscathed.

Brother Reynolds gave up. He told Connors to sit in a corner and say nothing. Connors grinned through the gaps in his teeth. He was happy to sit in the corner. He could see the school clock from there and he counted the minutes until it was time for Brother Reynolds to dismiss us for the day.

Some days, after school, Connors and I went for a walk down the Marina. We climbed on to the quay wall and begged pesetas, drachmas and French francs from the crews of foreign ships. We could see the world from there. The ghosts of corn and timber sails. The flags of nations we would long to visit. The gulls circling over Sweden and Finland, Russia and Scandinavia, and beyond to Egypt where the pyramids stood as a monument to vanity and the death of kings.

We played hide-and-seek beneath the jetties. Dived naked from the slipway steps. Swam in the dull grey waters of the Lee. And then lay on the grass beside Dunlops and Fords to dry out under the last rays of the afternoon sun.

On our way home we paused to see the *Innisfallen* leave its berth. We saw it turn and move out, drift slowly past Blackrock Castle and head towards the Atlantic. We saw it enter the night, its decks crowded with emigrants from Cork – most of whom were destined never to return.

Connors often talked about emigrating from Cork. He'd seen Ronald Colman in *Under Two Flags* at the Savoy cinema and was determined to join the French Foreign Legion. He changed his mind later when he saw Gary Cooper in *The Lives of a Bengal Lancer*. That made him want to join the British Army and defend the Empire on the northwest frontier of India.

His mother encouraged him. She wanted him to go to Australia or Burma, Mongolia or the Gobi Desert, or anywhere as long as he was out of the house. Mrs Connors wasn't pleased with her son. And her son wasn't too keen on her either. He was convinced she was trying to starve him to death.

"The food she gives me is rotten. I think she wants to be a nun."

Mrs Connors did want to be a nun. The convent beckoned her, but she was lumbered with her son. If she could have sent him into outer space, she would have done so gladly. She prayed for the Martians to come. She went down on her knees and offered up The Rosary for a merciful release. She closed her eyes, but when she opened them Connors was still standing there, staring her in the face.

"Does she have holy pictures in the house?"

"All over the shagging place," said Connors.

I had never been inside Connor's house. His mother wouldn't permit it. She was against visitors unless they were ordained priests or fully paid-up members of The Legion of Mary. She had the house consecrated to the Sacred Heart and a statue of Saint Anthony guarding the front door. There was no way past him.

"It's a wonder she lets me in," said Connors. "But she only does that to torment me."

Mrs Connors was always tormenting him. On weekdays, she made him his breakfast of tea and bread and dripping but only after she'd dragged him to early Mass in the South Chapel in Dunbar Street. In the evenings she made him a pot of soup, but Connors said you wouldn't know what she'd put into it and he was afraid to look.

Sunday, however, was her best day. She locked the larder

door then and spent the whole day fasting. She expected Connors to do the same, but he came round to our place and ate us all out of house and home. My mother thought Mrs Connors was demented – and she had grave doubts about her son. But she fed him when she could.

The house they lived in was small and dark and it stood close to the South Presentation Convent in Abbey Street. Mrs Connors could see the nuns from there and the light burning in the convent chapel.

"She says the light is the eye of God and if it goes out she'll die. I told her I'd blow it out meself if she didn't stop annoying me, but she takes no notice."

Connors hated the light. It shone through the window at night and he couldn't get to sleep. He tried counting sheep, and when that failed, he hid under the bed. But the light followed him, like a spectre cast from the runes, and there was no escape.

When his father was alive, the window had been blocked up. When he died, Mrs Connors had it opened again.

"It's like living near a lighthouse now," said Connors. "I've shifted the bed three times, but I'm still blinded."

"Didn't your father believe in God?"

"He did not! The only thing he believed in was land reform and capital punishment for people with religion. I didn't know what he was talking about at the time. 'Tis only dawning on me now. That's why she wants rid of me."

"Are you going to run away?"

"I will one day. But I'd hate to leave the Da. He's buried in Saint Finbarre's now and I go and talk to him sometimes. You'd think she'd do the same – but she never goes near the place. She says my father is in Hell and there's nothing she can do about that."

Connors survived his mother and when she died he buried her with the statue of Saint Anthony planted firmly

in her lap. Later, he had the window boarded up and slept
blissfully in a darkened room.

Eleven

The quays were black. My father was unemployed and the consensus of opinion was that I should look for a job after school. With Mr Goldman's help I applied for a job as a messenger-boy and was rewarded by an interview with a Mr Thomas A Grogan.

Mr Grogan was a butcher who also passed himself off as a grocer – and he required a strong lad who could climb mountains with a basket-load of groceries and the slaughtered remains of cattle and sheep. He was offering a salary of seven shillings and sixpence per week and the applicant was required to ride a bike. I could ride a bike – provided the wind was westerly. I omitted to mention this to Mr Grogan.

"You don't look very strong," he peeped.

"I'm as strong as a horse," I said.

"I'm not looking for a horse," said Mr Grogan. "Can you ride a bike?"

I looked at the bike. It was large, black, and clearly designed to withstand the abuses of legions of messenger boys. Mr Grogan waited.

"Well?"

"'Tis no trouble, Mr Grogan."

"We'll see."

He laid his hand on my head and steered me towards the bike. "I've had it specially made," he said.

I could see that. The handlebars were solid. The wheels were made of cast iron, and the carrier-basket, welded to the frame in front, was guaranteed by its makers to bear the maximum of weight with the minimum of strain to the bike – if not to the messenger-boy.

"I've had messenger-boys before," Mr Grogan groaned. "They were not up to it."

"Try me, Mr Grogan."

"Don't rush me. I'm thinking." Mr Grogan thought. His gaze wandered from the toes of my feet to the crown of my head. He was not impressed.

"How old are you?"

"Ten."

He shook his head. He walked round me. He examined my back, pressed down on my shoulders, looked at my hands and then opened my mouth.

"If you were a horse, I wouldn't give twopence for you."

I straightened myself up. I tried to look like the wrestler Dano Mahoney. I said I was a personal friend of Jack Doyle, the boxer. I said that his wife, Movita, had recommended me. Mr Grogan shook his head again – and he went on shaking it until I thought it would fall off.

Presently, he said – "I must be mad in the head, but you're falling apart and my heart goes out to you. You can start on Monday."

"Thanks, Mr Grogan."

"And remember this – I pay seven shillings and sixpence a week and I expect value for that."

"Yes, Mr Grogan."

I backed away. I was now an employee. I kept my head low.

On Monday afternoon, I arrived at Mr Grogan's shop. He was standing at the door, the bike beside him, and the carrier basket loaded with the day's deliveries. He handed me a list of names and addresses.

"You'll find most of those are for Saint Luke's and

Montenotte. The rest are for the Good Shepherd's Convent. I'll expect you back at five. Understood?"

"Yes, Mr Grogan."

He turned his back and disappeared into the shop.

I stared at the bike. It was overloaded and when I touched it, the saddle rose in the air and the rear wheel followed it. I pressed it down with my hands and managed to climb onto the saddle. But when I tried to reach the pedals, I found that my legs were too short. There was no way I could ride it.

I climbed down, pressed hard on the saddle with one hand and wheeled the bike along Prince's Street towards Patrick Street. By the time I reached Patrick's Bridge, I was exhausted.

I paused for a moment to catch my breath – and then I saw my friend Connors. He was leaning against the parapet of the bridge and he was smirking.

"Oh!" he says. "Working, are you?"

I hate people who smirk and there were times when I could have spat poisoned darts at Connors – but I restrained myself.

"You'll never make it," he said. "By the time you reach MacCurtain Street you'll be dead."

"You could at least give me a hand!"

"Sorry, old stock, but I'm not feeling too well. That's why I've been off school for a week."

"You don't look sick."

"I know. It's one of those foreign diseases. Doesn't show on the face. Who are you working for?"

"Grogan's."

"Holy Jasus!" exclaimed Connors. "Don't you know about him? He's a monster. Nosey Donaghue worked for him last year and he's crippled now."

"Who says?"

50

"I do. I went to visit him in the Union a couple of days ago and he can't even get out of bed!"

My heart blenched. There was a stabbing pain in my right leg. I felt distinctly unwell.

I knew Nosey. He was strong. He had muscles coming out of his ears. He could walk on broken glass. I didn't know he'd worked in Grogan's.

"Not any more he doesn't," said Connors. "He'll be on crutches for life. If I was you I'd go home. Push that bike into the river and run for it."

"I can't. I need the job."

Connors smirked again and gave a consumptive cough for the poor of Cork.

"Oh well," he spluttered. "I'll see you in the Union."

"Are you not going to give me a push?"

Connors paused. "I'll tell you what I'd do," he said. "You collect the bike every day from Grogan's. Wheel it round as far as Patrick Street and I'll wait for you there. I'll give you a hand as far as Saint Luke's."

"And then what?"

"After that, you make the deliveries. And when you've finished, you can sit in the basket and I'll ride the bicycle down the hill."

"How much?"

"A shilling a week from your wages. It's for nothing! I'm only doing it as a favour."

I agreed under pressure. My wages had been reduced by a shilling, but it was worth it to keep the job. And Connors kept his word.

Every day, he helped me push the bike up as far as Saint Luke's and when I'd completed my deliveries, I sat in the carrier-basket and Connors free-wheeled the bicycle down the hill. I might have known it couldn't last.

One day, the brakes gave out. The bicycle ran out of

control and we crashed into the front door of the Coliseum cinema at the bottom of the hill. I sprained an arm and Connors spent six weeks in the South Infirmary with a broken collarbone.

"I always knew working was a mug's game," he said. "Next time, get someone else!"

I didn't need someone else. When Mr Grogan saw the wreckage of the bike and my sprained arm, his heart went out to me again. He said I could work in the slaughter-house for a while and help the men to keep the floors clean. As an afterthought he announced that he would deduct part of my wages every week to cover the cost of repairing the bike.

Twelve

I had never been inside a slaughter-house.

The pens were filled with the sounds of death. The animals jostled and strained against the wooden fences and against each other. They sweated and steamed and their breath clouded the air above them.

A man appeared. He wore a black leather apron over his corduroy trousers and he wore wooden clogs. His footsteps echoed across the yard as he moved towards the enclosure.

The bull saw him coming. He pawed the ground and snorted, but the man ignored him. The bull snorted again, the white froth issuing from his mouth and hanging in trails from his lower lip. The man stared at him for a moment and then prodded him with a steel rod. The bull lowered his head, as if to charge, but there was no room.

The man circled the pen and approached him from the rear. He prodded the bull again, forcing him in the direction of a narrow gangplank leading to the slaughter-house. When the bull reached the gangplank, he stumbled, but the man continued to prod until the bull rose to his feet and stumbled again as he headed towards the slaughter-house door. Here he stopped. He could go no farther. The door was closed.

The bull tried to move back, but a steel gate had fallen behind him and he was trapped. He kicked at the gate with his hind legs. He rammed his head against the door of the slaughter-house, and he used all his strength in a vain attempt to climb over the side of the gangplank. But he was locked in, without room to manoeuvre, and in the end he fell exhausted before the door.

The man moved off and returned a moment later, carrying a long rope over his shoulders. He tied one end of the rope around the bull's neck and pushed the other end through a gap under the slaughter-house door. He entered the slaughter-house through a side entrance and pulled the rope through.

The slaughter-house was cold. The walls were painted white and an iron ring lay embedded in the centre of the concrete floor. The man drew the rope through the ring and threw the end over a stout beam directly above his head. He lit a cigarette and waited for the slaughterman to arrive.

Mr Cunningham was tall. He'd been a slaughterman for twenty-five years and was proud of his profession. He wore white overalls. He kept his fingernails clean and he carried a sledgehammer in his hand – the steel head pointed at one end. He nodded to the man. The man dropped his cigarette on the ground and stamped it out with his foot. Mr Cunningham looked at him with disapproval. He was against smoking in the slaughter-house. It was unhygienic.

When the slaughter-house door was opened, the bull rose to his feet and stared into the opening before him. He sniffed the air and he could smell the blood. He drew back, but the men pulled hard on the rope and dragged him down towards the iron ring embedded in the floor.

The bull roared. He twisted and turned and tried desperately to extricate himself from the choking rope, but the rope held him and the more he struggled the tighter it became.

He fell to the floor, his forelegs buckling under him, but the men continued to draw on the rope until the bull's head touched the iron ring and his hind legs rose in the air, kicking wildly upon an empty space.

After they had tied the rope securely to the beam above them, Mr Cunningham approached the bull. He picked up the sledgehammer from the ground beside him and struck the bull on the forehead with the pointed end. The bull's body convulsed with shock and Mr Cunningham struck him again on the same spot until a hole appeared and the blood gushed forth in a fountain of red.

Mr Cunningham lowered the sledgehammer. He wiped his hands with a clean white cloth. He inserted a hooked wire into the hole he had just created in the bull's forehead and then, very gently, he extracted the brain.

I stood at the slaughter-house door and vomited.

Thirteen

Every Sunday after Mass, the neighbours gathered in our tenement flat to sing and tell stories. My father played music and, sometimes, recited poetry he'd made up in his head. My father would never admit to having made up these poems. He said they were the work of great men long gone and now sadly neglected. My mother said he was the biggest liar in Cork – and he was. But he was also a poet. A poet is a man who tell lies, but in short lines and with style. My father had style.

Paddy Tom Kilroy also had style. He lived over in Frenches Quay and everyone called him The Captain because he wore a sailor's cap and had never been to sea. He owned a small fishing boat, too. It had been willed to him by his father and was moored near the South Gate Bridge, but Paddy had never set foot on it. He said the weather was too bad.

The weather had started to go bad fifteen years before when Paddy's father had died and left him the boat. It was still bad and there was no sign of an improvement.

Paddy leaned over the parapet of the South Gate Bridge and stared at the boat. The timbers were rotting. The seagulls were nesting on the deck and the barnacles were choking the hull to death.

Paddy looked at the sky. If only the weather would improve – but he knew it wouldn't. He'd read in the newspaper that morning that there was a storm brewing over Cork. He buttoned his coat. The weather was killing him. He could feel it in his bones.

One Sunday, Paddy arrived at our flat in Margaret Street and said he'd changed into a seagull. He didn't look like a seagull, and he still wore his sailor's cap, but my father invited him in and asked him if he'd seen a doctor. Paddy shook his head. There was no point. Doctors knew nothing about seagulls and, besides, he was happy enough the way he was. Come to think of it – he'd always wanted to be a seagull, but the boat got in his way.

My father thought he'd gone raving mad, but my mother was more sympathetic. She offered him fish. Paddy ate the fish and said he'd never tasted anything sweeter in his life. On his way out, he thanked my mother and said he'd remember her in his will. My father almost choked. He hated fish and he was convinced that Paddy would be in the madhouse within the week.

A few weeks later, Paddy returned to the house. My mother found him sitting on the stairs and there were tears in his eyes. He said the police were after him, and when my mother asked him what crime he'd committed, he said he hadn't committed a crime. All he'd done was to fly in and out of the South Chapel during Mass and screech "More Fish!"

The congregation was terrified and the Parish Priest had had a heart attack – but whose fault was that? A seagull was a perfectly harmless bird and all the congregation had to do was to say "Sorry, Paddy, we've run out of fish" and Paddy would have been satisfied and gone elsewhere.

When the police arrived, Paddy was wheeled off to the Bridewell and he spent a week in there flapping his wings about and claiming that under international law it was illegal to imprison a seagull. The guards at the Bridewell knew nothing about international law, but they insisted that under Irish law the police could arrest anyone for anything – even if he were a seagull.

Paddy applied for bail, and my mother had to pawn my father's best suit in order to raise the money to have Paddy released.

My father was a tolerant man, but when his best suit had to be pawned to have a seagull released from jail, things were getting altogether out of hand. He had nothing against seagulls – provided they let their droppings drop on someone else – but this particular seagull was getting on his nerves. He wanted his suit back – and he said so without music.

My mother laughed. She knew that Paddy was a genius, and if he felt he was a seagull, then that's what he was. After all, there were worse things he could be – like a policeman or a Blueshirt. My father didn't agree at all and was now beginning to worry about my mother. Any minute now and she'd be sprouting wings.

She didn't. She pulled her black shawl tightly around her shoulders and went to the courthouse the following morning to hear Paddy being charged with a breach of the peace. He pleaded "Not guilty" and when the magistrate asked him for his full name he replied: "Seagulls don't have full names. They're just called – Seagulls."

The magistrate nodded his head. He understood perfectly. Paddy was a poet. He dismissed the case and Paddy winged it from the court a free bird.

He was missing for months. My mother searched around his usual haunts, but there was no trace of him. Paddy had disappeared.

Then, one day, while she was sitting in a pub in Sullivan's Quay, having her usual bottle of stout, the door opened and Paddy walked in. She offered him a drink. Paddy accepted and sat beside her in the snug.

"You've been away?" she said.

"I have," Paddy declared. "Do you notice anything different about me?"

My mother wasn't sure. Paddy shook his head. He was no longer a seagull.

"That's a sad day for Cork, Paddy."

"It's a sad day for me too, Ma'am. But the fates were against it."

He finished his drink and turned towards the door.

"By the way," he said, "I've willed you the boat. Maybe your son will find a use for it."

"I'm sure he will," said my mother. "But you'll be with us for a long time yet, Paddy."

Paddy shrugged his shoulders. "I'll be going now," he said. "Thanks for the drink."

"Are you going far?"

"I'm going for a walk on the water," Paddy replied. "God knows when I'll be back."

The door closed behind him and a week later Paddy's body was found floating on the water close to Blackrock Castle. My mother wept – and the seagulls carried Paddy home.

Fourteen

My mother believed in poets. She said they were not born but invented by God to celebrate his angels. My father believed in my mother, but thought poets should be heard and not seen. The anonymous poem was the real poem. It belonged to everyone and not just to the messenger who happened to deliver a first copy. My father could be complicated at times. It was hard to know what he was talking about. My mother said it was best not to ask. It only made confusion worse confounded.

When he was a young man – and long before he'd met my mother – my father joined the British Army and served with the Royal Munster Fusiliers in India. You could tell he'd been to India because when he was drunk he recited 'Gunga Din', and when he was sad he talked about the foothills and the Ganges and the nabobs and the moguls who were presented with their weight in diamonds every time they had a birthday.

My father never celebrated his birthday – and he hated uniforms. And when I asked him why he had joined the British Army, he said he had no idea. He just happened to be passing by the recruiting office one day and heard a voice crying – "I Want You!" When he turned around, he saw General Haig standing there and he hadn't the heart to refuse him.

The General was polite enough. He wanted to know how old my father was and when my father said he couldn't remember, the General had him medically examined. The doctor looked through one ear and couldn't see out through the other – and my father was in. The General promised to meet him in France, but my father boarded the wrong boat at Southampton and the next thing he knew he was in Calcutta singing 'God Save the King', whom he'd never met.

When he tried to explain all this to my mother one day, she developed a migraine headache from which she never fully recovered.

My father liked India. He felt it was his spiritual home and he was happy to sit by the Ganges all day contemplating the Universe. The Army, however, had other ideas. They taught him how to box.

He ran five miles under the blazing sun every day and then he worked out in the gym. He developed muscles in places he never knew existed. He skipped and he danced. He rubbed salt on his face and steeped his hands in vinegar and brine. He punched leather until the gloves split, exposing the protective bandages underneath. And then he ran another five miles until the heat drained him of everything but fists and hard driving bone.

The Army was proud of my father. They said he was a natural in the ring. They promoted him to Corporal and entered him in competitions all over India. He stood against the best that the subcontinent could provide and in three years he had fought his way up to become Amateur Boxing Champion of the British Army in India. And then he quit.

He gave no reason. He offered no explanation. He simply hung up his gloves and walked away.

My father still maintained an interest in boxing after he left the Army and returned to Cork, but he refused to enter the ring and he never talked about his own experiences as a boxer. Instead he told stories about the great boxers of the past – of John L Sullivan and Jim Corbett – Jack Dempsey and Gene Tunney – Max Baer and Tony Galento – James Braddock – and the then current champion Joe Louis. He talked about Len Harvey, who was light on his feet and should have been a ballet dancer, and Jack Doyle, who could sing but wasn't hungry enough to be a great champion.

He knew about them all and could list their achievements and their failures. And he knew how they felt when the bell sounded for the first round and how they felt when the final bell heralded victory or defeat. He had tasted both and had not been counted out.

He said boxing was a poem. He said Jim Corbett created images with his feet and Joe Louis painted pictures with his fists. My mother couldn't understand a word of it and said the British had a lot to answer for. She could be complicated too and had her own way of looking at things.

She blessed the Irish Rebellion of 1916 and said that Connolly and Pearse were two of the greatest Irishmen who ever lived. My father thought Pearse was a lunatic and that Connolly was led astray by a lot of codology.

My mother supported the Russian Revolution of 1917. My father said she'd think differently when the Communists invaded Cork.

My mother sided with the diehards during the Irish Civil War and said that Michael Collins should have been shot dead the moment he returned from London, having signed the Anglo–Irish Treaty. My father thought it was better to settle for half-a-loaf than none at all.

My mother mentioned MacSwiney who died on hunger strike in Brixton Prison. My father remembered the funeral.

My mother thought we should burn everything British in Ireland except their coal. My father said he would burn anything if it kept the house warm.

My mother said he should never have joined the British Army. My father said he loved India.

My mother said he ought to be ashamed of himself. My father said he was not.

She wrote "La Pasionaria is the noblest woman on Earth" on the tenement walls.

My father couldn't read and had never heard of Dolores Ibarruri.

My father and my mother loved each other and they lived happily together for a time.

Fifteen

Lefty Thompson was my father's friend and, though he too had joined the British Army during the Great War, my mother admired him because he was now on the side of the Spanish Republicans and stood with Mr Goldman at the corner of Washington Street to protest against the Fascists. My father did not protest against the Fascists, but he wouldn't support them either. He said Lefty was his friend – and that was enough. Lefty understood. My mother did not. She said there were times when friendship wasn't enough.

She wanted him to stand beside Lefty and Mr Goldman and protest in a loud voice. She wanted him to paint slogans on the walls and declare who he was and what he stood for – but my father said no. He was not that kind of man. He could play the tin whistle. He would not deny his friends and he would keep open house for all those who could sing or play music, or appreciate a good story or a poem. That's who he was. That's what he stood for. That was my father.

Lefty was different. He could not play the tin whistle, but he could tolerate a good story and he could sing when his throat was oiled with a sufficient quantity of liquor. And he was taller than my father.

He stood six feet and six inches in height and the muscles on his arms stood out like the tow ropes on a battleship. My father said he could have been one of the great boxers of the age – if only he had two legs.

Lefty did have two legs at one time, but he lost one of

them during the Great War because he had no luck and boarded the right boat for France at Southampton, when he should have boarded the wrong one, like my father, and ended up in India.

Lefty would have enjoyed India. The French irritated him. And when he arrived in France and was met by General Haig, the General irritated him by trying to kiss him on both cheeks and saying, "You're just in time for the Big Push."

Lefty had heard about the Big Push, and he knew that the General had already lost about 40,000 men in a previous Big Push and the only thing he'd gained was fifty yards of mudflats. Lefty wasn't too pleased about that and thought the General was an idiot. He wanted to go home. But the General wasn't sending people home that day. He was sending them all to the Front to take part in the Big Push.

The General was beset with the Big Push – "Once more, Thompson, and we'll all be home by Christmas." But on Christmas Day, Lefty was still sitting in the trenches with his feet in three feet of muddy water while the General was playing leap-frog with his subordinates in the Officers' Mess.

When the General had finished playing leap-frog, he ordered everyone "Over the Top!" Lefty was so happy to get out of the trenches that he was first over – and the only thing he remembered after that was waking up in hospital and wondering where the rest of him had gone.

The surgeon didn't know. Lefty asked him twice – but the surgeon had amputated so many legs recently that he could no longer tell one from another and had no idea where he'd thrown the ones he'd cut off.

"It was the right one," said Lefty.

"It's always the right one!" exclaimed the surgeon. "I never amputate anything else. Was there a scar on it?"

"There was," replied Lefty. "I fell off me roller skates when I was five."

"It could be anywhere," the surgeon declared. "Better ask General Haig."

But when Lefty asked the General where his right leg had gone, the General didn't know either.

"Are you sure you had two when you went over the top?" he asked Lefty.

"Oh yes, Sir. I remember distinctly. Two legs. A right and a left."

"Most extraordinary. Well, Thompson, keep your pecker up. I'll enquire about the missing leg. In the meantime, congratulations. We gained ten yards yesterday. Unfortunately, we lost them again this morning – but we'll keep trying, eh!"

"Yes, Sir. May I ask about the number of casualties?"

"Of course. Good luck, Thompson. Jolly good luck."

And that was the last that Lefty saw of General Haig.

Two months later, Lefty was discharged from the Army and everyone called him Hoppy though he preferred to be called Lefty. He received a pension of eleven shillings a week and the British Legion provided him with a bread-voucher enabling him to obtain a free loaf every Friday at the local bakery.

General Haig did slightly better. He was made an Earl and the Government awarded him a grant of one hundred thousand pounds to help him cover his household expenses. When he vacated the house in 1928 and moved into the final No Man's Land, he was exhausted but fulfilled.

Lefty lived longer. He made himself a boxcar out of two planks of wood and four pram wheels and he propelled himself around the city like a child practising for the Grand Prix. He called himself "The Socialist" and was arrested for disorderly behaviour in Patrick Street when he made a speech advocating free love and the equal distribution of wealth. My father was all in favour of the latter, but the notion of free love gave him arthritis. My mother was more flexible – *Que Será, Será* ...

During the last days of his life, Lefty tried to make a living selling postcards of revolutionary heroes at two for a penny in the Coal Quay Market. He was not successful. When he died, he left his body to science with instructions that when they had finished with the remains they were to cast them into the nearest dustbin. He added a postscript to that: "Sorry about the missing leg, lads. But see what you can do with the remaining one."

He was buried at night, near the banks of the Lee, in a dustbin filled with red carnations.

Sixteen

Monday was murder-day. The schoolroom clock struck high noon and Brother Reynolds stood with his back to the wall and sniffed the air. He said he could smell treason. His nose twitched. His hands shook and his gaze wandered from desk to desk and from boy to boy. He studied our faces. He searched behind our eyes for traces of shame and guilt – and when he found them he smiled and ordered the unlucky ones to come forth. My friend Connors and I came forth. We admitted our guilt. We confessed our shame. We had not been to ten o'clock Mass the previous Sunday and we knew we were damned.

Brother Reynolds said we were damned. He said that on the final Day of Judgement we would stand before the Lord God of Hosts and He would say unto us – "Woe be to those who did not attend ten o'clock Mass on Sunday. Depart from me, ye cursed, into the everlasting flames of Hell which was prepared for the Devil and his angels."

Connors and I departed. We sank into Hell. The Devil was pushing red hot pokers into our ears and Brother Reynolds was beating us across the palms of the hands with a pure ash cane. Six slaps each and an extra one for Sunday because that was a holy day.

My friend Connors thought holy days were a cod and said his mother had invented them for the sole purpose of torturing his father. When he told Brother Reynolds that, Brother Reynolds beat him again until the cane split wide open – and then he told him to kneel on the floor and ask

God for forgiveness. My friend Connors did kneel on the floor and he prayed hard. But he prayed he'd grow up to be a millionaire so that he could afford to hire a hit-man and have his mother assassinated.

I prayed for Brother Reynolds. I prayed that his eyes would fall out and drop on the floor and we could all play football. But I forgot I'd given up praying and when there was no response, I sank deeper into Hell.

Brother Reynolds explained about Hell. He said he'd seen it in a dream and it had seven levels and the deepest level was reserved for boys who had bad thoughts and never went to ten o'clock Mass on Sunday. I had bad thoughts. I was in love with Mickey Rooney and I wanted to sleep with Ann Sheridan. Mr Goldman said I was confused.

Brother Reynolds was never confused. He had three ash canes and he used them with zeal on all those who had not been to ten o'clock Mass. And when those canes were broken on the hands of children who were forever damned, he'd send me down to the Institute of the Blind to collect more canes. I wondered about the blind. Did they know that they were making canes to beat people to death who could see? Brother Reynolds would know. Brother Reynolds knew everything.

He knew that I hadn't been to ten o'clock Mass on the previous Sunday because I sold newspapers in the street on Saturday nights and then went to the late-night cinema to see Ken Maynard riding a white horse. He knew that I slept late on Sundays and was too tired to get out of bed. He knew that I had a mania for the cinema and was crippled trying to walk like James Cagney. And he knew that if I had enough money, I would build a cinema of my own – and let nobody in but Connors and myself.

Brother Reynolds didn't approve of the cinema. He never sold newspapers in the street and he never tried to walk like

James Cagney. He would not be damned. He stayed up all night waiting for ten o'clock Mass on Sunday morning.

Brother Leary, on the other hand, did not concern himself with ten o'clock Mass. At another time, upon another level in Hell, he sat on a chair and struggled to teach us that two and two did not make five. He tried hard, but no one was interested and the knowledge burned him. So he turned to the bottle – and every day when he entered the classroom he carried a small flask of whiskey in his back pocket. That was his comfort and when he had drained the flask he sucked the neck of it dry and cried "Mama!" to the world and to all who could hear him. Brother Reynolds heard him and said he was a drunk, but the children were used to drunks and simply ignored him until he fell on the floor – and then they carried him to his desk where he slept peacefully with his head resting on piles of discarded jotters and sheets of pink blotting-paper.

You could feel sorry for Brother Leary. He was a small twisted little man with a whingey expression and a drooping moustache. He had hairs in his ears and when he spoke his teeth rattled like chaneys in a box. He said his life was sore and you wondered what he meant, but he knew you didn't care and that knowledge too filled him with despair.

Sometimes, Brother Leary tried to hide his drinking habits. He hid the flask behind the blackboard – covered the board with numbers and equations and then asked us to copy them all down in our jotters. When he was satisfied that we were all duly ensconced, he'd slip behind the black-board and help himself to a drink.

He didn't know about children and had forgotten how well they can see through blackboards and chalk. We could smell the whiskey. We could taste his sense of disillusion. He counted out the number of his days and found them all wanting.

When Brother Leary was young, his parents said he was born to be a priest. You could tell by the way he looked at you – and he had a halo round his head. But Brother Leary had no intention of becoming a priest. He was more interested in politics and in the War of Independence that was raging across the country. He joined the IRA and fought against the British Army in the hills around Cork. He organised ambushes and laid land-mines on the roads. He blew up bridges and was reputed to have personally executed two Black and Tans who were involved in the attempted burning of Cork in December 1920. The British put a price on his head, but he fled to America where he remained until the war was over. Then he returned to Ireland and found that those he had fought beside for so long were now killing each other in a murderous Civil War that was to last for years.

Brother Leary was sick. He saw his past as inglorious and the present a bogland of lost hopes and wasted aspirations. He sought refuge in the church and became a Brother in Christ, only to find that his remaining days would be spent teaching mathematics to children who were born to emigrate from the country he had fought to set free.

When Brother Leary drank, it was to relieve the pain and to blot out the agonies of disillusion. But the pain remained and the disillusion remained until a car he was driving crashed into a wall, and he died drunk at the wheel.

Seventeen

If there was a university in Cork in my youth, I was not aware of it. The cinema was my university and Mr Goldman said it was a great art – but only as long as the actors remained silent. The moment Al Jolson opened his big mouth in *The Jazz Singer* everything fell apart. Maybe Mr Goldman was right, but I was made for the talkies.

Any pocket-money I had I spent at the local cinema. And when I hadn't any pocket-money, I stood outside the Savoy and the Pavilion and gazed in wonder at portraits of the Hollywood stars. W S Hart riding the back lot range. William Boyd before he became Hopalong Cassidy. Paulette Godard bathing in ass's milk. Edward G Robinson discovering a cure for the unmentionable. James Cagney in *The Public Enemy*. Mickey Rooney staging a Broadway musical in his back garden. And most of all and most again – Ann Sheridan. I gazed on her with trembling heart and (I can reveal it now) we were married secretly in Cork by Pat O'Brien, who played the priest.

Is it any wonder then that when I saw an advertisement in the *Evening Echo* for a part-time Assistant Projectionist at our local fleapit, I applied at once? You can be sure I did. I was tailor-made for the job and the owner, Quasimodo, knew it.

His name was Quasimodo because at the beginning of each programme he charged through the cinema with a bell in each hand, shouting, "Sanctuary! Sanctuary! We'll begin in a minute." He was also in love with Lon Chaney and, in

72

later years, developed a passion for Charles Laughton. I understood how he felt, though all I wanted to do was to make love to Ann Sheridan and my loins ached from yearning.

Quasimodo had no interest in Ann Sheridan. If he'd had his way, he would have shown *The Hunchback of Notre Dame* twice a day and three times on Sunday. He would have sat in the cinema alone and he would have died for Lon Chaney.

When I arrived for an interview on the first day, Quasimodo asked me to spell Lon Chaney's name. I spelt it correctly and was hired on the spot. Quasimodo then explained the duties of an Assistant Projectionist – Evenings Only – No Alcoholic Beverages Allowed in the Projection Room:

"An Assistant Projectionist," he declared, "is a man – or, in your case, a boy – who sorts out the reels of film delivered to the cinema twice weekly by the renters of said film. He examines the reels. Numbers them in the correct order and then helps the Chief Projectionist to insert them into the projector. A very simple procedure, really. Anyone could do it."

"And what does the Chief Projectionist do?" I asked.

"Very little," replied Quasimodo.

"Could I speak to him?"

"Not at the moment."

"You mean he's not here?"

"He'll be back next week."

Quasimodo then took me by the hand and led me towards the projection box. He pointed out the two giant projectors bolted to the floor.

"There are one or two little things I forgot to mention," he said.

"Like what?"

"Well, to begin with, dear boy, all these films are highly inflammable. That means that they are quite likely to burst into flames at the slightest rise in temperature. And, secondly, each projector is equipped with two blue sticks of charcoal. These have to be lit and held closely together during the running of the film. If you allow them to drift apart, the screen will turn blue. If you push them too close together, the projector will overheat and the whole thing will explode. Are you with me so far?"

"I think so."

"Then there's the matter of the reels. Sometimes, they arrive broken. And sometimes the actual film may be damaged. You'll have to look out for that."

"Is it dangerous?"

"Not necessarily. The important thing is to be careful. If you insert a broken reel into the projector, the film will probably come to a grinding halt and the audience will throw missiles at the screen. They have, after all, paid fourpence."

"And the damaged film?"

"Ah – that's tricky. A damaged film may get caught up in the sprockets of the projector. In which case, the remainder of the film will spill out on to the floor and catch fire. As I say – the important thing is to be careful."

I promised to be careful and, once again, asked him when the Chief Projectionist was due back.

"Monday or Tuesday," replied Quasimodo. "The doctors have assured me that it shouldn't take longer than a week. In the meantime, do you think you could manage by yourself?"

I said I'd try. I pinned a photograph of Ann Sheridan to the wall above the projectors and pleaded with her for guidance. She did not let me down. Her eyes protected me. Her smile filled me with confidence. I approached the projectors.

"Now, the first thing to remember," said Ann, "is that there are two projectors and each reel of film lasts about twenty minutes. You insert Reel One into the first projector and Reel Two into the second projector – making sure beforehand that you have made a number of scratches near the end of each reel so that you'll know when it's about to end. I would suggest that you make these scratches on the top right-hand corner of the film."

"Yes, Ann."

"You then tie a piece of string to the shutter of the first projector and link it to the shutter on the second projector – and keep it tight. Then push the starter coil and away you go."

"God bless you, Ann."

"I'm sure He will. Now, during the running of the film it is essential to keep one eye on the screen and the other eye on the two burning sticks of charcoal. When you see the scratches appearing on the top right-hand corner of the screen – you pull the piece of string – shutting off the first projector and starting up number two. If you do this quickly enough, you will avoid 'End of Part One' appearing on the screen and achieve a fine sense of continuity."

"Beautiful."

"Finally – remove Reel One from the first projector and insert Reel Three. And so on until you reach Reel Eight. By that time the film should be completed and you can wrap up and go home."

"With you, Ann?"

"Natch, Sweetheart. And if an accident occurs – don't worry. I will always visit you in hospital."

But there was no need for her to visit me in hospital. The Chief Projectionist failed to return and I survived as an Assistant Projectionist until the cinema was closed because it was considered a potential fire hazard.

Quasimodo wept.

He sat in the stalls on that final day and watched *The Hunchback of Notre Dame* for the last time in his own cinema. "Sanctuary! Sanctuary!" he cried as I closed the doors and carried the photograph of Ann Sheridan with me into the night.

Where is she now? Where have they gone – the snows of yesteryear? Come home. Come home. All is forgiven. Come home …

Eighteen

I suppose, in some ways, you could say that my Aunt Bridget was a little mad. Certainly, many people thought so. She wore a flaming red blouse, a billowing black skirt, a pair of men's boots – and she told stories to children. It was night when I met her.

I was sitting on the pavement outside Miss Mac's sweet shop in Mary Street when she appeared round the corner carrying all her worldly possessions in a paper bag. She asked who I was. And when I told her, she said, "I'm your Aunt Bridget."

"The mad one?"

"That's what they say. Is your father at home?"

"No. They're all out."

"I'll sit with you then till they come back."

She sat beside me on the pavement and opened her bag. She removed a handful of sweets and offered me one.

"I'm not supposed to take sweets from strangers."

"I'm not a stranger," she said. "I'm your Aunt."

"My father said you were mad. You ran away from home and joined the gypsies. You were all right before that."

"Was I?"

"I don't know. They don't talk about you. Have you come home?"

"I think so."

"I'll take the sweet so. You can live with us." And so she did – until she found her own house at the bottom of Evergreen Street.

In her youth, my father said, Aunt Bridget was known as a very respectable girl. She went to Mass regularly, was educated in a convent and learned to bow her head demurely in the presence of the opposite sex. She spoke, but only when she was asked, and never interrupted when her elders and betters were engaged in serious conversation.

When she reached the age of forty, however, she took what my father described as a desperate turn for the worst. No one knows how it happened, but one day she looked at herself in the mirror and said – No. The following day she changed her clothes, bought herself a pair of men's boots, and announced that from now on she was going to wander the roads of Ireland and tell stories to children. She kept her word – and the stories she told were magic.

There was the joyous story of a young girl who found a butterfly who had lost its colours. The girl painted new colours on the butterfly and the butterfly flew away to create a rainbow over the city. And listening to my Aunt I could see that rainbow. It arced its way through the autumn skies and I could see its reflection in my Aunt's eyes.

Then there was the story of the young boy who climbed the highest mountain in the world and when he reached the peak he found the portrait of a woman etched deep in the rock. And the strange thing about the story was that no one had climbed that mountain before – or so it was said.

Oh, my Aunt could tell a story all right and leave it hanging there at the end to make you wonder at the mystery of it.

And there were other stories, too. Like the time she saw a woman buried in ice – or the time she saw a tree walking along the road, its branches filled with a myriad of clouds and its leaves glittering with blue stars. And she thought to herself: "What's a tree doing walking along the road when it could just as easily fly?" For trees could fly when they were not standing still and holding the world together with their roots.

Her technique was simple. The stories were true and they were filled with wonder. Not the kind of wonder that would be understood by an adult, but a child certainly. My Aunt had faith in children, and when she saw one in the street, she'd hold out her hand and the child would respond when it might never have responded to another human being.

In my Aunt's mind, children were unique. You didn't have to tell them that the world rested on the back of a giant turtle. Any child could see that – and that's why the world wobbled all the time and you had earthquakes and plagues and famine and whooping cough and chicken pox and measles. If it wasn't for the trees, which held the whole thing together with their roots, the world would have collapsed years ago and sunk into an abyss. My Aunt said so. And she was right.

She said the sky wasn't always blue either. It could be any colour you wanted it to be. She once saw a pink sky and she liked it so much she kept it that way for a week in spite of people telling her she was mad. The children didn't think she was mad. The sky belonged to my Aunt – and when she'd finished with it, she'd pass it on to them and they could paint it any colour they liked.

When my Aunt wasn't telling stories to children, she made children's clothes and sold them to the neighbours for whatever they could afford. Sometimes, all they could afford was – thanks. But that was all right, too. She'd manage.

And she made dolls – paper dolls from string and newspaper and glue she'd prepared herself. You could see it bubbling in the pot that hung precariously over the fire in the back yard of her house in Evergreen Street. She stood tall. She held a large potstick in her hand and as she stirred the glue I could hear her singing softly to herself – "If I was a witch now, I could change the world." But she wasn't a witch. She was my lone Aunt Bridget. An artist, a storyteller and a lover of children. When she died, the sky turned a bright pink and remained that way for a long time.

Nineteen

When my father had an accident on the Quays, we thought we were in for a fortune in compensation. Two years later, the compensation arrived – four hundred pounds – most of which he owed to publicans, grocers and solicitors who'd befriended him. With what remained of the compensation, my father decided to go into business. He opened a small coal-store at the bottom of Travers Hill and advertised in the local newspaper: "Coal and Blocks – Delivered Daily to All Parts of the City." When he omitted to mention was that he had no way of delivering the goods.

"We'll invest in a donkey and cart," he said. "It's the only solution."

He scoured Cork for a suitable donkey and cart and, finally, met a man in a pub who said he had the ideal thing for sale.

"Is it in good condition?" enquired my father.

"Perfect," replied your man. "The donkey is as strong as a battleship and the cart was made by Chippendale. You can have both for a fiver."

My father handed over the fiver and we were all set to deliver coal and blocks to the citizens of Cork. The donkey, however, had other ideas.

When my father locked him in the stable for the night, he kicked the door down with his hind legs – and then kicked my father and almost crushed him to death against the stable wall.

"He's a bit frisky all right," said my father. "But once he

starts work he'll be grand." My father was an optimist. The donkey had no intention of starting work. He stood rock solid in the stable yard and kicked anyone who came near him.

"What we need here," my father said, "is an expert."

Cork is full of experts. And Poncho Sullivan was the greatest expert of them all.

"When I was living in the Argentine," he said, "sleeping rough on the pampas, you know – I used to watch the Gauchos training wild horses. It's no problem."

My father wasn't sure. "This is a donkey," he said, "not a flaming horse."

"Same thing," declared Poncho. "It's entirely a matter of breathing. You approach the animal from the left-hand side, breathe gently up its nostrils and it will immediately see how friendly you are."

Poncho did his breathing act and was discharged from hospital three weeks later on crutches with a bandage round his head. "Is it possible," he wrote to his solicitor, "to sue a donkey?" The solicitor never replied. They're like that when it comes to anything simple.

One day, after school, I went along to the coal-store to help my father promote the business of delivering coal and blocks to the citizens of Cork without any means of transport.

The donkey was standing in the yard, daring anyone to come near him, and my father was talking to Pyramid Reilly. He was another expert. He'd studied the pyramids of Egypt for years and could now prove, beyond doubt, that the Lost Tribes of Israel were living in Evergreen Street. He looked at the donkey, examined the shape and the size and the way it was now standing with his rear end facing the sun, and shook his head.

"It's a conundrum," he said.

"I beg your pardon?"

"A puzzle. But I've got the measure of it now. It's not a donkey at all. It's a frustrated racehorse."

"Are you sure?" asked my father.

"Certain," declared Pyramid. "I won't go into the mathematics of the thing – it would only confuse you. But you've only to look at his behaviour. He's upset. Now, if you were a racehorse and someone tried to pass you off as a donkey, wouldn't you be upset?"

"You have a point there, Pyramid."

"Well – there you are then. Take my advice and buy a racing saddle. Put the saddle on his back and go and find yourself a jockey."

My father looked at me and I pleaded for a merciful release. But two days later I was glued to the saddle and the donkey never looked happier. We were now in the racing business. My father sold the coal-store, fed the donkey on porter and oats and set me on a diet of onion soup and barley.

"In a week," he said, "you'll be thin as a rake and light as a feather. Ideal for a jockey."

I didn't want to be a jockey. I wanted to live in Tibet and be a monk with a bald head and eat goat's meat. I prayed that the donkey might have a stroke. I promised to give up swearing and stop staring at girls and wondering what they looked like under their skirts. I promised anything and everything if only God would put an end to it all. But God wasn't talking to me then. I'd denied Him too often and said He was deaf as a post.

We went into strict training. Two hours in the morning before school. Two hours in the evening after school. The donkey was in his element and I was suffering from nervous exhaustion.

The end came suddenly. I was sitting in the Lee Fields

one day, resting my weary bones, and the donkey was eating grass from a small patch near the Lee Road. At the far end of the field a group of boys were playing hurley. I watched the ball rise high in the air and then fall directly on the donkey's head. The effect was miraculous. He reared up on his hind legs, brayed as if he'd swallowed a foghorn and bolted straight down the Lee Road. I followed – slowly – and by the time I reached Washington Street the city was at a standstill. Traffic was held up. Pedestrians were fleeing in all directions – and four policemen, with a rope, were struggling to put the donkey under restraint. By the time my father arrived, they had managed to do so.

I glowed with relief. The donkey was dragged on to the back of a lorry and my father was taken to the Bridewell where he was charged with being in possession of a dangerous animal. He was fined ten pounds and ordered to get rid of the beast. The donkey was sold. My racing days were over and I believed in the Holy Spirit for a week.

Twenty

My paternal grandmother, Lizzie Baron, sat by the window of her room in Mary Street and watched the children playing handball against the side wall of Miss Mac's sweet shop directly opposite. She sat there every day now – ever since my grandfather had died and she had decided not to leave the house anymore. I went to visit her often, but she seldom spoke. She seemed content just to sit there, watching the children playing handball and waiting to be reunited with my grandfather.

"He was a big man," she said. "Biggest man in the world. He was not to be dead."

She paced her words. Measured them out slowly, one at a time, and laid them down before me – a pavement to her mind.

I wanted to know about my grandfather. I wanted to know where they had met and whether it was true that she was Greek and my grandfather had rescued her from a band of marauding Turks. But she shrugged her shoulders, as if it were of no consequence, and continued to stare out of the window.

Presently she said: "He talked to the stones. He wished to be buried in a wall. Your people did not do that. It was not right."

"Do you want to be buried in a wall?"

"I lie with him," she said.

I looked at the room. When my grandfather was alive, it seemed large and airy. Now it was small. The window was open, but the room smelled of old clothes and stale food. In the sink beside her, the unwashed crockery and china plates lay piled high – and on the floor near the fire my grandfather's boots lay turned on one side as if drying out after a day in the rain. Above the fire, the mantelpiece was bare. She had removed the clock that had stood there for years and now there was no time in the room and the only sound was that of the ball bouncing against the wall across the street.

In a corner of the room, my grandfather's bed stood as it had always stood – close to the wall and covered with a dark red quilt. But she had made the bed and my grandfather's nightshirt, neatly ironed, lay folded carefully across two pillows. It was the only task she performed daily. Everything else was unimportant. When I asked her about her past, she said that was unimportant. And when I asked her how she felt now about those who had persecuted her when she had first arrived in the city, she said she had seen worse and so had my grandfather, but she would not say where and asked me to change the subject. I changed the subject and asked her why my grandfather wanted to be buried in a wall.

"Did he like walls?"

"No," she said. "He did not like walls." And left it at that.

My mother was right. Trying to get information from Lizzie Baron was like pulling teeth. I tried again.

"If he didn't like walls," I said, "why did he want to be buried in one?"

She turned her head, studied me for a moment and replied – "Stones. There is truth in stones. Can you swim?"

"Swim?"

"Your grandfather could swim. He was a fine swimmer. I saw him. He rose from the water like a bird. He lay on the sand naked. He was naked in the woods. Always naked. Always beautiful. Not to be dead."

I looked at her face. I had no idea what she was talking about. I couldn't imagine my grandfather being naked. I had never thought of him as being beautiful and I had never seen him swim.

"Why was he naked?" I asked.

She smiled. And for a moment I thought she was mocking me. But her eyes were sad, and when I looked down at her hands they were held tightly together and the knuckles glowed white from pressure and tension.

"Why?" I persisted. But she refused to answer and lowered her head.

I felt guilty then and knew that, somehow, it was wrong to question her. She was struggling for words. She didn't want to answer questions anymore. She had said enough.

"I'm sorry," I said. "I won't ask you again."

She raised her head, paused for a moment, and then moved towards the bed. When she reached the bed, she knelt on the floor beside it and pulled out a tin box from beneath. Opening the box, she withdrew a number of tattered and faded photographs. She handed them to me. They were photographs of walls.

On the ground beside one wall, a group of people lay dead. The wall above them was pockmarked with bullet holes. Against another wall, two children stood facing the camera. They looked puzzled and hungry. A third wall was blank, apart from what appeared to be a list of names scratched along the side in a language I did not understand. A fourth showed a man and a woman standing beside it, holding hands. And the last photograph was of a wall covered with photographs of men, women and children.

The photographs frightened me and I wondered what they meant and why she was showing them to me now. She said nothing and just sat there on the floor watching me as I turned them over and looked at them again.

"The children," I said. "Who are they?"

"No questions," she said. "Just look."

I looked at the one showing the man and the woman holding hands. I wanted to ask who they were too, but I knew she wouldn't answer me.

The woman was small. Her eyes stared at the camera and out beyond it to something far off in the distance. She wore dark clothes and her long black hair hung loosely over her shoulders and down her waist. The man beside her was tall. He was wearing a pair of short trousers. His chest was bare and his feet were bare. He was looking at the woman and in his right hand he carried a revolver.

I turned to the remaining photographs, but my grandmother stretched out her hand and said "Give them to me now." I gave her the photographs and she held them in her hand for a moment before replacing them in the tin box and returning the box to its place beneath the bed. Then she rose to her feet, crossed the room again and resumed her seat near the window.

I sat close beside her and together we watched the children playing in the street. We heard the sound of the ball as it bounced, backwards and forwards, against the wall of Miss Mac's sweet shop.

Twenty-one

You could feel the air. And if you stood close to Miss Mac's window in Mary Street you could taste the fruit. It was laid out in long wooden trays and there were apples and oranges and pears and bananas and currants and sultanas and you knew it was Christmas. The cold air rose to a mist and if you held your breath and then let it out again in one great gush, it would cover the window and you could write your name on it. Miss Mac wouldn't be pleased and sometimes she'd shout at you – but she tried not to because she knew it was Christmas too and everyone spoke kindly to each other then.

Miss Mac was kindly. She handed out free bags of sweets to the children and then went to Midnight Mass and sang hymns to the Virgin Mary. The Virgin Mary had a baby in her arms. Miss Mac wanted a baby of her own, but my father said no one would marry her because she had consumption and you couldn't have babies when you had consumption. Other people had consumption too, but at Christmas you didn't think about things like that. You played happy. Everyone played happy. The rich spoke to the poor and a star shone in the South Chapel and the poor didn't feel poor anymore because it was Christmas.

It was Christmas in the kitchen. My mother made the Christmas pudding and said you had to be careful with pudding because it was difficult to make and if you didn't do it properly it could explode all over the place and make holes in the ceiling. My mother was careful. She laid a pillowcase on the table and filled it with fruit and a handful of suet and my father added porter. You could smell the porter. And when the pudding boiled black in the cast-iron pot, there was steam everywhere. It penetrated the walls and clung to the rafters and you could feel with the tang on your tongue that now it was Christmas.

You didn't grow at Christmas. You stood perfectly still and your height remained the same and the mist covered time because you wanted everything to stay exactly as it was now and it would always be Christmas. Your father didn't grow either and your mother was young and there were no grey hairs in her head because she'd dyed it with henna. My father dyed his hair too, but would never admit it, though everyone could see because he'd done it with boot polish.

My father drank whiskey at Christmas. He paid twopence for *The Echo* when it only cost a penny because the newsboy deserved a tip and he knew it was Christmas. My father's friend Murty knew it was Christmas too, and my father said he deserved something as well, though he never paid for his drink, but you could forgive that around Christmas.

When my mother saw Murty in the Street, she bought him another drink and Murty was drunk and fell all over the place and swore to God and his Holy Mother that he would never touch whiskey again until next Christmas. Then she went to visit Mrs Barrett, who lived across the street and was sick and bought her a whiskey too because she needed it to kill the germs. Mrs Barrett was old and some people called her a witch, but at Christmas she changed into an angel.

The city was filled with angels. You could see them in Patrick Street and above the altar in the South Chapel and they all had wings and, sometimes, it snowed. You waited for snow and if the snow failed to arrive, you could always buy pretend-snow and sprinkle it on the windows where it glittered and shone and felt cold and then warm and crinkly-toed and blessed with Christmas.

It was Christmas everywhere then. With Maisie Sweeney and me as we sat on the stairs of our tenement house while she read aloud from her book crammed with ghosts and goblins and fairies and things that went scrump in the night. It was Christmas in corners. It lit up the dark and filled you with light and turned on the stars on a giant Christmas tree.

You believed in ghosts, but you weren't afraid of them because they all ran away at Christmas and you knew you were brave until you were foolish enough to ask Maisie why they had chains on their feet and she told you.

Maisie Sweeney knew all about ghosts, and the reason they had chains on their feet was because they'd forgotten to give presents to children like Maisie Sweeney and now they were suffering the torments of the damned. You would remember Maisie Sweeney and make sure to buy her a present for Christmas and sprinkle it with holy water.

When I told my friend Connors about Maisie Sweeney, he said that the only thing she deserved for Christmas was a poisoned apple. He deserved a poisoned apple too, but you couldn't say that because he was your best friend and you never knew what he planned to give you for Christmas. Connors didn't believe in Christmas. He gave his mother a box of chocolates one year and when she opened the box, there was an explosion you could hear all over Cork.

I was wedded to Christmas. I sang in the choir at Christmas. And when we arrived back at the house after Midnight Mass in the South Chapel, there was porter on the table and a chicken from the chicken factory where my mother worked over the season. She stuffed the chicken. She filled it with breadcrumbs and spoonfuls of sausage-meat and drenched it with porter just to give it soul. I wasn't interested in soul. I was drunk on Razza and bottles of Kia-Ora and my stomach was bubbling with excitement from Christmas.

There'd be presents in the morning. They'd be lying at the foot of my bed and packed in my stocking and there was bound to be a train-track and an apple and a penny and a bag full of sweets.

It was warm by the fire. The night cradled me. And when I woke up in the morning, the room was a golden glow and the day that was in it sang Christmas.

Twenty-two

Salty O'Cleary was a small whiskery little man who never married because he saw no sense in courting danger. He didn't live in a house either because the walls stifled him and he couldn't see the stars at night. But every Sunday, after church, Salty would visit our house. He'd give a loud knock on the door, step back three paces, and wait for the door to open.

Inside the house, Salty's signal was clearly understood. My mother would disappear into the kitchen and my father would open the door.

"Come in," he'd say. "You're more than welcome." And Salty would reply – "I was only passing."

Salty was always only passing. He never went anywhere directly and never intended stopping off when he arrived. But he'd come inside anyway, peer anxiously around the room and then head straight for the fireplace. Only then was my mother permitted to leave the kitchen. Salty was safe – his back to the fire – the roaring flames protecting him from women.

"In the old days," Salty declared, "the world was ruled entirely by women and they made an awful mess of it. Things are different now, thank God, but you still have to be careful." And when Salty said that, he made sure to move closer to the fire and throw another sod of turf on it.

In a distant corner of the room, my mother sat and listened. She thought Salty was great. A little cracked in the head maybe, but a grand story-teller. I never knew what to think and laughed – until Salty put the fear of God in me with tales of headless coachman and the great God Mog, who ate children for breakfast and kept their bones in a bag to feed his four mad Alsatian dogs.

My father, as usual, said little. But when the stories became too outrageous he'd take down his tin whistle from its place above the mantelpiece and play a jig or a reel and everyone would dance – except Salty. He moved closer to the fire. There were far too many women about and he wished to God they'd stay at home and keep the door locked.

Presumably, at some stage in his life, Salty must have had a mother, but he never mentioned her. The idol of his life was his father – and when he died, Salty took to the roads. He piled his few meagre belongings onto a handcart, pushed it before him, and swore that he would never live in a house again.

On summer nights Salty slept in the fields, and during the long winter months he slept in a makeshift tent with a hole in the top so that he could see the stars. He slept alone, avoided all contact with women, and if you asked him why, he'd cry – "Disaster!"

Sometimes, Salty would talk of other things besides women – but it didn't last. Like the time he was pushing the handcart along the road and the ground opened up and swallowed him. Salty had often prayed for the ground to open up and swallow him, but he never expected to be taken seriously. When he recovered, he found himself in an open grave. It took him half an hour to climb out and it put years on to him. Salty didn't like graves because you never knew who they'd put on top of you. It could be a woman. When Salty died, he wanted to be buried in a tower with a perpetual fire blazing all round him. Women were afraid of fire. Salty knew that from his father.

When his father was alive, Salty used to ask him about women. He never saw one in the house and when he passed one in the street his father told him to keep his eyes shut. Salty kept his eyes shut and was forever being run over by horses and people riding bicycles along the footpath. His father said women were a screed. You couldn't be up to them. If you looked at them crooked, they'd poison you. And if you looked at them straight, they'd read you and you'd fall over yourself and break a leg.

"Best not to look at all," said his father. "Keep well away from them." And Salty did – and his father nurtured him.

Salty had faith in his father and when his father told him that he had once had the misfortune to marry a woman, Salty asked him what had happened to her. But his father wouldn't tell him – "It would only upset you," he said. And Salty was grateful for that because he really didn't want to know about his mother.

He was happy with his father. They went for walks in the country. They went fishing down the Marina. And, in the evenings, they sat by the fire and his father told him stories.

The stories were about men. Good men. Decent men – and how they were all plagued by the hauntings of women. Salty listened. He didn't know that his father had killed his mother. He didn't know that his mother lay in an unmarked grave in another part of the country. He moved closer to the fire. The shadows lengthened across the room and his father held him.

The last time I saw Salty he was pushing the handcart before him along a country road in West Cork. It was a warm summer's day, but Salty was dressed in a long black heavy overcoat and, for the first time in his life, he was wearing a hat. He looked old and tired. And when I asked him where he was going he said – "Nowhere. I'm only passing." I wished him luck and he moved on. I never saw him again.

Twenty-three

Paul Muni was appearing in *Black Fury* at the Savoy cinema and my mother said he was the greatest actor in the world and *Black Fury* was the best film ever made. It was also the only film she'd seen, so her judgement was crucial. I was determined to see it.

My father, however, had turned against the cinema. He said it was a corrupting influence, invented by Lenin to confuse the people of Cork. When my mother suggested it was time he consulted a doctor, my father went down on his knees and offered up The Rosary for the salvation of her soul. Then he went to Mass.

He went to Mass twice a day now – ever since he saw God in his cups and gave up the drink and turned to religion. He had the house consecrated to the Sacred Heart, he offered up novenas for the conversion of Russia, and on Sundays he played hymns on the tin whistle when he should have been playing jigs and reels. He was also convinced that he'd seen a burning bush in the back yard, but by the time he'd reached it, the bush had disappeared. I was praying that my father would disappear so that I could go to the Savoy cinema and see Paul Muni.

Paul Muni was a star. The Savoy cinema shone with stars. They were built into the ceiling and when the lights were dimmed, the stars twinkled above your head and heaven was only an ice-cream away.

Fred Bridgeman was a star. He played the organ. He sat at the keyboard in full evening dress, and the organ rose from the ground through a fountain of light, and the words of the songs appeared on the screen and we all sang 'Mexicali Rose' and tried to sound like Gene Autry. My father wouldn't appreciate things like that. He was too busy talking to God – though the only films God ever appeared in were diabolical.

On Sunday afternoons, when the neighbours had departed with the music of Mother of Mercy still ringing in their ears, my father retired to bed. My mother went to visit her mother's grave in Douglas and I sat cross-legged on the kitchen floor, dreaming of the stars. On this particular Sunday, I was dreaming of Paul Muni.

Earlier in the day, I did happen to mention to my father that I wanted to go to the pictures to see Mr Muni and he replied, with his usual breathtaking clarity, "I'll give you bloody pictures!" and then retreated to the bedroom. It's at moments like that that you begin to wonder how anyone ever manages to understand the English language. He removed my shoes, too, and planked them under his pillow. "You won't go far without shoes," he said. "Not on a Sunday anyway."

Sunday was important in Cork. On any other day of the week you could walk the streets of the city in your bare feet and no one would notice. Sunday was different. That's because it was God's Day and God had a fetish about shoes. He wanted everyone to wear them. My father said that – and he knew. He was now in direct communication with God and God told him everything.

You could feel sorry for my father. He'd forgotten I was an atheist and didn't give a hang about shoes. My only interest was the cinema. So while my father slept, I opened the front door, and ten minutes later I was standing in the queue outside the Savoy cinema. A few committed Christians stared at my bare feet and a number of others made some disparaging remarks about the effects of the Russian Revolution on the children of Cork – but I stood firm. I was now a dedicated atheist and I did not have to wear shoes on Sunday. I had read that in a book.

I had just about reached the head of the queue when my father appeared waving an ash-plant above his head. Anyone could see he wasn't happy and before I knew where I was he was all over me shouting, "The curse o' God on ye – and that fella Muni, too! I'll anoint the both of ye!" There was no point hanging around listening to that kind of talk, so I ran.

My father chased me across Patrick Street – up Winthrop Street – and I had just managed to reach the Post Office in Oliver Plunkett Street when I ran straight into Mugsy Corrigan. He was from the North Side and was reputed to be a boxer, but he'd never met my father and he hadn't a notion of who I was. When I ran into him, he almost had a stroke.

"Oh!" he cried – raising me three feet in the air by the scruff of the neck – "Oh! And what the hell do you think you're doing, ye thick?"

I was about to offer a perfectly reasonable explanation when my father arrived on the scene.

"Let me at him!" he roared. "Just let me get me two hands on him!"

"Control yourself," said Mugsy. "Control yourself! What's the matter with ye? Sure he's only a child."

"A child? What child? He's me own son, isn't he?"

Mugsy looked at me. "Is that thing your father?" he asked.

May Paul Muni forgive me, but I took one look at the ash-plant and denied everything.

"I don't know who he is," I said. "He's been following me all day."

My father choked. Mugsy turned pale, lowered me gently to the ground and placed a protective arm around my shoulder. He glared at my father.

"You ought to be ashamed of yourself," he said. "An old goat like you, chasing little boys."

That was too much for my father. He removed his jacket, laid it carefully down on the pavement, then tried to split Mugsy over the head with the ash-plant. Mugsy retaliated by punching my father on the jaw, and before you could say trapstick or Nobbling Thomas, a crowd had gathered and Mugsy and my father were battling it out in front of the Post Office.

By the time the police arrived, my father's shirt had been torn to ribbons and some committed Christian had stolen his jacket. He was not amused. And while the crowd were regarding Mugsy as the hero of the day, my father was bundled into a police van and driven off to the Bridewell. I watched from a distance – and then ran all the way home and hid under the bed.

Three days later, my father was released from jail. I developed a severe dose of flu when I heard he was coming home. He arrived wearing a borrowed shirt. My mother made him a cup of tea. She made me a cup of tea. We sat by the table – and the silence was deafening.

Twenty-four

My cousin Beatrice was fish. She never married. And for thirty-one years she sat by her stall in the Coal Quay Market and sold fish. She sold mackerel and herring, pollock and hake, whitefish and crabfish, salmon and skate. My cousin Beatrice slept with fish. And when she woke up in the mornings the scales clung to her.

"Is it any wonder I never married? I belong to fish."

My cousin Beatrice talked of fish. And the room she lived in at the corner of Grattan Street was an ocean of fish. She spoke with fish. She knew them by name and by stream – and when their seasons came and the fish gathered in shoals along the River Lee, she sang with fish.

"Is it any wonder the world envies me? I sing with fish."

My cousin Beatrice dreamed of fish. She knew where they lived – in sunken castles a thousand fathoms deep – and in her dreams she'd visit them. The sharks pleasured her. The whales carried her on their backs and the salmon waltzed with her.

"Is it any wonder the people persecute me? I dance with fish."

But one morning my cousin Beatrice awoke from her dreams and knew that she hated fish. The hate grew on her breast. A dark stream weeping through her skin. She could see it in the mirror. She could smell the stench. She could hear the sea rising through a green mist to cover her.

"Is it any wonder the sea haunts me? I drown in fish."

My cousin Beatrice rose from her stall in the Coal Quay.

Market and renounced fish. She bought perfumes and herbs, ointments and soaps, and a wire brush to scrub herself clean. But the stench remained. She could feel it under her fingernails and on her hands. She could taste it in her mouth and her clothes reeked of it.

She burned her clothes. She removed the bedclothes from the bed and she burned them, too. She opened the window of her room and screamed out at the people in Grattan Street – "People of Cork – I abjure all fish."

My cousin Beatrice grew nightmares of fish. She sat in a courtroom surrounded by fish. The judge was a fish. The prosecuting council was a fish. And the jury, stretched out like sardines in a tin, were all fish.

She was accused of slaughtering fish and selling their bodies for profit on the Coal Quay Market. She pleaded for mercy. She said the fish were already dead when she received them. She said she was only a poor woman struggling hard to make a living. And she asked what was the harm now in selling dead fish?

"But you can't argue with fish," she said. "They stood on their tails and said I'd murdered their fathers and their mothers and the pride of their unborn children. The sweat stood out on me like beads of glass and I woke up screaming."

My cousin Beatrice became fish. The doctors said so and they pointed out how she gulped in the air through her sides and wriggled on the floor when the nightmares were over. They wrapped her in a canvas bag filled with sea-water. They fed her on food fit only for fish. And when she wept, they comforted her.

"Is it any wonder the fish tortured me? I abandoned fish."

My cousin Beatrice was fish. And when her season was over, the sea opened in waves and treasured her remains.

Twenty-five

It was one of those long blue and lazy afternoons in autumn and along the Mardyke the trees were shedding their leaves for the last time in Mr Goldman's life. He knew it would be the last time and he said so without rancour or regret.

"I grow old," he said. "What else is there for me to do but to die gracefully."

"Are you a hundred?" I asked.

"Maybe two," he replied. "And you?"

"I'll be twelve in August."

"You're growing old too," he said. "Soon now, you'll be as old as I am."

We sat on the park bench and watched the leaves falling from the trees. They formed a glittering golden scatter along the pathway and he said:

"You'd never think to look at them now, that they were once green and springing." He shook his head, opened his newspaper carefully and stared at the headlines. I could tell he was old. The grey lines of his time wrinkled his forehead and the brown spots on his hands mirrored his days. He read the small print with a magnifying glass and I could almost hear his bones creak.

"They're dying in Madrid," he said. "It'll be over soon. Have you been to school today?"

"No."

"Mitching again? You should go to school. You might learn something there. I can't teach you everything."

"You've taught me a lot."

"Maybe. But there's always something more."

"Like what?"

"I don't know. But something."

He folded his newspaper with extreme care and raised his head. I could see the tears in his eyes.

"The important thing," he said – and paused. "The important thing now is to know what's happening in the world. The Spaniards know about things like that. Would you like to go to Madrid?"

"Would you?"

"I'm too old. I was even too old when the war started. But I should have tried to go anyway instead of standing at street corners protesting. That's easy."

"You did what you could."

"Maybe. But it's too late now anyway. Franco will be in Madrid in no time at all."

"My father says the war will be over then."

"And what does your mother say?"

"She thinks there'll be an even bigger war later on."

"She's probably right. Let's go for a walk."

He placed the folded newspaper inside his overcoat pocket and held me by the hand. We walked towards the bandstand.

"Sometimes," he said, "they play some wonderful music there. It fills the air. Do you like music?"

"Yes. People come to our house every Sunday and play music all the time."

"Of course. I'd forgotten that. It's a nice custom."

He paused, leaned against the bandstand and said: "You know, when I was in Spain, many years ago, I used to sit in the cafés every night and listen to the Spaniards playing the music of their lives. I don't suppose they're playing a great deal of music now."

"Do you like the Spaniards?"

103

"Very much. They're a remarkable people."

The bandstand was closed. There would be no music that day. Not until the weekend. It was not a holiday. A number of unemployed dockers were lying on the grass, enjoying the afternoon sun, and a group of children were playing rounders close to the Western Road.

"One of these days there'll be an accident there," he said. "It's too close to the road. Do you want to go home now?"

"I think so. I feel sad today, for some reason."

"Me, too. Try and go to school tomorrow. Perhaps I'll see you afterwards. It's a pity about the music."

"Yes."

He turned away and I watched him walking slowly back towards the park bench. When he reached the bench, he sat down again and removed the folded newspaper from his overcoat pocket. He looked at the headlines, studied the small print with the aid of a magnifying glass, and wiped his eyes with a clean handkerchief. He moved on. *Viva La Quince Brigada,* old stock. *Viva La Quince Brigada.*

Twenty-six

Chrissie Watson wasn't bad,
She gave her husband all she had,
But when she saw he wasn't dead,
She cut his throat and went to bed.

Chrissie Watson lived in Blue Boy's Lane and everyone said she was a demon because when her husband died she refused to attend the funeral – and looked ten years younger the following day when she went to collect on his insurance policy.

"The curse of God on them!" said Chrissie. "After forty years of marriage, I deserve ten insurance policies."

Chrissie's son Michael didn't attend the funeral either, but that was because Chrissie locked him in the cupboard and said she'd only let him out if he promised to dance on his father's grave. Michael managed to escape through the back window, but by the time he reached the graveyard the funeral was over and his father was under six feet of clay.

"I tried me best," he told his father. "But you know what she's like."

"I do indeed," replied his father. "May she fall in a ditch."

"Are you comfortable down there?" Michael asked him.

"I am not!" his father moaned. "Did you see the coffin she bought me? She must have got that in a second-hand shop."

"I'm sorry, Da, but she wouldn't spend the money. I'll bring you flowers tomorrow."

"You'll do nothing of the kind! Haven't I enough to contend with without you sticking flowers all over me? Go home to your bed."

"Yes, Da."

"You're a good boy – but you have no bloody sense."

"I know that, Da. But can I come back and talk to you sometimes?"

"You can if you want to. I'll hardly be moving house."

"That's true, Da. Goodnight, so."

"Goodnight! And mind yourself on the way home. That mother of yours may have put a curse on you."

Michael walked sideways from the graveyard and kept his fingers crossed all the way home in case Chrissie had put a curse on him.

When Michael was young, his mother was always putting curses on him. "And when I criticised her one time, she caught hold of me tongue and for weeks afterwards I couldn't speak or pass water." Michael gave up criticising after that and spent most of his years wandering around graveyards and sleeping rough under headstones.

"You'll catch your death of cold out there," said Chrissie. "Are you demented, or what?"

"I like graveyards," Michael replied. "I feel safe out there."

"Safe? You're thirty-eight years of age. Can't you think of something better to do?"

"I talk to me Da."

"And does he answer you?"

"He does, Ma."

Chrissie shook her head. "I always knew there was a knot in your brain. Get into the cupboard."

So Michael entered the cupboard and Chrissie locked the door on him and he sat there in the dark thinking about his father.

One day when Michael arrived home from the graveyard, where he had been sleeping rough beside his father's grave, he found his mother in what he described as her witch's mood. He wasn't sure what he meant by that, but she was very solicitous. She'd baked him a cake. She made him some tea and she hovered about him, tending to his every need, as if he were an invalid and expected to die at any minute. And, true enough, he didn't feel at all well after drinking the tea. His mother, on the other hand, never looked better – but he noticed that only as he was leaving the house.

"You're going now?" she asked.

"I am," replied Michael.

"And may I enquire where you're going."

"You may. I'm going to visit me Da's grave."

"That's a good boy," said Chrissie. "He could do with the company."

Michael left the house and walked slowly towards the cemetery. When he reached his father's grave, he sat on the gravestone and spoke to his father.

"She was very good to me today," he said. "Best ever."

"Oh, yes?" groaned his father. "Kind, was she?"

"Yes, Da. Falling over me with kindness she was."

"That's a bad sign," said his father. "She was kind to me, too. Now look at me."

"Did she poison you, Da?"

"She did that. And then tried to cut the head off me with a knife."

"Maybe it was an accident, Da."

"Accident be damned! I was in mortal agony. How do you feel?"

"Queasy, Da."

"Queasy? I thought as much. The Lord help you. You'll be joining me soon."

Michael rose to his feet and resolved to sleep in the graveyard that night and every night from now on.

It was a week later when the parish priest found Michael lying face down on his father's grave. It has been raining steadily over the past few days and Michael was now suffering from pneumonia. The parish priest called for an ambulance and Michael was removed to the South Infirmary, where he died two days later.

When Chrissie heard the news, she said she was devastated, and on the day of the funeral she retired to bed and refused to leave it. She said she was ill and would never be the same again.

It was my father who attended to the funeral arrangements and it was our next door neighbours who carried Michael's coffin to the grave. He was greeted by his father.

"Didn't I say you were done for?" his father said. "Didn't I warn you?"

"You did, Da. She's done for us both now."

"Move close beside me, like a good boy. We'll haunt her together."

"I'd prefer to do it meself, Da."

"Well, if that's what you want. But do it properly. There's no point in employing half-measures."

On their way home from the graveyard, my father said he saw Michael's ghost coming from the direction of Chrissie's house. His friend Murty was convinced he'd seen it too. If it wasn't him, he said, it was the dead spit of him. My father suggested keeping the news to themselves – for the time being anyway.

When they arrived at Chrissie's house they found the front door open, and entering the kitchen they found Chrissie lying on the floor with her mouth open and a look of horror on her face. They carried her to the bedroom and Murty went to fetch a doctor. Presently, Chrissie opened her eyes.

"Did you see him?" she asked my father.

"Who?"

"Michael. I was lying on the bed and I heard the front door opening below. He called out to me, but by the time I got downstairs he'd gone."

"Did he say anything."

"He said I'd killed him. He said I'd killed his father, too. Me! His own mother. How could I do a thing like that?"

When the doctor arrived, my father left the house and Chrissie fell into a deep sleep from which she never recovered. She was buried between her husband and her son. There were no mourners.

Twenty-seven

A dark-haired woman arrived at our front door one day and offered to read my fortune if I crossed her palm with silver. I didn't have any silver and offered her the top of a lemonade bottle instead. She said I'd die of drowning. Three weeks later I fell into the River Lee near Parnell Bridge and had to be rescued by my friend Connors.

"That's the second time you tried to drown yourself," he said. "This could get monotonous."

Connors didn't know about the fortune-teller – and when I told him he said she was a cloth-head. "And you're worse for believing her. I thought you said you were an atheist?"

"I am."

"Then next time she calls give her a cup of tea and put weed-killer in it. That's what I would have done."

"You would not."

"I would so!"

And you could believe Connors. He had faith in weed-killer and regarded all fortune-tellers as lunatics who ought to be put down.

I wasn't sure about fortune-tellers. And when I asked my mother about them, she said some people were gifted with second sight and you had to accept that – though she herself had never been to visit one and neither had my father. He believed in cats.

If he saw a black cat on the road, he knew it was going to rain. If he saw a white cat at the front door, he was sure there was going to be a war. Sometimes he was right. Sometimes it rained. And, sometimes, the war fell on us here.

On our side of the city there were few cats, but the fortune-tellers prospered, though their predictions were limited. They never forecast the ending of the world or the dawning of a new Ice Age – and they seldom committed themselves to anything beyond the misery of hope. They charged a shilling for that and an extra sixpence for whatever personal future you were desperate to secure.

If you were an unmarried woman – then all you needed was a man. If you were a married woman – all you required was faith and the prospect of a constant job for himself in Dunlops or Fords. The crystal ball would take care of that. The tarot cards would chart the course and the tea leaves would reveal the day and the hour when the postman would arrive with a special letter. When that special letter failed to arrive – well, you could hardly blame the tea leaves for that. Perhaps your faith wasn't strong enough or the light was bad. "Shall we try again, dear?"

And why not? We thrive on hopelessness, and witness in the lifeline of our hand the poverty and ignorance of our times.

Sometimes, of course, the fortune-tellers of Cork aspired to be healers or doctors and, in truth, perhaps they were. Is your asthma bad? Is there consumption in the house? A bereavement in your life or a broken dream? You stand outside the Penny Dinner House in Hanover Street and you count your dreams. You haven't got them anymore. You haven't a shirt to your back or a shawl to wrap round you and the shame consumes you. Can a fortune-teller cure that? She can – and more. She can hold your hand and, like the leper of old, you'll be grateful for a human touch.

And, I suppose, in a way, that's what it's all about. We gaze into our crystal ball and we search for the light.

"Carry it with you, dear. It will see you through. The pain will go." And sometimes it does. But only sometimes.

When I was growing wild in Cork, the city was filled with dreams and poverty abounded. It clung to the walls of tenement houses. It pervaded the streets. It was etched into the bones of children and adults and it conquered the spirit and aspirations of men. We needed our dreams and we cried out to our fortune-tellers – for who else could provide a future at the turn of a card?

There was Toesy Hanlon from Cove Street. She sat in her bare feet and touched the sick, the blind and the maimed with her left foot and they felt better for it. She counselled the poor, provided new dreams and rich futures, read tea leaves for the girls, and saw her own death revealed in the bottom of a cup. She raised her prices after that because she hadn't long to go. But she lived to be a hundred and died rich – and nobody blamed her because that was her way and she had brought them hope.

The Stanley sisters also provided hope. They worked in tandem and never left a client without some light in the darkness.

"The man who loves you is married, dear – but the wife is not well. We'll offer up a novena." And so they did.

But best of all was Nostra Keegan. She sat in a heap in her tent – held fast to her crystal ball – and offered nothing but the truth. She said Fords and Dunlops would soon be no more. She said the quays would lie black, the dole queues would lengthen and there would be a great war which would engulf us all.

"I won't be around to see it, dear, but it's misty in the ball. Have you tried emigrating – or a holiday in Bermuda?"

We tried emigrating. Nostra remained at home – and when she died they carried her to the cemetery in Douglas, still clutching her crystal ball.

"I may not need it up there, dear, but it's as well to be prepared."

Nostra was always prepared and raised her umbrella long before it rained.

I could believe in Nostra. I could believe in all the fortune-tellers and all the clairvoyants and I was born when Pluto was in conjunction with Mars. What more did I need? Connors would have said "Weed-killer." But I wasn't sure about that. For the poverty remained. And darkly darkly sang the tenements of Cork.

Twenty-eight

If you looked closely at the face of the clock, standing on the mantelpiece in our house in Margaret Street, you would see that it was made by Hilser's of Cork. And if you opened the sideboard drawer, set in the kitchen, you would see a small box with a broken hinge. The box belonged to my mother. She treasured the contents – and if you were brave enough to open the box you would discover a dark brown medal bearing the following inscription: *Seachtain Na Casca – 1916*. On the lining of the box, you would see the name of the jeweller who had supplied it – M Roche, 61 Patrick Street, Cork.

Sometimes, on those long Sunday afternoons when my father had retired to bed and my mother had gone to visit her mother's grave in Douglas, I wondered about that box. Where had it come from? Who was the medal presented to and for what service? But when I asked my mother about it she would say, "It's a long time ago. Leave it now." And I would leave it there, locked in a drawer, safe among shadows.

When you are very young, shadows have meaning and their substance fills you. Stretch out your hand and you can feel the flesh. Probe deeper and you touch grieving bone. When you look at the clock, the hands tell you nothing. Only the shadows are real – and a small box with a broken hinge.

When my mother returned from the graveyard that day, her hands were stained with earth and moss and her skirt was damp from kneeling on wet grass.

"I was cleaning the headstone," she said. "I planted some flowers, too. The old ones are dead. It looks better now."

"Does it?"

"Much better. Will you promise me something?"

"If I can."

"When I die – bury me beside my mother."

It's hard to think of your mother being dead. She wears a black shawl, fringed and tasselled and she will live forever. But when you look at her face now, you can see the years and you know that she is not the same woman who suckled you when young. You're still young. You're twelve years of age, but you feel older and the years weigh on you.

There was a time when I didn't feel like that. I sat high on my father's shoulders and he carried me into the English Market and down the Marina and I felt a thousand years young and filled with expectation. When we arrived home, my mother would be there. She'd be baking a cake or washing the clothes or cleaning the house and, sometimes, she'd be painting slogans on the walls. She didn't do that anymore. She went to her mother's grave, laid flowers on the earth, and when she returned home she sat by the fire and counted her beads.

"You're growing up now," she said. "You must learn to take care of yourself. I can't do it anymore."

She shivered with cold, pulled her shawl tightly around her shoulders and let the beads fall silently on to her lap.

"You've let the fire go out," she complained. "You're as bad as your father."

I raked the fire, nursed it with sticks, and covered the flame with a handful of turf. I sat beside her.

"The medal in the drawer," I said. "Why don't you tell me about it? Who does it belong to?" She shook her head, moved closer to the fire and warmed her hands.

Through the bedroom door I could hear my father beginning to wake up.

"You'd better make him some tea," she said. "You know what he's like at this time of the day."

I filled the kettle, settled it carefully on the rising fire, and waited for the water to boil.

When my father entered the room, I made the tea and offered them both a cup. My mother refused, but my father accepted and, with the cup in his hand, he moved over to the window and stood there looking down on to the street. Presently, he said: "In India – I was some champion." He paused for a moment, sipped his tea, and repeated – "Some champion."

My mother ignored him. His photograph stood on the dresser in the kitchen and it was framed in gilt. He wore a British Army uniform and he held a rifle in his hand.

"It's been ages now," he mused, "but the Ganges filled me."

My father was a big man and when he walked up Mary Street and Margaret Street, the neighbourhood children danced in his wake and called him Gianty. He didn't mind about that. He was proud of his figure, proud of his past, and felt the name suited him.

"Six-foot-four," he said, "and no stooper."

My mother stared into the fire and continued to ignore him.

In the bedroom, where they both slept on a large double bed that shaped the room, there were two photographs – one of James Connolly and another of Padraig Pearse.

"They were both shot," my mother said. "Murdered by the British. I want you to remember that." I promised to remember it.

"In India," my father said, "the natives burned their dead."

116

His photograph stood on the dresser in the kitchen and the rifle bore the legend – Lee Enfield. Point 303. Standard issue.

He turned from the window and looked at my mother. "The Ganges," he said, "is a holy river. I washed my face in it."

"So you did," said my mother. And rose from her seat beside the fire. She entered the bedroom and the door closed firmly behind her.

"I was some champion!" my father said. "Some champion. Remember that, too."

I lit the lamp. The room was silent. I was twelve years old and the world was ending.

Twenty-nine

On an evening shortly after my mother's death, my father knelt on the floor of the bedroom they had shared throughout their married life and prayed for her soul. Her photograph stood on the table beside the bed. Her shoes, recently polished, lay under the bed, and her black shawl still hung from a nail behind the bedroom door.

When my father had finished praying for my mother, he rose to his feet and stood for a moment looking down at the white mourning-sheet now stretched across the bed. He had made the bed. He had swept the floor and moved all his personal belongings into a small room at the rear of the house. Nothing more remained to be done. My mother was dead. My father left the room, locked the door securely behind him and never entered the bedroom again.

Six months later, my father moved his belongings from the room at the rear of the house into the kitchen. He locked the back door, slept near the kitchen fire and, like his mother before him, refused to leave the house.

"It will see me out," he said. "We were married here. She died here. It will see me out."

He sat by the fire, close to the bed, his personal belongings scattered about him.

"She left the rosary beads to you," he continued. "I don't know why. Sure, you don't believe in anything."

"I'd still like to have them," I said.

"They're hanging on the wall. You can have that tin whistle, too. I don't play it anymore."

"I'm sorry to hear that."

"Nothing to be sorry about. Everything goes in the end."

He reached up and removed the tin whistle from its place above the mantelpiece. It was covered in dust.

"I haven't cleaned it. I haven't cleaned anything in here. Mrs Barrett comes in sometimes, but you know what she's like."

He handed me the tin whistle and moved closer to the fire. On the dresser beside him, his photograph, framed in gilt, was also covered in dust.

"You can have it, if you want to," he said. "There's nothing else I can give you."

His image smiled through the dust on the photograph, and in his British Army uniform, he looked brave and soldierly.

"India blest me," he said. "Did I tell you that? Reached down to my soul and blest me. Your mother didn't understand that."

"She married you."

"We married each other," he said and lapsed into silence.

Presently, he rose to his feet and moved over to the sideboard. He opened the drawer and removed a small box with a broken hinge. He raised the lid and stared down at the medal resting inside.

"You'd better have that, too," he said. "It belonged to her brother."

"I didn't know she had a brother," I said. "What happened to him?"

My father looked at me for a moment and handed me the box. "He died in jail," he said. "What else would you expect?"

He turned away, moved over to the bed and sat on the edge of it. I read the inscription on the medal: *Seachtain Na Casca – 1916.* "Politics," he said. "Politics and remembrance. They bleed us dry."

"You had the two days," I said.

"Yes. We had the two days. And I'm grateful for that. Maybe we'll have two more in the next world. I pray we do. But you don't believe in things like that, do you?"

"I'll hang on to the medal," I said.

"And the other things? The photograph, the rosary beads and my tin whistle?"

"Those, too."

"You're odd," he said. "I said that on the day you were born. You haven't changed. Your mother was the same. Odd as bedamned – and a champion of lost causes."

"You were some champion yourself," I said.

"Yes, wasn't I? Some champion. And I washed my face in the Ganges. Not many can say that."

"Not many."

He lowered his head, covered his face with his hands and remained there for a little while, waiting for the dark.

Postscript

Once upon a time, in the city of Cork, a famous battle took place. It became known as 'The Wonderful Battle of the Starlings'. On a bright day, a very bright day with the sun dancing in the sky, the starlings gathered over the city and fought each other for possession of the people of Cork. The battle lasted three days and three nights, and when it was over the streets of the city were covered with the dead bodies of millions of starlings.

Then, mysterious fires broke out. The wooden houses of the Marsh caught fire and the city of Cork was burned to the ground. But the people of Cork rebuilt their city – a capital city which now stands on the banks of the River Lee. Here I was born to evening music and the sound of traffic moving through the streets.

Song for a Raggy Boy
A Cork Boyhood

To my children

*My voice is a
stone child in a
dark reformatory*

Raggy Boys

Raggy boys are tall and thin
Raggy boys are small and fat
Raggy boys are not like us
We're class.

Raggy boys are born in sin
Raggy boys wear raggy clothes
Raggy boys smell
And that's that.

Raggy boys don't go to Mass
Raggy boys are thick in school
Raggy boys should be slapped
And then strapped.

Raggy boys stay out all night
Raggy boys lead you astray
Raggy boys curse
And much worse.

Raggy boys will cut your throat
Raggy boys will blind your eyes
Raggy boys don't bleed
They breed.

Raggy boys are black of heart
Raggy boys wind up in jail
Raggy boys don't mind
They eat their kind.

Prologue

The handcuffs were large. My hands were small. And the policeman sitting beside me in the second-class railway carriage was stained and jowling. His chin was blue, his fingers dark from nicotine, and the ash from endless cigarettes lay scattered over his waistcoat and coloured the knees of his baggy trousers.

Sergeant O'Donnell was fat and when he sighed deeply, as he did from time to time, his mouth opened, his waistcoat expanded and his neck bulged under the stiff collar of his faded blue shirt.

"Mazawatte tea," he said. "I should drink more of that." And I hoped that he would and maybe choke or have a stroke. But I said nothing and stared out of the window at the newsboy selling the *Cork Examiner* on the station platform and the porter loading baggage on the train.

Sergeant O'Donnell sighed again and with his right hand reached into his pocket for another cigarette. He placed the cigarette in his mouth and was about to use his left hand to reach for a box of matches when he realised that we were both handcuffed together.

"I suppose you could slip out of those without any bother," he said. "Could you?"

I could, but I didn't want to disillusion him. Sergeant O'Donnell had faith in handcuffs. He had faith in keys. They hung from a chain in his waistcoat pocket and he caressed them like a saint fingering a relic.

"The handcuffs are classic," he said. "I had them

specially made. But they're not meant for children. I'll take them off when the train starts."

He fingered the keys, chewed on his cigarette and looked down at the handcuffs.

"If I removed them now, would you make a bolt for it?" he asked, but I refused to answer him and continued to stare out of the window. Sergeant O'Donnell shook his head. The cigarette fell from his mouth and landed on the floor. He stooped to pick it up and pulled me forward.

"Sorry about that," he said, "but it's your own fault." He leaned back in his seat, returned the cigarette to his pocket and closed his eyes.

"I hate this journey," he said. "Do you know that? Always did. Especially with children."

We sat in silence. The newsboy was still selling the *Cork Examiner* on the station platform and the porter was still loading baggage on to the train.

It began to rain, and at the far end of the platform an elderly nun raised her umbrella and hurried towards the train. When she reached the carriage we were sitting in, she opened the door, lowered her umbrella and stepped inside.

"It's not reserved, is it?" she asked. And Sergeant O'Donnell opened his eyes and studied her.

"No," he replied. "It's perfectly all right. You can sit over there."

"Thank you. You're very kind."

"Not at all, Sister. There's plenty of room."

The elderly nun placed her umbrella on the rack above her head and closed the carriage door.

"Dreadful weather," she said – and sat near the window. "If it's not cold, it's wet. I almost missed the train."

"Are you going far?"

"Not too far," she answered. "But I dislike being late – and everything is so slow nowadays."

Sergeant O'Donnell nodded his head. "It's the European situation," he said. "There'll be a war soon. You can be sure of that."

The elderly nun looked puzzled. "A war? Do you really think so? But surely it won't affect us?"

"It's affecting us already, Sister. You can hardly buy coal now for love or money. And this train is running on turf."

"I didn't know that," she said. "I'm a little out of touch. But I remember the last war. And Spain, of course."

She lowered her head, kissed the crucifix she was wearing round her neck and then crossed herself.

"Poor Spain. Sometimes I despair. Isn't that dreadful?"

Sergeant O'Donnell didn't reply – and the elderly nun looked away and then turned towards me.

"Would you like a sweet?" she asked. "I've got some here."

Sergeant O'Donnell grunted. "There's no point talking to him, Sister. He's like a dummy."

"You can speak to me surely," she said – and held out her hand. "How old are you?"

"He's thirteen," muttered the Sergeant. "And no saint, I can tell you that."

The elderly nun reached into the pocket of her habit and produced a bag of sweets. "Have one of these," she said. "They're home-made."

Sergeant O'Donnell tugged at my wrist and almost pulled the handcuffs over my fingers.

"You could at least say thank you," he growled. "She's only offering you a sweet."

My wrist hurt, but I stretched out my hand for the sweet she was offering and, for the first time, the elderly nun could see that the Sergeant and I were handcuffed together. She looked embarrassed. She coughed. The bag of sweets fell from her hand and lay scattered over her lap.

"I'm sorry," she said between coughs. "I'm so sorry. That was clumsy of me."

She picked up the sweets, returned them to the bag, and then handed them to me.

"Say thank you," ordered Sergeant O'Donnell – "before I brain you."

The elderly nun stared at me for a moment and then moved closer to the window. She looked at the sky and at the rain falling heavily on the station platform. The porter had disappeared. The newsboy was sheltering in the doorway of the Station Master's Office – and the newspapers under his arm were damp and staining.

I felt the train begin to move. It pulled slowly out of Glanmire Railway Station, entered the mile-long darkening tunnel out of Cork and headed north.

*

"You're growing up now," my mother said. "You must learn to take care of yourself. I can't do it any more." Her voice haunted me. Her grave, neglected in Douglas, still disfigures me. I remember her eyes, the gentle touch of her hands. I remember her face – and her black shawl hanging from a nail in the bedroom door. I made so many promises and never kept one of them.

One

Late upon a June evening, William Franklin stood at the doorway of Saint Jude's Reformatory School for boys of a certain disposition and pulled hard at the well-oiled bell wire stapled to the wall. From a long way off he heard the bell ringing somewhere within the building. He pulled on the bell wire again and waited for the door to open.

Franklin was thirty-five. He had spent three years in Spain, fighting on the side of the Republican forces, and when he returned to Ireland he found that there was little welcome for those who had fought on the losing side.

A teacher by profession, he had applied for many jobs but had always been turned down for reasons which, though never stated in writing, were clearly understood. When he applied for the post of teacher at Saint Jude's, he expected a similar response and was surprised to be offered the post without even having to attend an interview.

Now he was here. He had walked two miles from the nearest railway station and, though he had enjoyed the walk, in spite of the weight of the suitcase he was carrying, he was now tired and in no mood to be kept waiting at the front door. He was about to pull the bell wire again when he heard footsteps echoing along the corridor and, presently, a key being inserted in the lock and then the door opened. He was greeted by Brother Tom.

"Yes? What is it? I can't be everywhere at once you know."

"I'm sorry," Franklin said – and wondered why he was

apologising. He could smell the whiskey on Brother Tom's breath and the smell irritated him.

"Franklin?"

"That's right."

"We expected you earlier. Come in. I'm Brother Tom."

"The Prefect?"

"No. Brother John is the Prefect. I help."

"Well, perhaps you could help me with this suitcase then."

"Of course."

Brother Tom struggled with the suitcase and Franklin followed him into the hallway.

"Can you manage?"

"I can manage very well," said Brother Tom as the handle of the suitcase slipped from his hand and the suitcase dropped to the floor.

"Oh, dear! You'll have to carry that yourself. It's too heavy."

He closed the door, fumbled for a moment with the key, and when Franklin tried to help him, he muttered something about an insane world, and what could you do about it anyway and it was no fault of the young. Franklin had no idea what he was talking about and waited for him to turn the key in the lock.

"You were saying?"

"I wasn't," Franklin replied. "But if you're finished fiddling with the lock, perhaps you could direct me to the Superior's Office."

"Oh, yes. Father Damian's Office. He's at Benediction now. You'll have to wait until the morning before you can see him. Would you like something to eat?"

"No, thanks."

"I'll take you to your room so."

Franklin picked up the suitcase from the floor and followed Brother Tom slowly along the corridor.

Brother Tom was old. The grey hairs on his head were scarce and falling. His flesh was old – and when he walked he could feel his bones protesting and his heart weeping for a rest. But most of all his shoes were old and Brother Tom resented that – because shoes gave a man dignity, especially when new and highly polished. The shoes he was wearing now were polished almost out of existence. The heels were worn down, the leather stretched beyond endurance, and no matter how often he had applied to the Prefect for a new pair, there were always some excuse – like funds are low or the oven in the Bakery had to be repaired again or maybe he was too old and shouldn't be walking around in highly polished new shoes anyway because he might fall and break his neck. Brother Tom would have been delighted to break his neck, if only he could have had the dignity and comfort of a new pair of shoes before he died.

But you couldn't explain that to Brother John. Like you couldn't explain why the world tormented you and why your only faith now was in the young who might see God as he had once seen Him, casting a gentle light upon the world. John had no time for the young. He did not believe in being gentle. He believed in a strong hand and an avenging spirit and maybe that's why he was Prefect and wore patent-leather shoes that shone brightly and never seemed to wear out. Brother Tom envied him the shoes and, sometimes, his age – but nothing else.

He thought about Franklin's shoes. It was the first thing he noticed when Franklin entered the hall. They were badly worn and he was about to say something to Franklin about the need to take care of them, but he forgot because he'd had a few drinks and too many things to do and he could see that Franklin was irritated. People were always being irritated. The world was irritating. There was no light and his feet hurt.

He heard Franklin walking behind him. He tried to hurry along the corridor but he was afraid of falling because he knew that Franklin would think he was drunk. But he wasn't. He'd had one or two, or maybe three, and that made him forget things but he could still walk, and run if need be, if Brother John would provide him with a decent pair of shoes.

He was getting tired of Brother John. He was getting tired of all the excuses people made for doing nothing, and when they did do something, invariably getting it wrong. Maybe Franklin would get things right. At least he was new and he wasn't a Brother in Christ.

When they reached the end of the corridor, Brother Tom opened the back door and beckoned Franklin to follow him across the yard. They passed by the school chapel and Franklin could hear the voices of the school choir singing at Benediction. Brother Tom entered the Old Prison, a large Victorian building once used to house political prisoners.

"It doesn't look very nice," said Brother Tom, "but you'll find it quite comfortable."

They climbed the stairs and in a narrow cell, recently prepared by Brother Tom, Franklin was presented with his room. There was a bed, a bookcase, a bedside table with a lamp and a wash-hand basin in the corner.

Brother Tom pointed to the wall. "You'll find the lavatory in the cell next door. Will that be all right?"

Franklin placed his suitcase on the bed and sat beside it. "It'll have to be," he replied without humour. "What part of the building is this?"

"The old cell block. It used to be a prison in the old days, but it's hardly used at all now."

"Except for lay teachers?"

"I tried to make it as cheery as possible, Mr Franklin."

"I'm sure you did."

"Will there be anything else?"

"No, thanks."

Looking a little disappointed, Brother Tom was about to leave when Franklin said: "I'm sorry. I'm a little tired."

"Of course. I quite understand. You must be exhausted after your journey. Did you walk from the station?"

"Yes. I enjoy walking."

"So do I. But not when I have to carry a suitcase. You should have telephoned for a car. Brother John would have collected you."

"Maybe next time."

"I hope there won't be a next time, Mr Franklin. Goodnight."

He moved towards the door and looked back at Franklin, who was sitting awkwardly on the edge of the bed.

"Do you think you'll be happy here, Mr Franklin?"

Franklin smiled and gestured toward the room. "I have no idea," he said. "Why do you ask?"

"Well, you're the first lay teacher we've had here. We could do with a change."

"From what?"

"From many things. We're all brothers here – except for the Father Superior, of course. We've been here a long time."

"I see. Is that why you drink?"

"I am not drunk, Mr Franklin. Just old. It's one of the penalties of being born."

"I can think of a great many more," Franklin said – and Brother Tom stared at him.

"Do you believe in God?"

"Not very often."

Brother Tom nodded his head. "It's not easy. I grant you that. But we must try. Sleep well."

"And you, Brother Tom."

Brother Tom left the room and as Franklin listened to

him moving slowly down the stairs he wondered what he'd let himself in for.

He rose from the bed, opened his suitcase and looked around for somewhere to hang his clothes. No wardrobe. He opened the door, stepped out into the landing and entered the cell next door. He relieved himself in the lavatory, washed his hands under the tap and returned to his room. He stood near the window. He could see the Recreation Square from there, a low wall dividing it in the centre, and he could see the light shining in the chapel. The singing had stopped and Franklin stood there for a long time staring at the light.

*

"There's a valley in Spain called Jarama
It's a place that we all know so well
It was there that we gave of our manhood
And most of our young lives as well ..."
Do you remember the songs? The slogans you painted on the wall? The music in the room on those long summer afternoons. I remember your voice. The ghosts of corn and timber sails. You are far away and I am closing the door upon a silent room.

136

Two

Inside the chapel the boys had settled in their seats and Father Damian stood in the pulpit and smiled down at them. He'd had a hard day, but it was over now and all that remained for him was to speak to the boys before they retired to their beds and then retreat to his office and have a quiet drink with Brother Tom before meeting the new boy and, possibly, Mr Franklin.

He didn't know about Franklin. There had been many applicants for the post of lay-teacher at Saint Jude's – the usual scattering of ex-seminarians, disguised prison officers, Army leftovers and Pioneer-raging fanatics who were more interested in creating a nation free of alcohol than in taking care of its children. Father Damian had seen enough of those. They haunted his days and made him long for the Mission Fields where he had spent four years sharing the Gospel and finding God.

Franklin, he hoped, would be different. He had never met the man, but he had heard good reports about him from those who had known him as a teacher before he resigned and went to Spain. True, he had fought on the Republican side in that lamentable conflict, but that was his own business. Father Damian wasn't interested in politics. He wanted a dedicated teacher, a man who had seen something of the world and was not intimidated by the prevailing winds. He chose Franklin.

There were objections, of course. He expected that. The local parish priest reminded him of the atrocities committed

137

by the Republicans in Spain – and the Bishop informed him that anyone who fought against General Franco could not possibly be a fit person to teach in a Catholic school – even if it was a reformatory.

The Bishop had a signed portrait of General Franco hanging on the wall above his desk and Father Damian had a tough time avoiding his disapproving gaze, too. But he finally managed to persuade the Bishop, by agreeing to accept full responsibility for Mr Franklin's appointment and promising to provide a weekly report, in writing, on "… this person's good behaviour – if any."

There was only one other obstacle to be overcome and that was the Prefect. He had deliberately avoided telling Brother John about Mr Franklin's background, and he prayed that Franklin would have the good sense not to mention it. But Brother John was bound to find out sometime and then, as Brother Tom would say, life could prove a little difficult.

It was difficult enough now, in all conscience, but Father Damian continued to smile, because that's what he always did when standing in the pulpit before the assembled congregation.

He smiled at the boys. He smiled at Brother Tom who had just entered the chapel, late as usual, and he smiled at Brother John who was never late and stood at the sacristy door, hands in his pockets, and hanging from his wrist the leather strap with two coins embedded near the end. Brother John said the coins were for decoration, but Father Damian suspected otherwise and knew that one day he would have to confront that problem too.

And then there was Brother Mac, huddled in a corner beside the statue of Saint Augustine, and suffering the torments of the damned for all those imaginary sins he had committed. What was he to do about him?

Father Damian lowered his head, blessed the congregation with an easy hand, and dreamed about the Mission Fields.

"My dear boys, this evening I would like to speak to you about The Little Flower. Now – who was The Little Flower? It may seem a strange question to ask. For who, in all creation, has not heard of this most appealing of saints? Even the primitive tribes of Africa have heard of her.

"As many of you know, I was once a missionary in that dark continent. And, one day walking through the jungle, I was confronted by an apparition from the darkness. I was about to flee for my life when I heard a voice cry out – 'Flee not, O White Father – for I too have heard of The Little Flower.' I turned, amazed to find that the apparition I had feared was nothing more than a simple African native.

"I asked him how he had come across the story. And he told me – in his own language, of course – that he had heard it from an Irish missionary, the first white man to have set foot in that part of Africa. He asked me to repeat the story. So, there and then, in a jungle clearing miles from civilisation, I sat down and related the story of The Little Flower.

"I told him of her life and of her death – and of that great moment when God, who so loved this child, sent down from Heaven a shower of roses. And when I had finished, this simple native rose to his feet and cried – 'My God! My God! I am so grateful to the Christian churches for having brought me this most remarkable of stories.'

"Of course, these were not his exact words. But the meaning was clear. This man had been so moved by the story of a loving child that his whole being was possessed with the spirit of enlightenment. And it is this spirit of enlightenment which I should like to pass on to you thisevening. Jesus loves the simple soul – the obedient servant. So let us be obedient in all things and humble of heart. So that God, in his mercy, may send us too a shower of roses at the moment of our death."

Father Damian crossed himself and hurried from the pulpit before the boys had risen to their feet – to be marched off to the dormitory.

*

My friend Connors knew all about reformatory schools. "When you walk in there," he said, "they take all your clothes away – and they give you a grey uniform – and then you have to pray. That's all they know about, praying and beating the knackers out of people. I knew a fella once who died in a place like that. He had pleurisy, but they said he was just shamming and they sent him out cutting turf in all kinds of weather. At the funeral they prayed. They had all the boys standing round the coffin and the priest went on about how your man had now been forgiven for his sins and was safe in the arms of God. My old man was right. They should blow up places like that and stuff the Brothers down a boghole."

Three

When Brother Tom arrived in the Superior's office, he found Father Damian sitting at his desk, sipping a drink which he had just poured himself. The bottle stood on the desk and there was an extra glass. Father Damian motioned towards the bottle.

"Help yourself, Brother Tom. I'm sure you could do with it."

"I've had one or two already, Father."

"I can see that. I don't know why I bother to hide it myself all the time. Go ahead."

Brother Tom filled his glass and then sat in the well-cushioned armchair close to the fire. Father Damian sat at his desk.

"It's one of the few moments in the day I look forward to," he said – and sipped his drink. Brother Tom nodded his head – and both men sat in silence for a moment staring into the fire.

"Has the new teacher arrived yet?"

"Yes, Father. He was a little late – and I didn't think you'd want to see him after Benediction, so I took him straight to his room."

"What's he like."

Brother Tom paused. "His shoes could do with a polish," he said. "And I don't think he liked his room very much."

"Tetchy?"

"I think that's the word."

"That's a great help! I hope I've made the right choice here, Brother Tom."

"You usually do, Father."

"Not lately. Remember that Brother Regan from Limerick? I put him in charge of the Bakery and he turns out to be a raving lunatic. Every loaf of bread in the shape of a cross. And at Christmas his special Babe in the Manger cake. I thought I'd never recover from that."

"He wasn't your choice, Father. The Bishop appointed him."

"Maybe so. But what I should have done was to lock him in a cupboard somewhere, not put him in charge of the Bakery."

He reached for the bottle, filled his glass again, then offered the bottle to Brother Tom.

Brother Tom hesitated. He wasn't sure if he wanted another drink as the heat from the fire was beginning to make him feel drowsy. He covered his glass with his hand and shook his head.

"I don't think I should, Father. I'm not as young as I used to be."

"You've got a long way to go yet," Father Damian admonished, "but I won't press you."

Brother Tom looked relieved. He was happy sitting there. He'd had enough to drink today and he didn't want to spoil it by getting drunk and falling asleep. Not that Father Damian would mind. He knew that, but there were others who would mind if they happened to walk in and find him stretched out on the chair.

He was fond of this chair. He was fond of Father Damian. The room was aglow and the flames from the fire played shadows on the wall and he could stretch out his legs and warm his feet and forget about his shoes. What did he want with shoes anyway? He could remember a time when he ran around in his bare feet and nobody bothered him and he felt all the better for it. But that was a long time ago. Things were different now. Shoes were important. Shiny shoes were even more important. He must speak to Father Damian about that. But not tonight. He would do it tomorrow when his feet hurt and his shoes damned him again.

Father Damian looked at Brother Tom, and was suddenly conscious of his age. Brother Tom was a very old man. Father Damian had never thought of it before. Or maybe he just didn't want to think about it. He depended on Brother Tom whom he felt was the only member of the staff possessed of a titter of common sense. He would have liked to have seen him made Prefect, and had in fact gone out of his way to try to arrange it, but the Bishop had said he was too lax, drank too much and was not suited. Now he was too old. Brother John was in charge. And Brother Tom drank even more and, sometimes, fell asleep in his chair.

Father Damian wondered if he was asleep now. The empty glass was still in his hand and he sat perilously close to the fire. His eyes were closed.

"Are you all right, Brother Tom?"

Brother Tom opened his eyes. "I'm fine, Father. Just warming the bones, that's all. But I'd like to go to bed now, if you don't mind."

Father Damian helped him to his feet. "Of course. It's very selfish of me to keep you up so late. You should have been in bed ages ago."

"Not really, Father. The old don't need that much sleep. An hour or so will do me."

"I'll see you to your room."

"I'd rather you didn't. But if you'll point me in the right direction …"

143

Father Damian opened the door and directed Brother
Tom to his room at the far end of the corridor. He walked
slowly, his hand pressed against the wall for guidance, and
Father Damian watched his figure until he disappeared out
of sight and the room door closed behind him.

Father Damian returned to his office. He sat by his desk
and poured himself another drink. He would have liked to
have retired to bed himself, but there was still the new boy
to see when he arrived from Cork, and God knows when
that would be. The boy would be tired. He would probably
have to be fed – and so would Sergeant O'Donnell. Brother
Tom usually took care of things like that, but there was no
point disturbing him now. He would sleep till dawn. He
looked at his watch. The door opened and Brother Mac
walked in.

"Ever thought of knocking, Brother Mac?"

Brother Mac looked at the glass in Father Damian's hand
and at the near empty bottle standing on the desk.

"I'm extremely sorry to interrupt your … meditations,"
he said, with obvious disdain, "but the matter is of some
importance."

"Yes?"

"I wish to protest."

Father Damian swallowed his drink and poured himself
another. He felt he was going to need it.

"Go ahead, Brother Mac. What is it now?"

"You know very well what it is, Superior. You deliberately sent Brother Tom to spy on me."

"Did I?"

"I saw him! I was kneeling there in my room and he was
skulking at the window."

Father Damian put his hand to his head as the weight of
the world descended upon him.

"You're letting your imagination run away with you," he

said wearily. "Brother Tom was nowhere near your room."

"Are you suggesting that I am making this up?"

"I'm not suggesting anything at all, Brother Mac. Sit down."

"I prefer to stand."

"Sit down!"

Brother Mac sat in the chair and folded his arms defensively across his chest. Father Damian looked at him.

"What were you doing in your room, Brother Mac?"

Brother Mac turned his head away. "Penance," he mumbled. "I was doing penance."

"For what?"

Brother Mac didn't answer. Father Damian rose from his chair and moved over to the fire.

"Do you know what year this is, Brother Mac? It is 1939. We are not living in the Middle Ages."

"I am aware of that."

"Then why go on punishing yourself in this degrading manner? I have instructed you before. I will not do so again. You will not scourge your body."

"Is that an order, Superior?"

"It is more than that, Brother Mac. I am placing you under a vow of obedience. Is that understood?"

"Perfectly. But I will write to the Bishop."

"You will write to no one! I am the Superior here, and you will do exactly as I say."

"Have you any further instructions – Superior?"

"Not for the moment. But now that you are here, I would like some information. During your tour of duty in the Square today, there was an accident involving the boy Davitt. What happened?"

Brother Mac paused. "I have no wish to discuss the matter."

"I have. What happened?"

"An obscenity."

"The boy said that you struck him violently across the head when he asked your permission to go to the lavatory."

"There was another boy already in that – establishment."

"And you attacked Davitt because of that?"

"I will not allow two boys to enter that … building … at the same time."

Father Damian shook his head. "I don't know what we're going to do with you, Brother Mac. There are over two hundred boys in this reformatory – and if we have to provide a separate lavatory for every one of them, we shall require half the country to accommodate us."

"You have no conception."

"Maybe so. But as from this moment I am relieving you of your duties in the Recreation Square. You will take charge of the Carpenter's Shop. And I doubt that even you will be able to detect a sin of impurity in a block of wood."

"Will that be all, Superior?"

"Yes, Brother Mac. You may go."

Brother Mac rose from his seat and looked directly at Father Damian.

"You have no conception," he repeated. "None whatever."

He lowered his eyes and swept out into the darkness.

*

It was twilight, and my father lit the lamp in our tenement flat in Margaret Street, where we moved closed to the fire.

"Let me tell you about names," he said. "You have a good one. It's the same as my own. Don't make a mock of it."

I promised I wouldn't.

"In my day, people were proud of their name – and they would only give it to you if they thought you were as good as themselves, or they could trust you in some way. Names were

important to people. There was a fella in Cork one time who lost his name. He went raving mad and spent the rest of his life wandering up and down Patrick Street looking for it.

"'Has anyone seen me name?' he'd ask. 'Surely to God, someone must have seen it?' But nobody had and nobody could remember what it sounded like, or if he ever had one in the first place. But he had one all right – and it must have been a good one from the look of him. He's dead now. Buried in East Cork somewhere and there's nothing on his grave but a number."

"Is that true?"

"As true as we're sitting here," my father replied – at which my mother almost fell into the fire. She kept her own name when she married my father and I understood now why she did.

Four

"Name?"

Brother John stood at the top of the Recreation Square with his hands deep in his pockets and looked over my head. It was my first morning at Saint Jude's School and it would last a lifetime.

We had arrived at Saint Jude's at eleven thirty the previous evening. The building was dark, except for a single lamp that shone brightly in the window of the Superior's Office. The Superior said we were late and Sergeant O'Donnell blamed the European situation.

The taxi that had brought us from the local railway station was still standing at the door. Sergeant O'Donnell asked the driver to wait and the driver said he would, but it was double fare after midnight. Sergeant O'Donnell told him to watch his step and we both entered the Superior's office.

Inside the Superior's Office, Sergeant O'Donnell removed the handcuffs from my wrist and asked the Superior to sign for the body. The Superior signed a copy of the committal form and then asked if we were hungry. Sergeant O'Donnell said we were not. We had already eaten on the train and he was now in a hurry to reach his hotel.

The Superior nodded his head. He was familiar with the routine. Sergeant O'Donnell would stay at the local hotel. He would be supplied with free drink after hours and he would leave in the morning without being asked to pay his bill.

He shook hands with the Superior. He patted me on the head. He said he was dying to get back to Cork – and the Superior escorted him to the front door.

I watched from the window as he entered the taxi, the handcuffs still in his hand – and the keys, hanging from his waistcoat pocket, now shining brighter than ever. The Superior waved him off and then returned to his Office.

"I'll bet you're glad to be rid of him," he said. "He's a terrible man, but you mustn't blame him. He's only doing his duty."

The Superior was being dutiful too. He walked me to the dormitory. He said I wasn't to worry because there were lots of boys in Saint Jude's like me and I would meet them all in the morning. He said I must be tired and he helped me to undress. He said *Now I lay me down to sleep*. He said I must pray to Saint Jude and he covered me with a blanket. I had never heard of Saint Jude and I slept until the bell rang.

It was seven o'clock. I woke up, dressed myself, and stood to attention at the foot of the bed. I was imitating the other boys. The bell rang again and we made our beds. I looked at the other boys. No one looked at me. They were standing to attention again, staring at the wall.

It was a morning like any other morning after the bell rang in Saint Jude's.

Brother Mac stood at the door. He shouted "Fall In!" and we moved into line. He cried "Quick march!" and we marched into the wash-house. He clapped his hands and we washed our faces. He clapped them again and we scrubbed our fingernails. Then he inspected us.

He said cleanliness was next to Godliness. He said young boys were disgusting objects. He said the world was on fire with obscenity and sin. And then he clapped his hands again and we all marched to the refectory.

The refectory was long and narrow. We sat eight to a table and thanked God for what we were about to receive. We ate porridge in silence and bread in silence and one boy poured tea silently into our cups. We thanked God we were able to drink it. We thanked God when we'd finished it. We thanked God when we stood up and thanked Him again because we had the strength to stand up and had not been stricken by some fearful disease like some boys had because of the impurity of their thoughts and the abomination of their desires.

I could see God painted in bright colours on the ceiling of the refectory. I could see Saint Patrick painted in green. He had a crozier in his hand and he was driving the snakes out of Ireland.

Brother Mac shouted "Fall in!" and we all fell into line. He cried "Quick march!" and we marched.

It was a morning like any other morning after the bell rang in Saint Jude's.

On our way to the Recreation Square, Brother Mac pulled me aside and told me to wait near the Superior's Office until Brother Tom arrived with the roll book under his arm.

"I should have done this last night," Brother Tom said. "But I was asleep when you arrived. Did Father Damian take care of you? I'm sure he did. What's your name? It's only for the register, you know. I'm not going to steal it."

I didn't care if he was going to steal it. I wasn't going to give it to him.

"Ah well, it doesn't matter. I can get it from your committal form. Come on inside."

He opened the door and I followed him into the Superior's Office. He placed the roll book on the desk and searched through the in-tray for the committal form.

"I see from your papers that you're a bit of a demon. You'll have plenty of company in here. The place is full of demons. We'll have to find you a trade of some sort. How about the Metal Workshop? That might be useful later on if you wanted to open a safe. No? Well, there's the Carpenter's Shop. How about that? Jesus was a carpenter, you know."

I did know – and look what happened to him.

"The only other thing I can suggest is the Laundry, but that's not very exciting, washing clothes all the time. Personally, I'd go for the Metal Workshop, but it's up to yourself. You don't have to decide now."

He opened the roll book and entered my name. He placed a number beside it and wrote – "Three years". He closed the book and held my hand as we left the Superior's Office and walked towards the Recreation Square.

At the entrance to the Square, Brother John was on duty. He was lean and tall, he had stubble on his chin, and I could see the wide strap hanging from his wrist. He looked over us.

"Good morning, Brother John. Isn't Brother Mac on duty this morning?"

"As you may clearly observe, Brother Tom, he is not. The Superior has seen fit to place him on other duties. Who is this creature?"

"This is the new boy. He arrived last night."

"I believe our new English teacher also arrived last night. What's he like?"

"As God made him, I expect. A worthy soul."

"You'll be the death of me, Brother Tom. You know nothing about the man."

"I assume the Father Superior does. Otherwise he wouldn't be here."

"We shall see. What's this creature in for?"

"I haven't studied his papers properly yet, but I'm sure he's a nice boy."

151

"There are no nice boys in here, Brother Tom. If he was a nice boy, he'd be at home minding the house. Isn't that so, boy?"

Brother Tom patted me on the shoulder. "He's not very talkative, Brother John – but give him time."

Brother John smiled. "He'll talk to me," he said. "That's what I'm here for."

Brother Tom turned away and walked in the direction of the chapel. Brother John watched him for a moment and then looked over my head.

"Name?" he asked – as if speaking to the horizon.

I made no answer – and Brother John's hand flashed from his pocket and his fist almost fractured my jaw. I fell to the ground where I could taste the blood issuing slowly from the corner of my mouth.

"Get up," he said quietly. "Take your time."

I rose to my feet and Brother John glanced at my face.

"I will repeat the question. Listen carefully. Name?"

"Galvin."

Brother John struck me again, but this time with the back of his hand, on the side of the head. I staggered against the wall.

"When you speak to me," he almost whispered, "you will address me as 'Sir'. Do I make myself clear?"

"Yes, Sir."

"Now then. Your name is Galvin. What are you?"

"I don't know, Sir."

"Then let me enlighten you. This is a reformatory. It is not a nursery. It is not a school for young ladies – and it is not a pleasure garden. It is a reformatory school for hooligans. And that's what you are, Galvin. A hooligan. A dirty, degenerate and filthy little hooligan. Do you agree with that description?"

"If you say so, Sir."

"I do say so. I do indeed. Are you a wise boy, Galvin? I trust not. Because if you are, let me warn you. The woods are filled with wise boys. They get eaten up. Swallowed alive. Torn limb from limb. Is that what you want?"

"No, Sir."

"Then behave yourself. I shall be keeping a sharp eye on you from now on. Mercier!"

He shouted in the direction of the Square and Mercier appeared almost at once. He was about sixteen years old and he spoke through his teeth.

"Sir?"

Brother John stared at the horizon. "This revolting creature is new," he reported. "Remove him from my sight and show him the ropes."

Mercier winked at me and I followed him to the centre of the Square where we were joined by Peters, who was small and fat and wide-eyed at the sight of blood.

Mercier looked at my jaw. "It's not broken," he grinned. "You've got blue blood. That's what probably upset him."

"Will he die?" Peters asked, his two eyes almost falling out of his head.

Mercier ignored him. Wiping the blood from the corner of my mouth with the sleeve of his jacket, he then rubbed his sleeve along the edge of the wall.

"He's a bastard," he said. "They're all bastards in here. You'll have to get used to that. Where have they put you to work?"

"In the Carpenter's Shop, I think."

"Brother Mac is in there," Peters said.

"Since when?"

"This morning. He's been taken off the Square."

Mercier shook his head. "Another bastard. Don't ever ask him for permission to go to the bog. He'll kick you to death."

"He kicked Davitt yesterday," Peters announced with mounting enthusiasm. "I saw him. Kicked him in the legs and then bashed him over the head with his fist. I think Davitt's dying."

"He's not dying! He's got concussion, that's all."

"That could be fatal, Mercier. If he dies, we might all have to go to his funeral. I hate funerals."

"Oh, shut up, Peters! Why do you always have to make a mountain out of everything?"

Peters remained wide-eyed as Mercier looked to another boy who was moving slowly in our direction.

"Oh, Christ! There's that scabby Rogers again. Don't talk to him."

Rogers approached. He was pale-faced and his mouth was open. Peters said he was twelve and that his mother had died in agony. Mercier shrugged his shoulders and said that Rogers should have died with her. He regarded him with scorn.

"Piss off!"

"I just want to talk to the new boy, Mercier."

"Well, he's not talking to you. No one is talking to you. Move!"

"I haven't done anything."

"You're a spy. A stinking informing creeping ghett of a spy. Go hang yourself. And do it now before somebody else does it for you."

"That's not fair, Mercier. I never informed on you."

"The day you do, I'll tear your arm off. Now, shag off."

Rogers had tears in his eyes. He turned away and I watched him walk to the far corner of the Square where he stood with his back to the wall, ignored by everyone.

Peters looked uneasy. He remained silent for a moment, then said: "You shouldn't talk to him like that, Mercier."

"Why not?"

"What if he goes to Brother John?"

"Let him."

"It's not worth it, Mercier. Besides, I feel sorry for Rogers."

"Are you kidding? He's an informing ghett."

"Well, I don't know …"

"I do. Now, belt up – and let's go and play football."

Mercier ran ahead across the Square, and Peters and I followed. He was standing with the ball in his hand when we arrived.

"Kick it!" he shouted through his teeth. "Kick the bloody thing!"

He threw the ball at my feet and I kicked it high in the air.

*

"What is important," Mr Goldman, my friend in Cork, wrote, "is not names, but papers. They can take your name, lock it away in a book, or bury it deep under a mile of concrete, but they can't remove it from your head. And even if they could, what does it matter? You can always invent a new one. Papers, on the other hand, are a different matter. A man without papers doesn't exist.

"When I was younger than I am now, I travelled all over Europe – and I could do this because I had my papers in my pocket. But, one night, in Hamburg, I was attacked and beaten up by a gang of anti-Semitic thugs. I reported the matter to the police and they immediately demanded to see my papers. I said that I didn't have any papers. They had been stolen in the attack. And, from that moment on, I ceased to exist. I became a non-person. A man who could be dumped on a train – shunted from one country to another – made to lie in a ditch and beg for his food.

"A man is a nothing without papers. He's like a child locked

*in a cell and the only thing he can do is scratch his name upon
the wall and hope that, one day, someone will remember it. I
send you my love. I keep your name close to my heart — and the
room glows with remembrances of our times together."*

Five

"A reformatory school, Mr Franklin, is very different from a National School. You will find that the problems here are very different."

They had walked far from the Recreation Square, as Father Damian was showing Mr Franklin the lay-out of the school.

"Many of these boys come from the most deplorable backgrounds," he continued, "but we do our best. We give them a trade, religious instruction – and, hopefully, a sense of moral responsibility. But, alas, the chances are that most of them will end up in jail."

"We could change that."

"Oh?"

"Affection. Knowledge. A feeling that someone actually cared what happened to them."

A pained expression crossed Father Damian's face. "Don't be a saint, Mr Franklin. I've got enough saints here already and most of them are demented."

"Get rid of them."

"I wish I could. But I have to obey orders. Mr Franklin. A man of your background should be able to appreciate that. Were you long in Spain?"

"Long enough."

"I can imagine."

He paused for a moment and looked across at the entrance to the Square. He could see Brother John there, head high, hands in his pockets, walking backwards and forwards, close to the wall. He could hear the sound of the boys playing football and he wondered if Mr Franklin played because that could be useful in addition to his other qualifications. He was glad Franklin was here, but he could foresee the problems.

"Let me be honest with you, Mr Franklin. Apart from Brother Tom, the staff here were very much opposed to your appointment."

"On what grounds?"

"Oh, nothing political. Let me assure you of that. They know nothing of your activities in Spain – and I have made quite a point of not mentioning it. But they do feel that the responsibility for these boys is best left in the hands of the Church."

"And you?"

"I am responsible for your appointment, Mr Franklin. Does that surprise you?"

"A little. I would have thought that the Bishop would have had something to say about it."

Father Damian smiled. "Oh, you can be sure he had!" But, sometimes, even Bishops can be persuaded of the need for change. Let me show you something."

He moved closer to the Square and Franklin stood beside him.

"Do you see that wall over there?"

"Yes, I noticed it last night."

"It runs right across the centre of the Square," Father Damian said. "That was one of Brother Mac's ideas. He felt it prudent to separate the younger boys from the older ones."

"And you agreed?"

"Yes, Mr Franklin. I agreed. But I'm getting tired of walls – aren't you? Let's move on and I'll show you the rest of the building while there's still time."

He moved away and as Franklin walked close beside him he could see the lean figure of Brother John peering at them from the distance.

Brother John looked at his watch. It was almost time for the work period to begin and he was curious to meet this new teacher whom the Superior had foisted upon him. He didn't approve of lay-teachers, particularly in a house like Saint Jude's. They were not committed – and their ideas of discipline were more suited to an academy for young ladies.

What would someone like Mr Franklin know about the revolting elements he had to contend with at Saint Jude's? Not that he knew a great deal about Franklin, but he could imagine the type. Riddled with those modern ideas that were lately bringing anarchy to the world. There would be no anarchy in Saint Jude's. He would not permit it.

He looked at his watch again. It was a silver pocket watch bearing Caesar's face, its Roman numerals clearly visible. He wound it up. He did so every morning at the same time and every evening when the bell rang for the Angelus. It kept perfect time.

He returned the watch to his pocket and headed towards the centre of the Square. He moved noiselessly, appearing, in his patent-leather shoes, to glide rather than walk. The boys moved out of his way as he passed between them – like a silent ship sailing through a darkening canal.

Either side of him were the elements it was his duty to keep in order – but he kept his eyes on the horizon until he reached the exact centre of the Square and then he stopped. It was time for the work period to begin.

He clapped his hands and waited a few moments for the boys to fall into line. When he looked at the line, it was not straight. Putting his hands in his pockets, he waited until it was. Then he motioned with his head and the boys moved off in single file, making their exit from the Square.

*

I can see the sky from here. Pale blue and not a cloud in sight. I walk from wall to wall and count the stones. It would take a year to count them all. My grandfather wanted to be buried in a wall. He's buried in Douglas now, deep in the earth, and no one sings for him.

The walls are grey here. So is the uniform I wear. Only the Brothers wear black. I miss the colours. My face reflected in the waters of the Lee. The rainbows in Evergreen. I am not like my grandfather. I mourn his passing. But I should not like to be buried in a wall.

Six

When Franklin entered the classroom at Saint Jude's for the first time, he found the room cold, the window open, and Brother John waiting impatiently at the desk.

"Brother John?"

Brother John looked at his watch. "May I remind you, Mr Franklin, that your duty in this classroom begins at ten o'clock precisely. It is now two minutes past."

"Sorry about that, Brother John. But the Superior was taking me on a guided tour of the school."

"So I observed. But that is hardly an excuse."

He put the watch back in his pocket and wiped his hands with a pure white linen handkerchief.

"I believe you once taught in a National School. Is that correct?"

"It was some time ago, Brother John."

"And what have you been doing since?"

"Travelling. It broadens the mind."

"I have never found it so. But since this is your first time on duty in this establishment, let me give you some advice. The creatures you are about to teach, if that is the word, should not be confused with intelligent human beings. They are hooligans. Degenerate, unnatural and unholy. That is why they are here."

"I'm surprised you can stand the strain, Brother John."

"I can stand it, Mr Franklin, because it is my duty before God to stand it – and for no other reason. When you have been here as long as I have, you will find that the only thing these creatures understand is strength. Should you fail to employ that strength they will eat you alive."

"Thank you for the advice, Brother John. I think I'll be able to manage."

"I hope so, Mr Franklin. I will leave you now. Your charges will appear in one minute. I have been obliged to keep them waiting in the hall."

He circled the desk, to avoid passing close to where Franklin was standing, and left the room.

Franklin closed the window and placed his briefcase on the desk. He looked at the room. There was a statue of the Virgin Mary standing mindfully in a corner and a picture of the Sacred Heart hanging on the wall above the desk. Pulling the desk forward, he placed the blackboard in front of the picture. Then he looked at the chairs. They were laid out in neat rows at the back of the room, and for a moment he thought they were fixed to the floor. He brought them forward, rearranging them into a semi-circle round the desk, then waited for the boys to arrive.

They entered the room in single file and stood to attention at the rear of the class. Franklin was leaning against the blackboard.

"All right. Find yourselves a seat and sit down."

There was a scramble for seats and Franklin waited until the boys had sorted themselves out and were finally seated. He then moved forward and sat on the edge of the desk, facing them.

"We shall begin at the beginning," he said. "My name is Franklin. Mr Franklin. This is my first day at Saint Jude's and I do not intend that it shall be my last. So – should any of you wish to challenge me, physically or otherwise, then I suggest that you do so now – and let's get it over with."

He paused and looked around the room. There were no challengers.

"Good. Then that's settled. I'm a fair man – but don't be under any illusion. I've got eyes in the back of my head and I can move like greased lightning. Are there any questions?"

Peters stood up and Franklin studied him for a moment, before deciding there'd be no problem with him.

"What's your name?"

"Peters, Mr Franklin."

"You have a question?"

"Yes. What's a nice man like you doing in a place like this?"

Everyone laughed – and Franklin let the laughter continue for a moment before raising his hand.

"That's a good question, Peters. Why do you think I'm here?"

"Because you couldn't get a job anywhere else?"

Everyone laughed again – and Franklin let that continue too until they stopped laughing and Peters sat down.

"Any more questions?"

"You haven't answered the first question yet," Peters persisted. "Why not?"

Franklin looked at the remainder of the class. They were waiting for an answer – and Franklin knew that there would be no more questions and no co-operation until he'd answered Peters.

"Very well," he said. "I will tell you why I am here. I am here because I am a teacher. I have been a teacher for many years and I think I'm a good one. We will teach each other. But before we begin, let us get a few things straight. Your reasons for being here are no concern of mine. My concern is what you will do when you leave here. But, while you are here – in this room – you may ask any questions you like and I will try to answer them. If I cannot answer them, I will say so. I am on your side. Remember that."

He paused, opened his briefcase and removed a book.

"Now then. Can you all read?"

There was no response and Franklin turned to Peters again.

"You, Peters. Can you read? Well, can you or can't you?"

"No, Mr Franklin."

"Why not? Come on, Peters. Why can't you read?"

It was Mercier who answered. "Because no one ever taught him – that's why."

Franklin could feel the contempt in Mercier's voice, but decided to ignore it. When he looked at his face, Mercier was smiling.

"What's your name?"

"Mercier – Mr Franklin."

"Can you read?"

"Yes."

"Good. Then you will teach Peters. You will spend one hour with him every day and you will teach him all you know about the art of reading."

"Why should I?"

"That's another good question, Mercier. Think about the answer. Are there any more in the class who can't read? Come on, it's nothing to be ashamed of. Stand up all those who can't read."

And to Franklin's surprise, most of the boys in the class rose to their feet.

"I'm not teaching all that ignorant lot!" Mercier protested. "That's your job."

"We will do it together, Mercier. You will come here every evening after Benediction – and we'll see what we can do. Now read this."

He handed Mercier the book. "Page twenty-one – 'Lycidas' – and let's have it loud and clear."

Mercier opened the book and read:

Lycidas

Yet once more, O ye Laurels, and once more
Ye myrtles brown, with ivy never sere,
I come to pluck your berries harsh and crude,
And with forced fingers rude
Shatter your leaves before the mellowing year.
Bitter constraint, and sad occasion dear,
Compels me to disturb your season due:
For Lycidas is dead, dead ere his prime,
Young Lycidas, and hath not left his peer:
Who would not sing for Lycidas? ....

Seven

Brother Mac sat on a hardback chair at the door of the refectory and counted his beads. He was praying for deliverance and he kept his head low.

At a nearby table, Mercier was explaining the refectory rules. He sat at the head of the table and I sat beside him. It was lunchtime and we were permitted to speak. That was refectory rule number one.

"Rule number two," said Mercier, "is – keep your voices low so that the lunatic at the door will not be disturbed while he prays for his release from Purgatory. All other rules at this table were invented by me."

He paused and gestured towards Rogers. "At the foot of the table," he continued, "we have Scabby Rogers. I did not invent him. He was found in a rat hole."

He turned to me. "You're Fish," he said. "Last in. I'm Jack. Here for years. Ding-dong."

"Can we eat now?" I asked.

"Not yet. As you can see, there are four loaves of bread on the table – to be divided between the eight of us. But, as you can also see, the loaves are not in equal size. That's because Peters here works in the Bakery and can't see straight. So what do we do?"

"Kill Peters?"

"I'll have to think about that. In the meantime, we have a system. It's called Jack first – Fish last. Which means the guy who's been here the longest gets first choice. He shares with the guy who's been here second longest – and so on down the line. I share with Peters."

"And who do I share with?"

"Rogers."

"I don't mind."

"You hear that, Peters? The fish doesn't mind sharing with Scabby Rogers. Rogers is a dog."

"I am not a dog," Rogers whispered almost to himself. "I am not a dog."

Mercier ignored him. "He is also a survivor. And do you know how he survives? By eating his friends. Make sure he doesn't make a friend of you."

"I don't need any friends."

"That's a good policy. You're learning fast. Now, we can eat."

He reached for the largest loaf on the table, cut it expertly into two equal parts, and let Peters grab his share. I waited until the other boys had made their choice and then looked at Rogers. He was waiting patiently at the foot of the table, and suddenly I didn't feel hungry anymore. I pushed the remaining loaf along the table towards him.

"You need to watch him," Peters said. "He's a desperate cutter."

I watched Rogers cutting the loaf. His hand shook and the two pieces of bread were not of equal size.

"I'm sorry," he said, and offered me the larger piece.

"Keep it," I told him. "I don't want any."

"Then put it in your pocket," Mercier said. "Don't leave it on the table."

"He's not supposed to do that," Rogers cautioned. "It's against the rules. All uneaten bread must be left on the table."

Pretending not to hear, Mercier continued to address me.

"Let me tell you something, Fish. If you leave bread on

167

the table, do you know what will happen? Brother John will come along, or Brother Mac, or another one of these bastards – and they'll say, 'Fucking hell! We're giving those boys too much to eat. No wonder they're getting fat.' And tomorrow morning there'll be less grub on the table."

"That's not true," Rogers said. "Leave the bread on the table. If you don't, you'll get into trouble."

"How?" Mercier asked – looking directly at Rogers for the first time since we'd sat down. "How will he get into trouble? Will you tell Brother John?"

"No, I won't. You keep saying things like that about me, Mercier. But I never informed on anyone."

"You're a dog," Mercier said. "You're a frightened dog. Scared out of your pants because you think you'll never get out of this place if you don't play ball with that lot. But there's no ball, Rogers. Nothing! We're fighting a war in here. All of us. And we're on our own."

"I'm …" said Rogers – who looked as if he were about to be sick. He put his hand to his mouth and rose from the table.

"He's going to puke!" exclaimed Peters, covering his bread with both hands. "He's going to puke!"

"Then he can fuck off!" Mercier said. "And puke outside."

Rogers rushed from the table and headed for the door. Brother Mac let him pass and then followed him outside.

There was silence at the table. But Mercier continued to eat, as if nothing had happened. He was the only one to do so. I felt angry when I looked at him – and I felt pity for Rogers, who, shunned and frightened, was now vomiting in the yard outside. I was about to speak when Mercier said: "Don't! You know nothing about this."

"He's sick, for Christ's sake!"

"Rogers is always sick. He was born that way. But before

you go wasting your sympathy on him, just remember all those he's informed on since he came here."

"Like who – for instance?"

"Duggan for one. He was flogged. And so was Murphy. Who else, Peters? You tell him."

"I don't know, Mercier."

"You know bloody well. Tell him."

"I didn't hear Rogers tell Brother John. It was McGovern told me."

"Bollox!"

Mercier paused for a moment and then said: "There were two lads kissing in the dormitory. They were 'All-One'. Peters was there and so was McGovern. But it didn't bother them. Why should it? Then along comes Rogers. He saw what was happening. And the next morning he went and told Brother John."

"I saw him talking to Brother John," Peters said. "But I didn't hear anything."

"McGovern did. And you were standing right there beside him. What's the matter with you?"

"What happened?" I asked.

"Brother John went to the dormitory that night, dragged those two lads out of their beds, and flogged them. You can still see the scars."

"That's true," Peters admitted. "There was blood every-where."

"And you want me to cry sorrow for Rogers? I'd cut his throat ten times over. And so would you – if you had any sense."

I didn't know if I had any sense. I didn't know how I felt. I saw Brother Mac return to the refectory with the rosary beads still in his hands. He stood at the table and looked down at us. I had nothing to say – and neither did anyone else.

*

There was a man one time who spent his whole life searching through books. He was looking for a word – a single word that would explain everything. He discovered it at the moment of his death and was amazed to find that there was nothing to explain.

Did Mr Goldman know that? My grandmother did. She never explained anything. She stood back and saw what she could see and she believed in herself.

I am looking for a sound and spend my days listening.

Eight

The walled garden at Saint Jude's was Brother Tom's oasis. And whenever he had time, or the weather was good, or for no reason at all, he would sit there on the garden seat and think about his feet.

Sometimes he thought about other things, but today he was thinking about his feet. They were sore from standing. They were sore because his shoes were old and no longer fitted properly. They were sore because he was old, and old people often suffered from sore feet. And while he was thinking about them, the garden gate opened and Franklin entered his oasis.

"I hope I'm not disturbing you, Brother Tom?"

Brother Tom was disturbed – but that was the way of the world. Everyone disturbing everyone else.

"Not at all," he said. "Do sit down."

Franklin sat on the seat beside him. The oasis was getting crowded.

"It's a most attractive garden, Brother Tom. Did you landscape it yourself?"

"With God's help. But I leave it to Mercier now, who seems to take quite an interest in it. You wished to see me about something?"

"Yes. About Mercier – as a matter of fact."

"He's a very intelligent boy."

"I'm aware of that. What's his background? Are his parents alive?"

"His mother died some years ago. Cancer, I believe. But his father is still alive."

"Does he visit the boy?"

"I'm afraid not. Are you interested in Mercier?"

"I'm interested in all the boys, Brother Tom. But Mercier seems to be a cut above the average. Have you any idea what he intends to do when he leaves here?"

"Knowing Mercier, I suspect that his only ambition is to be a master criminal."

"You're probably right. When does he leave?"

"Oh, quite soon now. In a couple of months, I think."

"A pity."

Brother Tom smiled. "I don't think Mercier would agree with you there, Mr Franklin. He can't wait to get out of the place."

"We can't blame him for that, I suppose. At the moment, I've got him teaching some of the other boys to read."

"That's a good idea. Would you like to see more of the garden?"

"If you wouldn't mind, Brother Tom."

Brother Tom rose to his feet. They were still sore, but his knees were getting stiff now and he had to move.

"I come here to sit, Mr Franklin – but at my age one can only sit for so long, no matter how pleasant the weather."

"I understand."

Brother Tom was convinced that he didn't, but there was no point in explaining further. Only the old understood what it was like to be old – and only the very young could appreciate them.

"Are you interested in gardening?" he asked. But Franklin didn't answer. He was staring at the wall and at the initials scratched here and there along the stone. He could see Mercier's initials and the date – and there were many going back over the years.

"I knew them all," said Brother Tom. "And, sometimes, I wonder what became of them."

"And now?"

"Now more than ever, Mr Franklin. Do you think there will be a war?"

"The war started a long time ago, Brother Tom."

"In Spain?"

"Yes."

"The Superior mentioned you were there. Were you involved in the fighting?

"Yes."

"So many deaths."

Franklin nodded his head and Brother Tom looked at him. "You don't believe in prayer, do you, Mr Franklin? Why did you go to Spain?"

"I think I was under the illusion that the meek were about to inherit the earth."

"They will one day, Mr Franklin. You can be sure of that. Does anyone else know you've been to Spain?"

"Just you and the Superior."

"Then I should keep it like that, if I were you. I don't think Brother John would approve. He tends to regard General Franco as a saint."

"And you?"

"I try to believe in God, Mr Franklin. I know very little about saints. Shall we go in now? The boys will be coming in off the Square soon – and I have many things to do."

"Of course."

Brother Tom opened the gate and waited until Franklin had left the garden and was heading towards his room in the old cell block. Then, he closed the gate, turned the key in the lock, and moved off slowly in the opposite direction.

*

Dear Mannie,

Sometimes, I would like to tell of a bird that sings in the garden. And how I am finding a new voice – but my lips are held tightly together by an old vice. I don't feel pain, nor do I suffer the despair which you might expect. I am standing back, looking for words, struggling to remember the ones you taught me. Innocence, you said, dies rapidly at the moment of birth. Mine lasted a little longer – but it is dying in Saint Jude's.

It is hard to express what they do to you here. It has nothing to do with names or pieces of paper. But the result is probably the same. You become a nothing, a face to be blanked out, a revolting element. One of these revolting elements died recently. His body lay in the chapel and his parents arrived from the country to take his remains home after the service. It was the first time they'd come to visit him. They must have forgotten he was here. Now I have forgotten his name and I have no idea what part of the country he came from.

Do you remember those Russian novels you used to read to me? I never understood what they were about, but I liked the stories, and I was carried away by the sound of your voice. The man who killed the money-lender. What was his name? I can see him standing on the landing of the tenement building, his face in shadow, listening for the dark. Is there a sound in that? Or is he still waiting to find out? I write from memory.

Nine

Mercier stood two feet from the dividing wall in the centre of the Recreation Square and watched the younger boys playing 'Release' on the other side. He winked at Watson, who was aged twelve and wore his hair long. Watson moved closer to the wall, smiled shyly at Mercier, then carried on playing with the other boys.

Mercier had never spoken to Watson. They worked in different parts of the school. They sat at separate tables in the refectory. They slept in opposite dormitories, and the wall in the Recreation Square – created in darkness and cement by Brother Mac – kept them farther apart.

Mercier hated the wall. It was low – no more than four feet in height – and every section of it could be clearly observed by whatever Brother was on duty at the entrance to the Square. And in the late evenings it was well-lit at both ends by two giant street lamps.

Only in the centre was there a shadow, and it was here that Mercier could reach over the wall and touch Watson and feel the warmth of his hand. He felt like doing that now, but it was too early and Brother John was on duty and looking directly at him. Mercier moved another two feet away from the wall and turned his back. Brother John stared at him for a moment and then looked towards the horizon.

"He's like a snake," Mercier said. "If I had a knife I'd skin him."

I felt like skinning him too, but decided to walk around in circles instead. Mercier joined me.

"Have you seen Peters?"

"Not since the Angelus," I replied. "He was heading towards the Superior's Office then."

"What the hell for?"

"He didn't say. Maybe he's gone to confession."

"Jesus Christ! That's all I need. Peters catching a dose of religion!"

"That won't happen to you."

"You can bet your life on it. I've seen enough religion in here to last me a lifetime."

We continued to walk in circles until, presently, he said: "What do you think of Watson? Doesn't he look like a girl?"

"Yes," I said. "He looks like a girl."

Mercier paused. "I've been here two-and-a-half years," he said. "It's a long time."

At the entrance to the Square, Brother John took his eyes off the horizon and moved purposely in the direction of the dividing wall. When he reached it, he stood close beside it and looked over at the younger boys playing 'Release'. He beckoned to Watson, who approached with his hands clutched nervously behind his back. Brother John looked over his head.

"You are aware, I take it, of the rules governing this wall?"

"No, Sir."

"They have not been explained to you?"

"No, Sir."

"Then let me explain them to you now. I will do so once and I will not repeat the explanation. Is that understood?"

"Yes, Sir."

Brother John placed his hands in his pockets and then spoke to the horizon.

"The wall," he announced, "is made of concrete. It was built for a purpose. That purpose is clearly defined. It is to separate the boys on this side of the wall from those on the other side. The wall is not to be touched by hand or foot. It is not to be leaned against. And it is not to be written upon by hooligans and degenerates who have nothing better to do. You are a degenerate, Watson. You are also a hooligan. If you were not, you would not be here. Am I correct?"

"Yes, Sir."

"Then let me explain further. On both sides of the wall there is a gap of two feet of solid ground. And upon this ground no boy is permitted to set foot. Should he do so, by accident or design, I will personally see to it that he is in no fit condition to do so again. Do I make myself clear?"

"Yes, Sir."

"Then depart – and get your hair cut – short!"

Watson backed away and Brother John looked at the ground. He removed a pure white linen handkerchief from his pocket, wiped his hands clean of Watson, and then walked, slowly, along a two-foot path of clearly defined earth on our side of the wall.

As we watched him from a distance, Mercier said: "I know every word that bastard is going to say before he opens his mouth. I can read into him."

"Can he read into you?"

"No one can. He watches me though. He's watching me now – and Watson – but he'd have to be up very early to catch me. He's nabbed Peters once or twice. Beat the shit out of him."

"What for?"

"Being too close to the wall. The magic two feet. I sometimes wonder why Brother Mac didn't place land-mines along it."

"Maybe he has."

"No such luck."

I looked at Brother John. He was still walking, backwards and forwards, along the magic two feet of ground on our side of the wall. I prayed for a miracle – but there were no land-mines.

When Peters arrived in the Square, his mouth was open and he carried a brown-paper parcel under his arm.

"Been shopping?" Mercier asked. "Or is this someone's birthday?"

Peters closed his mouth, but kept his eyes wide open.

"Well?"

"I've just had a visit," he screamed. "Would you believe that? A bloody visit!"

"Oh, shut up, Peters. Who came to visit you – Saint Jude?

"Very funny, Mercier! My old man came to see me, that's who. I haven't seen him for a year. And there he was."

"He must be going to die," Mercier said. "It could be your lucky day."

"I don't feel lucky," Peters moaned. "I feel sick."

"You'll get over it. What did your Old Man have to say?"

"Nothing much. He just apologised and said he wasn't a good father."

"You didn't contradict him, I hope?"

"I didn't know what to say, Mercier."

Mercier shrugged his shoulders. "Probably wouldn't have listened to you anyway. Parents and teachers! They're all the shagging same."

"Franklin doesn't seem so bad," I said. "At least he's on our side."

"That's what my old man used to say – Trust me, Kid. I'm on your side. But when I was being sentenced to this lot, he didn't even turn up in court. He was drunk."

"What about your Ma?"

"Died years ago. Bollox to it. What's in the parcel?"

Peters opened the brown-paper parcel. "It's a pullover,"

he said. "My mother sent it."

"Throw it over the wall," Mercier sneered. "That's what I would do."

"No, you wouldn't."

"Try me."

I looked at Mercier. He meant what he said. Peters folded the pullover again and wrapped it carefully in the brown paper.

"I think I'll hang on to it for a while," he said. "I might be able to flog it later on. Would you like a bit of chocolate?"

"Who gave you that? Your Old Man? Must have broke his bloody heart."

Peters shared the bar of chocolate among us and Mercier turned and looked directly at the dividing wall.

"Visitors!" he said with disgust – and shook his head. "The only visitor I ever had here was a scabby old social worker. And do you know what she said? – 'Be a good boy, Mercier, and mind your prayers.' Stupid bitch!"

He ambled off, stopped short at the edge of the magic line, and stood there staring at Watson.

Brother John paused in his tracks. He gazed steadily at Mercier. Then he clapped his hands.

"Fall in!"

Peters shrank visibly as he crossed himself. "Slave-time," he moaned – and we all fell into line.

Brother John had inspected us, and was about to issue the command to move forward, when someone close behind me belched loudly. Brother John's face turned a bluish-grey and his mouth tightened.

"Who made that noise? Who made that revolting noise?"

There was no answer – and Brother John looked from one boy to another and then at me.

"Was it you?" he hissed through his teeth. "I am asking

you a question, Galvin. Was it you?"

"I didn't hear a thing."

I suddenly heard the rattle of keys, however, and felt the flesh near my left eye split open. I fell to the ground, the blood streaming from the ragged wound. Brother John stood over me.

"The next time I ask you a question, Galvin, you will answer me in the proper manner. Now get up and fall into line!"

I rose to my feet and with my hand held to my face, I fell back into line.

"By the left – quick march!"

I could see the blood now, as we moved forward, staining the front of my shirt, as we marched quickly out of the Recreation Square.

*

My father wrote to me today. He said it was raining in Cork. Mrs Barrett wrote the letter. My father dictated the words. He said the house wasn't the same without me and enclosed a shilling postal order.

"There's a madman living next door now," he said. "I think he's a Protestant. He keeps ripping up the floorboards, and only stops when I play the tin whistle. I tried to talk to him today, by tapping on the wall like they do in prisons, but he refused to answer me. You'd like him I'm sure. He has no family and lives on his old-age pension but the nuns come in once a week and force him to clean up the house. I think they should leave him alone. It's his house, after all, and if he wants to live in a heap, that's his business. People interfere too much. I'll tap the wall again tomorrow and see if he'll talk to me. Mrs Barrett is writing this because, as you know, I haven't the art. But I hope you're all right. It's still raining."

I haven't told Mercier about the letter.

Ten

Mercier sat on a chair under the window in Franklin's room and read aloud from an anthology of verse that he had just discovered among Franklin's collection of books.

The legions march
Across the olive groves of Spain.
Their feet are guns
Their eyes are bullets in my lungs —
Remember Spain.
I cried to you
When the first flame arose
In Andalusia.
Now the flame is a fire
That burns the Pyrenees —
Remember Spain.
I will not yield
I will not fall
I will eat dynamite
And one day I will explode
Like a volcano —
Remember Spain.
Listen!
They are bombing Guernica.
Arrows fall from the skies
Bayonets grow in the fields
The children are bleeding —
I will not weep.

Remember Spain
Remember Spain …

He was about to set the book aside when he noticed the dedication: *To Comrade John Franklin – Spain 1937*. He read the poem again.

"Talking to yourself, Mercier."

Mercier lowered the book and saw Franklin leaning against the half-open door. He had obviously been listening.

"I like reading aloud. Can I borrow this book?"

Franklin entered the room and glanced at the anthology. "I expect so," he said. "What are you doing in my room?"

"You asked me."

"Did I? Oh, yes. I've got a number of books here I'd like you to take over to the classroom. Where's Galvin and your friend Peters?"

"They'll be here soon. Have you read all these books?"

"Yes."

Mercier rose from his seat under the window and moved towards the door.

"You were in the Spanish Civil War," he said. "What side were you on?"

Franklin hesitated before answering. "Do you know anything about the Spanish Civil War?"

"A little."

"Who told you that I was involved?"

"No one. I just noticed a dedication to you in that book I was reading. Are you a Communist?"

"Would it make any difference if I was?"

"I don't know. But I heard Brother John talking about the Communists. He said that they had burned all the churches in Spain – declared war on God – and that they'd be no Spain at all now if it hadn't been for General Franco."

"And no God either, I take it." He paused, moved close

to the window, and looked out on to the Recreation Square.

"Let me tell you something, Mercier. The war in Spain was between those who were overdue to inherit the earth – and those who were determined to prevent it. Do you understand what I mean?"

"No."

"Then let me put it this way. There are two classes in this world. The rich and the poor. The rich hold power-position – and all the authority. The poor hold nothing. Not even the graves they lie buried in. Don't you think it's time we changed all that?"

"Yes."

"Then we understand each other. You were reading a poem just now. What did you think of it?"

"I liked it."

"Why?"

"It says what I feel in one verse: *I will not yield. I will not fall. I will eat dynamite. And one day I will explode like a volcano.*"

"Against what, Mercier?"

Mercier looked at him. "Against these four walls," he said. "Isn't that what Spain was all about?"

Franklin waited a long time before answering. He remembered the poem. He remembered the dedication – written in a bombed-out café in the back streets of Barcelona. He remembered Spain and said: "Maybe. But don't take it too far, Mercier. Life is a little more complicated that that."

Mercier smiled. "Is it, Mr Franklin?"

"Yes," Franklin replied defensively. "You'll have to read more. A great deal more. Tell me about the books you've read. Where did you get them?"

"I swiped them."

"From the public library?"

"From bookshops. I used to go into the public library. It was warm there – and I read some of the books – but I never swiped any from there."

"I see. And what did you learn from reading those books?"

"Nothing."

"What kind of books were they?"

"Rubbish."

It was Franklin's turn to smile. "Well, that's something to know. You can borrow some of my books, if you like – and perhaps you can tell me whether you think they're rubbish or not."

"I don't promise to read them."

"You don't have to promise me anything, Mercier. Just help yourself."

Mercier held the poetry anthology up in his hand. "I'll take this," he said, quietly, and turned to leave when Franklin said: "You've forgotten why you're here, Mercier. I want those books taken to the classroom."

He pointed to a large number of books, arranged in neat piles, in a corner of the room. Mercier pushed the anthology into his pocket, but made no move towards the books in the corner.

"Have you transport?" he asked sarcastically, but before Franklin could reply there was a loud noise in the corridor outside, as if someone had knocked over something metal and was now cursing the idiot who had placed it in his way. Mercier ignored the commotion, but Franklin rushed towards the door as Peters entered, looking more wide-eyed than ever.

"I nearly broke me shagging neck!" he exclaimed. "There's a dustbin out there!"

"Are you all right?" Franklin asked. Then, seeing that Peters was still in reasonable condition, he added – "Where's your friend Galvin?"

Peters winced, "Didn't you know? He's having his face stitched."

"I beg your pardon?"

"Stitched! Brother John split him across the face with a bunch of keys. There was blood everywhere!"

"All right, Peters. Calm yourself. You didn't tell me about this, Mercier. Why not?"

Mercier shrugged his shoulders. "No reason to. It's happened before. Brother John likes hitting people. He's a lunatic."

"That's enough, Mercier. Cut that."

"And you should see his strap!" Peters cried suddenly, as if the vision might give him a heart attack. "It has four coins at the end of it and …"

"I said – that's enough!" Franklin shouted, cutting him short. "Now let's get on with moving these books."

There was silence for a moment before Peters said – "Galvin could be dead, Mr Franklin."

"Peters! Are you trying to provoke me?"

"No, Mr Franklin."

"Then move these books. You too, Mercier."

"Galvin won't be able to read them anyway," Peters muttered under his breath, as he and Mercier moved towards the books. – "If he lives at all, he'll probably be blind …"

Franklin was tempted to kill him – but decided against it.

*

When spring comes, Brother John leads us to the nearby stretch of bog and we cut turf for the winter. We march through the village and the people stare at us and some of them turn their backs. They know who we are. They resent us marching through their village. They pity Brother John, a holy man, having to deal with the likes of us.

The turf is wet. We lay it on the ground to dry and the March winds sweep over and round it. We cut deeper and the colour changes from brown to black. Forest roots, brown leaves, an old bone and a cow's horn.

There was a man murdered here. The trunk of his body was buried in the bog and, two years later, the police dug it up, the flesh still clinging to the bones, the marks on the skin clearly visible. Everything preserved.

When they had identified the victim, the police arrested the brother. They had fought over an acre of land and it ended in death. The body chopped up, the limbs fed to the pigs, the trunk buried deep in the bog.

The bog is alive. It holds you in its roots. We dig deeper and the March winds shiver and consume us.

Eleven

In Brother Tom's eyes, the small room that passed as an infirmary in Saint Jude's was nothing more than a small room where he kept aspirins and cotton wool. It contained a table and a few shelves, and a wash-hand basin in the corner, but the tap was broken and only gave water when Brother Tom struck it with a hammer, and then it did so in a series of explosive convulsions, culminating in a whine of atrophy and rust.

Sometimes, Brother Tom hid a bottle of whiskey in the infirmary. He covered it with cotton wool and tried to convince himself that it was strictly for medicinal purposes. But he knew that it wasn't – and so did his fellow Brothers in Christ. They regarded Brother Tom as a drunk who should have been retired years ago – and would have been if it hadn't been for the weakness and foolishness of his friend, the Father Superior.

But if Brother Tom were a drunk, he wasn't drunk now – as he wiped the blood from the side of my face, and examined the wound with care and sensitivity.

"It's nasty," he said. "Very nasty. Another inch and you'd have lost an eye. What did you do to deserve that?"

"Nothing, Brother Tom."

"Nothing? You must have done something, boy. What was it?"

"Someone belched," I said, "and Brother John thought it was me."

Brother Tom reached for the bottle of whiskey, opened

it carefully, and poured a little of it over a ball of wool.

"It'll sting like mad," he apologised, "but I have to disinfect it."

He dabbed at the wound with the whiskey-smelling cotton wool as my face contorted in agony and tears.

"By rights I should put a few stitches in it," he said, "but I've got nothing here – except a plaster. Keep that on a few days and then I'll have another look at it."

"Will I have to go to hospital?"

"I don't think so. The one in the village is hopeless. The only thing they know about is bullocks and cows and you're hardly one of those."

He covered the wound with a square of lint and sticking-plaster and smiled benignly.

"You know, in some countries of the world it's considered polite to belch – but that's only after a meal."

"I didn't belch. And he had no right to hit me."

"Never mind. Don't think about it any more. How are you getting on in the Carpenter's Shop?"

"All right. But the only thing I do there is stick bits of wood together with glue."

"Is that all? Well, maybe Brother Mac will let you do something more interesting later on. I used to be a carpenter, you know. I liked working with wood – shaping it and giving it back some of the life that it lost when it was taken from the soil. But I'm too old for that now. Too old for many things, I'm sure. Run along with you."

As I turned towards the door he added – "Are you hungry? I'm sure you are. There's a couple of sandwiches on a plate in the kitchen. Collect them on your way out."

"Thanks, Brother Tom."

"And get rid of that shirt. Take it over to the Laundry and ask Brother Whelan for a new one. You can't go around with blood on your clothes."

"Yes, Brother Tom. Goodnight."

"Goodnight, boy – and God bless."

I left the room, collected the sandwiches from the kitchen, and as I passed the window on my way to the Laundry, I could see him leaning against the infirmary table, his head lowered, and the whiskey bottle close to hand.

It was growing dark now and the lights were shining at both ends of the Recreation Square and in the windows of the chapel. It would soon be time for supper and then Benediction. Hurrying towards the Laundry, I saw Peters scurrying around the rear entrance to the Bakery. I heard the door close and saw the light switched on – and then off again. I waited for a moment, but Peters had disappeared – and there was no sound but that of my own footsteps as I crossed the churchyard and entered the Laundry building.

Inside the building, Brother Whelan stood with his back to the boiler. He said blood was difficult to wash off – and then enquired about the weather. It was the first time I'd ever seen Brother Whelan, who was known as 'The Phantom' because he never appeared in daylight. Instead he spent most of his time closeted in the Laundry, with his eyes closed and his ears cocked for the slightest irregularity in the sound of the engine that powered the water supply.

When darkness fell, Brother Whelan turned off the engine, but only for fifteen minutes, during which he went for a walk in the garden. But he kept his face covered, and he spoke to no one, preferring instead to communicate with the Almighty in silence and in dread.

As he spoke to me now, he sounded like Lazarus rising from his tomb, his voice hollow and echoing round the Laundry.

When I repeated my request for a new shirt, he said, again, that blood was difficult to wash off. He then enquired about the weather again and waited for an answer. I said the

189

weather was bad and he moved closer to the boiler. I said the weather was very bad and he almost fell into the boiler in an effort to escape it.

I removed my shirt and exchanged it for a new one. I tossed the old one into the Laundry basket and thanked Brother Whelan for his assistance. There was a crackling noise as he nodded his head – and a death-rattle as he embraced the boiler.

I retreated from the Laundry building and fled towards the Recreation Square.

Franklin was on duty now, but he said nothing as I ran past to join Mercier, who was sitting on the ground, two feet from the dividing wall.

"You're alive," he said accusingly. "Peters will be upset. He was looking forward to the funeral."

"Were you?"

Mercier didn't answer. "Sit down," he said. "You look like something Boris Karloff dug up from the grave. How many stitches did you have?"

"None."

"You can't be too bad so," he said as I sat beside him.

We sat in silence. He was looking at Watson, who was playing in the light cast by the giant street lamp, on the other side of the wall. And, presently, he said: "He's had his hair cut. That's a pity. Does your face hurt?"

"A little."

"You got a new shirt out of it anyway," he said. "It suits you."

"Thanks!"

Mercier patted the back of my hand. "Don't let the bastards get you down," he grinned. "That's what they want. Have you ever walked along an empty beach all by yourself?"

"Yes."

"You don't know how lucky you are. Let's move away from here."

We rose to our feet and Mercier directed me to a far corner where there was a minimum of light and only two of the boys playing handball against the outer wall. We stood in the corner and Mercier said: "We'll wait here for Peters. I sent him to the Bakery to swipe some bread."

We waited for Peters – who, when he finally appeared out of the darkness, looked as if he had just been sentenced to death by a firing-squad.

"Never again!" he complained. "Don't ask me, Mercier. I was almost nabbed by Brother John. And then I almost roasted meself!"

"I thought you were dead?" he said then, looking at me.

"Not yet," I apologised. "Maybe next week."

"Did you get the bread?" Mercier asked impatiently. "That's all we want to know."

"I did! But there was nothing in the cupboard – and I had to risk me life taking it from the oven."

"Where is it?"

"In me socks."

"In your what?"

Peters raised the legs of his trousers and displayed two loaves of doughy bread protruding awkwardly from the raggy tops of his navy socks.

"Holy God!" Mercier exclaimed. "You don't expect me to eat that? It's got hairs all over it."

Peters looked at the hairs. "They're mine!" he argued. "And you're lucky to get it, Mercier. If Brother John had seen me, I could be hanging from the wall."

"That's where you should be," Mercier said with conviction. "Let's have it."

Peters handed Mercier one of the loaves of bread and offered part of the other loaf to me. I declined gracefully.

191

"At least it's warm," Mercier said as he brushed the hairs from the doughy bread with the sleeve of his jacket.

Watching them eat, I was glad that I had already eaten the two sandwiches so generously provided by Brother Tom.

As I turned aside, I could see Rogers wandering aimlessly from one group of boys to another at the near end of the Square. He approached cautiously and Peters almost choked on the bread he was eating.

"Hello, Rogers," he coughed. "Would you like some bread?"

Rogers shook his head. "No thanks, Peters. I'm not hungry."

"You won't tell anyone, will you?"

"No."

"If he does," Mercier said coldly, "I'll kill him."

Rogers backed away, his head down and his hands deep in his pockets, and walked slowly towards the entrance to the Recreation Square.

"He'll split, Mercier! He's going to tell Franklin!"

Mercier was unmoved. "Not this time," he said. "I know him too well. He's going to the lavatory now – and he'll sit there on the seat and his guts will fall out."

Rogers reached the entrance to the Square and we could see him speaking briefly to Franklin. Franklin nodded his head – and Rogers rushed towards the lavatory.

It was quiet in the Square. The lights shone at both ends of the dividing wall and in the centre there was a shadow. It was darker now, and two boys, from opposite sides of the wall, reached over and touched each other.

*

"There's a golden rule in Saint Jude's," Mercier declared. "You do not ask anyone why he was sent here. But it would be nice to know who sent the Brothers here and what crimes they had

committed – and are still committing against us."

I am standing in the dark.

"The reason they send most kids into places like that," said Connors, "is because their shagging parents want to get rid of them. They send orphans there, too – and eegits who break open gas-meters, or smash a couple of windows, or maybe rob a few orchards here and there. I knew a fella once who broke into a cake shop in Oliver Plunkett Street. He spent all night sitting on the floor eating cakes – and he was still there the following morning when the owner came to open the shop. What kind of codology is that, for Jasus' sake? No wonder they locked him up."

I am standing in the dark.

"It makes no difference," Mr Goldman wrote. "The walls are there because you are there. When you go, the walls will disappear. Only the jailers remain. They need their walls. What else have they got?"

There's a light in the chapel. There is no Benediction.

Twelve

"Bless me, Father, for I have sinned."

Father Driscoll sat in the darkness of the confessional and listened to Brother Mac making his confession from the other side of the screen.

Father Driscoll was new to the village and this was his first visit to Saint Jude's to hear confession. He listened carefully, but found it hard to make out what Brother Mac was saying.

"You'll have to speak louder," he pleaded. "I cannot hear you. What sins have you committed since your last confession?"

"Impurity. My mind is filled with impure thoughts."

"And do you take pleasure in this?"

"No."

"Then what are you confessing, my son?"

"The existence of my body."

Father Driscoll lowered his head. He was tired listening. For two hours now he had been hearing confessions, first from the boys and then from the Brothers, and he was beginning to lose patience with grown men suffering from scruples when they should be out playing football or serving their time in the Foreign Missions.

He could understand the boys. Their sins were of the usual kind – bad thoughts and self-abuse – and he was prepared for that and no longer shocked, as he used to be when he had first entered the priesthood and was closer to God. Now, he was well into his sixties and this kind of confession, if anything, bored him – and all he could offer, by way of penance, was a cold bath and a good night's sleep with the arms folded tightly outside the blanket.

The Brothers were a different matter. Their sins, if sins they were, were more complex and he wondered if some of the Brothers, at least, were making them up simply to confuse him. Others, of course, were suffering from scruples and Father Driscoll had heard enough nonsense about that. And here, he was convinced, was another one with scruples.

"Have sense!" he said. "The body is a creation of Our Divine Lord. There is no sin in that."

Brother Mac paused. "You do not understand," he whispered. "I wash my hands until the skin is raw, but I cannot clean them. I spend my days fasting and my nights in prayer. I scourge my body until the blood runs cold. But in the morning the wounds are dry – and the flesh remains to mock me for another day. I cannot endure the burden of my own breath."

"Have you spoken to your Superior about this?"

"I can only speak of it in the dark."

Father Driscoll sighed deeply and moved closer to the screen. "What is your position in this place? Is it one of responsibility?"

"I am responsible to God."

"But you are in charge of young boys. Is that correct?"

"Yes."

"And how have you lived up to that responsibility? Have you abused it in any way?"

"No."

"You are quite sure of that?"

Brother Mac fingered the rosary beads in his hands and Father Driscoll waited for an answer.

"I watch them sometimes. The very young. And I think how beautiful they are. How pure and innocent. I want to

195

reach out and touch them. But the feelings last for only a moment. Because the young are not beautiful. They are not pure – and they are not innocent. Between the wide eyes – locked under that pale skin – there is obscenity and evil.

"When I was first appointed here, I did not think so. I thought an angel of God hovered over the bodies of the young. It is not so. The body of a young boy is a temple of corruption. The dwelling place of Satan. That is why I was forced to build a wall across the Square."

"A wall? What do you mean?"

"My tour of duty ended shortly before Benediction. I was standing alone at the entrance to the Recreation Square. It was a warm night, the air heavy on my hands and face.

"I did not notice it at first, but as darkness approached I could see the boys gathering in groups and in shadowy corners. I could taste the impurity. The corruption on the skin. The very stones reeked of it. I was sick. And all that night I lay on the floor of my room and vomited."

"Did you report what you had seen to your Superior?"

"Yes. He said that I had imagined it. An illusion. But the Devil is no illusion. He is always there – whispering. I begged the Superior to let me build a wall across the Square and, in the end, he agreed."

"I see."

"Do you, Father? Or do you also think that what I saw in the Square that night was an illusion?"

Father Driscoll didn't know what to think. He believed in God and he believed in the Devil, but he had seen neither and could rely only upon faith.

"I think that the world itself is an illusion," he said. "And sin is the axis upon which it revolves. I cannot help you. I can only warn you against excess. A wall of stones is no barrier against the wickedness and snares of the Devil. And there are more sins committed in the mind of man than were ever conceived of by the Devil or Almighty God."

Brother Mac left the confessional, returned to his room, and prostrated himself upon the stone floor.

He prayed for forgiveness. He prayed that, one day, he might see God as clearly as he had seen the Devil. He heard the bell ringing for Benediction – and in the shadow of the dividing wall, two boys, from opposite sides, leaned over and kissed each other.

*

My dreams enfold me. My mother's face. My father's hands. A tin whistle resting on the mantelpiece. A man with style changing into a seagull.

I can fly now. I can touch the clouds, circle the walls and look down upon a church steeple. I can screech "More Fish!" – and when they ask for my name I can say, "Seagulls don't have names. They are just called seagulls."

"Whatever you do," my mother said, "don't fall in the river." I have wings now. I can rest on the water. I can sing with fish.

"Your cousin Beatrice was here. She knows all about fish."

And when the bell rings in the morning, I shall not be found. My bed empty. My shoes on the floor. White feathers circling the dormitory.

There's a ghost in here. He hides under the blankets.

Thirteen

The morning began like any other morning. The bell rang in Saint Jude's. We made our beds and Brother Mac marched us to the wash-house. We attended Mass and then we marched to the Recreation Square.

We did not have breakfast – Peters said that the boiler had broken down and others said that a war had been declared and maybe we were all going to be sent home.

It was cold in the Square. We stood in groups. We huddled in corners. We rubbed our hands together and we shared our breath. Brother Mac kept his hands in his pockets and stamped his feet upon the frosty ground.

Brother John appeared. He placed two chairs at the entrance to the Square and stood between them.

"Fall in!" he cried – and we all moved into line. "In four lines," he added, "and face me."

There were over two hundred boys in the Square and we formed up into four lines and paraded in front of him.

"We are here to witness," he said – and called out two names. There was a moment's pause and the two boys stepped forward from the ranks. Brother John indicated the chairs and the two boys sat with their backs to us.

Brother John looked at them with disgust and then nodded to Brother Mac.

"To the bone," he said – and Brother Mac removed a pair of hair-clippers from his pocket and stood over the two boys. He proceeded to cut their hair. The hair fell over the shoulders of the boys and down onto the frosty ground. He continued to cut, until nothing remained on the boys' head but blotched skin and a raze of stubble.

He stepped aside – and Brother John commanded us to view. "Look well on this!" he cried. "And remember what you have seen."

There was silence in the Square – and then Brother John pointed to the ground. The two boys rose from their chairs and knelt before him.

"Remove your shirts and let your trousers down."

The two boys removed their shirts and let their trousers fall about their knees – exposing their backs and their buttocks to the cold morning air. Brother Mac moved out of sight – and Brother John addressed us.

"It is a shameful thing," he said. "A disgusting thing – when the behaviour of man descends to the level of the beast. It is an affront to God. A blasphemy of the soul. And Hell is not hot enough to punish the guilty.

"The punishment you are witnessing now is merely the beginning. In the hands of Almighty God lie future punishments – and those punishments will be more terrible than anything you have ever imagined."

He raised the strap and brought it down, viciously, upon the back of one of the boys. The boy screamed – and Brother John struck at the second boy who fell forward and cried "Oh, God! Oh, Jesus God!"

Brother John continued with the flogging, moving from one boy to another. And we could see the red stripes forming on the flesh and the blood streaming over the buttocks and down onto the backs of the legs.

Mercier turned his back on the scene and shouted "School! About face!"

Nobody moved – and Mercier shouted again – "About face, you bastards! What are you looking at?"

We all turned and faced in the opposite direction. Brother John stopped flogging the two boys.

"Mercier! What are you doing? You will face me! You are here to bear witness!"

"No flogging!" we chanted in unison. "No flogging! No flogging!"

Brother John raged. "I'll crucify you! I'll crucify you!"

We continued to chant and Brother John raised his strap again and resumed the flogging. He flogged until his arm ached and dropped to his side with exhaustion – and he stood there, in the freezing cold, with his body shaking and his face covered in sweat.

We were there to bear witness and we were pledged to remember.

*

They say that the cells in the old prison are haunted with the cries of old prisoners.
They say you can hear them at night or on rainy days.
They say some of them were hanged.
They say some of them were tortured.
They say some of them were flogged.
They say that was a long time ago.
Things are different now.
The cells are empty.
They are used for storing turf.

Fourteen

In the dining-room at Saint Jude's, Father Damian sat at the oak table and asked Brother Tom to fill his glass again from the now almost empty wine bottle standing on the sideboard. Brother Tom obliged and then offered a drink to Franklin. But Franklin refused. He was in no mood for drinking – and as he looked at the Superior and Brother Tom and then at Brother Mac, who was still pecking away at the remains of his dinner, he felt angry and dispirited.

Father Damian swallowed his drink and held the empty glass forward for Brother Tom to fill it again. Brother Tom did so and Father Damian smiled.

"You know, Mr Franklin – I was chosen for the priesthood, not by God, but by my mother. Does that surprise you? My mother, God rest her, was a very remarkable woman. She had six children and she was determined that one of us, at least, should become a priest. I was the fortunate one. Brother Tom, of course, would say that my mother was being used as a divine instrument. Isn't that so, Brother Tom?"

"Yes, Father."

"Well, there you are. But my mother was more practical than that, Mr Franklin. Having a priest in the family was like having money in the bank. The present is secure and the future holds promise of many dividends – we hope."

He sipped his drink and sat back in his chair. "I wonder, sometimes, about all those mothers who forced their sons to become doctors. If there's nothing on the other side of the grave, those people will be laughing their heads off at fools like me."

Brother Mac rose from his chair. "Excuse me, Superior."

"Yes?"

"I wish to be excused from the table."

"Sit down, Brother Mac! I have not given you permission."

Brother Mac resumed his seat as Father Damian finished his drink, and with a nod of his head, indicated that he wished for more. Brother Tom opened another bottle of wine and refilled his glass.

"Brother Mac thinks I've had too much to drink, Mr Franklin. What do you think?"

"It makes no difference to me, Superior."

And what about you, Brother Tom? Have I had too much to drink?"

"No, Father."

"And he's an expert, Mr Franklin. That's why he failed the priesthood. More booze than Latin in his brain. And I can tell you this – in the hands of Brother Tom the consecrated wine took on meanings that were never dreamt of in Holy Rome."

He turned to Brother Tom. "And yet, my friend, I think you would have made a good priest. Better than most. And why not? You know what sin is. I suppose it comes from having committed most of them yourself."

"Please, Father …"

"Don't be embarrassed, Brother Tom. In a way, I envy you. What do I know about sin? I'm like many another poor priest – a sinner by proxy. Oh, to be sure, we've heard of it. You can't sit in the confessional for long without becoming aware of at least one mortal sin. But do we know? I doubt it. We've never sinned deeply enough. And if we had, we would not take pleasure in it. And there's the rub. To spit in the face of Almighty God for the sheer pleasure of it. That's sinning – and I've never done that. I haven't the courage."

He paused and swallowed his drink. Brother Tom filled his glass again and Father Damian thanked him.

"I'm a bad priest, Father Tom. A failure. Not like Brother Mac here. He knows what sin is. Don't you, Brother Mac?"

"I do my duty, Superior."

"I'm sure you do. Perhaps you should have been a priest."

"I was not called."

"Perhaps you were deaf. Or maybe God, in his wisdom, had decided that the Church had suffered enough at the hands of incompetents like myself. We shall never know, Brother Mac."

"May I leave the table now?"

"You may not. Failure I may be, but I'm still a superior failure – and that must count for something in this world."

"You're drunk."

"Not yet, Brother Mac. But the evening is still young. Join me in a drink, Mr Franklin."

Franklin shook his head. "No, thanks."

Father Damian looked disappointed. "You're not a very religious man, are you, Mr Franklin? You don't have to answer that. You're a good teacher and that's the important thing. Were you in the Recreation Square today?"

"No. If I had been, that flogging would never have taken place. Have you any idea what those boys suffered?"

"I can imagine, Mr Franklin. I can well imagine."

"And what are you going to do about it?"

"There's very little I can do about it, Mr Franklin. Brother John is in charge of discipline."

Franklin scoffed. "Brother John is not fit to be in charge of anything. He's a Fascist thug. And Brother Mac here is an idiot."

Brother Mac lowered his head and Father Damian looked at him without pity. "And what do you say to that, Brother Mac?"

"I'm sorry," he whispered. "I turned away – but I was part of it. I'm so sorry."

"Well, that's a comfort!" Father Damian retorted – and drained his glass. "Pour me another drink, Brother Tom – and have one yourself."

"Not now, Father – if you don't mind."

"I do mind. Hold out your glass."

Brother Tom held out his glass and Father Damian filled it to the brim. He poured another drink for himself and glanced at what remained in the bottle.

"Is there another one?"

"Yes."

"Then open it – and leave it on the table."

Brother Tom hesitated – and then went to the sideboard and produced another bottle of wine. He opened the bottle and placed it in the centre of the table.

"Drink up, Brother Tom. If Brother Mac had his way we'd all be on vinegar and gall. The one mistake Christ made, Mr Franklin, was at the marriage in Cana. He changed water into wine. Brother Mac has never forgiven Him for that."

"It was an act of love," Brother Tom said, as he sipped his drink.

"You hear that, Brother Mac? An act of love. What have you to say?"

Brother Mac raised his head. "You have no interest in what I have to say, Superior. You're drunk – and you're trying very hard to provoke me. But I will not be provoked. I do my duty as best I can. And if I make mistakes, then I am sorry for them."

"Sorry? You offend me, Brother Mac. You age my soul.

You persuaded me once to let you build a wall across the Square. I must have been insane. Now, I want that wall removed. I want it taken down and destroyed!"

"It's too late, Father," Brother Tom said sadly.

"Too late? What do you mean – too late?"

"The wall in the Square, Father. The boys know why it was built now. They know what it means."

Father Damian felt sick. He pushed aside his wine glass and tried to rise from the table, but he was drunk now and slumped back into his chair.

Brother Tom rushed to his aid – and Brother Mac hurried from the room in disgust. Franklin remained.

"More wine?" he asked – "Superior."

There was no answer. And Franklin looked with distaste at the spilled wine, now spreading slowly across the dining-room table.

*

Letter from my father. Penned by Mrs Barrett.

"Since your mother died I haven't gone near the bedroom. I put a lock on the door. I'm sleeping in the back room now. I enclose a shilling. There's nothing on the quays. Not a boat in sight. I go down and lean over the South Gate Bridge sometimes, just to see the swans. I don't drink at all. Haven't touched it in years now, as you know. The man next door is like a demon, and he's still ripping up the floorboards, but I tapped on the wall last night with a spoon and he answered me with a hammer. I must invent a code so that we can talk properly. Have you a code in Saint Jude's? Send it on to me, if you can. Mrs Barrett is posting this. She'll be drenched doing it. It's raining again."

Letter from Mr Goldman. Penned by himself.

"When I was young my mother wanted me to be a Rabbi. Wasn't I the lucky man to escape from home! My brother in New York sent me a fiver for Christmas. The usual thing. But why Christmas, for Heaven's sake? Why not on the anniversary of the French Revolution, the Fall of the Bastille, or even Voltaire's birthday — though I've gone off Candide recently. Maybe I've read it too often. Zola hangs on."

Letter from my father. Penned by Mrs Barrett.

"I saw your friend Goldman yesterday. He was standing outside that old bookshop in the Marsh. He doesn't look at all well. He mentioned your mother and said she was a great woman. Talked about you too. I'm going for a walk now. The rain has stopped."

Fifteen

In loyal companionship let us unite
Happy boys are we.
A friend on the left and a friend on the right
Happy boys are we.
Happy, oh happy, oh happy are we
While we are here by the side of the sea
Happy are we – here by the sea
Happy boys are we …

It was late in the afternoon when Mercier stood at the head of the class and said that he had been charged by Franklin to teach those who could not read and write.

"Shut up!" he said. – "And just listen." We sat and listened.

There were over twenty boys in the class who had never learned the art of reading and writing – and in another room, at the rear of the building, Franklin was struggling to teach many more.

"We'll begin with you, Peters," Mercier said – and moved towards the blackboard.

"Why me?" Peters cried indignantly. "I'm not the worst."

"Can you read?" Mercier asked.

"No."

"Can you write?"

"No."

"Then you're one of the worst. So shut up and try to learn something of value."

Peters shook his head. He had no intention of learning. He folded his arms tightly across his chest and stared at the ceiling.

"I didn't want to come here at all," he complained. "I don't give a hang about reading and writing."

"You're an ignorant slob, Peters. What do you think is going to happen to you when you leave this hotel?"

"I'm going to be bloody happy!" Peters answered. "That's what."

We cheered loudly. We rose from our seats. We pounded the tops of our dilapidated desks. We stamped our feet on the bare boards and sang:

Vote, vote, vote for de Valera
Vote, vote, vote for all his men.
Though we're living in a sty
De Valera tells us why
And we'll never vote for Cosgrave
Anymore!

"Belt up!" Mercier shouted. "Knock it off – and sit down!"

We returned to our seats – and Mercier waited until the class was silent and there was no movement in any part of the room.

"That's better," he said. "Now, listen to me, Peters. Supposing, when you leave here, you wanted to forge a cheque?"

"I can read money," Peters proclaimed. "I could always read money."

"But the signature, Peters. What about the signature?"

"That's not reading," Peters countered. "That's writing."

"It's the same thing."

"No, it's not."

Mercier was becoming exasperated. "Are you going to co-operate?"

"No."

"All right. Be stupid all your life."

Mercier paused and looked hopefully at the remainder of the class. We did not respond – and Mercier turned to Peters again.

"Let's look at it this way, Peters. You want to be a success, don't you? Make lots of lovely money? Live rich?"

Peters regarded him with suspicion. "Yes?"

"Well, how are you going to do it? Robbing gas-meters? Bashing some old lady over the head and doing a bunk with her handbag?"

Peters thought for a moment and then, with a broad smile, answered "Yes."

We clapped our hands and cheered loudly – and we continued to cheer until Mercier ordered us to stop.

"That's not the proper attitude at all, Peters. There's no money in crimes like that. You want to know where the real money is? In books – bank books, post office books, stocks and shares. There's millions there, Peters. And if you're caught, you won't suffer any more than if you'd robbed a gas-meter."

"Who says?"

"I do. It's what they call respectable crime. The Fraud Mob. The Diddle Boys. The guys with pens in their hands and ledgers on the table. They wear posh suits and they've got bank accounts abroad. They don't need sledge-hammers. All they need is a pen."

"So?"

"So – in order to get into a mob like that, you have to be able to read and write. It's like basic equipment. Without it you're dead."

"Is that certain?"

"Positive."

Peters wasn't sure. He scratched his head. He tapped his

fingers against the side of the desk – and suddenly shouted: "Bollox! Teach me to read and write."

Mercier smiled – and turned towards the blackboard where he had already outlined the first lesson. He picked up the pointer.

"We'll begin with reading, Peters. Just follow the pointer. C-A-T – cat. M-A-T – mat. R-A-T – rat. Now, try it on your own."

Mercier pointed to each letter in turn and Peters repeated the letters and the words. He was filled with pride when he'd finished and we applauded his efforts.

"You're on your way to your first million," Mercier said – and Peters patted himself on the shoulder.

Mercier lowered the pointer. "Who's next?" he asked – and without waiting for an answer, pointed directly at Rogers. "You," he said – and the room was silent.

"I can read that," Rogers said nervously. "I don't need the cat on the mat."

Mercier ignored the remark. "Just follow the pointer, Rogers. That's all you have to do."

Mercier pointed to the blackboard and Rogers read, without pause, the letters and words outlined on it.

"Let's have that last word again, Rogers. I didn't hear you."

"R-A-T – rat."

There was no sound. We were looking at Rogers and his face was pale.

"That was lesson Number One," Mercier said quietly. "This is lesson Number Two – and it's called Who Killed Cock Robin? I said the fly – with my little eye. I killed cock robin."

We waited for him to continue. He sat at the edge of Franklin's desk and looked down at us. He held the pointer in his hand – and when he spoke, his voice was low and pleasing, as if he was telling a story to a group of very young children.

"Once upon a time," he began, "there was a large cage filled with golden robins. And these robins were guarded, night and day, by hundreds of enormous blackbirds. Terrible things, with steel claws, who would tear you limb from limb if you dared to open your mouth. So, what did these robins do? They kept their mouths shut and sat quite still in their cage.

"Now then, Kiddies. With all these robins housed together in one cage, something was bound to go wrong. They were all of the same sex, for one thing. They were Daddy Robins. And before long, many of these Daddy Robins started pairing off with each other. They played Postman's Knock and Pussy in the Corner and the like.

"Mind you, they didn't play these games openly. They weren't that stupid. All the other Daddy Robins knew about it, of course – but it was no concern of theirs. And, in any case, what were they expected to do about it? Tell the terrible blackbirds? No, Kiddies. Because the one thing you must never do is to betray a robin to a blackbird.

"But there was one robin who paid no attention to this rule. And, one night, when all the other robins were fast asleep, he crept out of his cage and told the Chief Blackbird all about it. The Chief Blackbird was furious. He wanted names – and this sneaky little robin provided him with names.

"The next morning, the Chief Blackbird entered the robins' cage and dragged out two of the robins. He shaved off their feathers – and then he flogged them until the blood flowed down their backs."

Mercier paused and then added – "That's the end of the story – except – what do you think should be done with the robin who betrayed his friends?"

There was silence for a moment. And then, from the body of the room, someone shouted: "Kill the bastard! Kill him!"

Rogers screamed. "I didn't do it! I didn't do anything!"

But we ignored his cries. We were listening to Mercier.

"Crush him!" Mercier roared. "Beat him to pulp!" – and brought the pointer down hard on the back of Rogers' hands.

Rogers screamed again as Mercier dragged him from his desk and forced him on to the floor. Then he kicked him – as we laughed and roared our approval.

We rose from our seats. We scrambled over our desks and we attacked Rogers. We punched and we kicked and we tore at his hair and his clothes as he continued to scream and cry out for someone to help him. But no one did – and we might have killed Rogers if Franklin hadn't entered the room at that moment and prevented us from doing so.

*

When you have removed my face
And replaced it with another
Do not tell me that this was your task
And I am better for it.
That is a lie.
When you have removed my lungs
And replaced them with others
Do not tell me that the air I breathe
Is cleaner now.
That is a lie.
When you have removed my tongue
And replaced it with another
Do not tell me that the songs I sing
Are sweeter now.
That is a lie.

When you have removed my eyes
And replaced them with others
Do not tell me that the land I knew
Is brighter now.
That is a lie.

Sixteen

After they had removed Rogers from the classroom at Saint Jude's and taken him by car to the local hospital, Franklin dismissed the class and ordered Mercier to report to him in his own room.

When Mercier did so, he found the door open and Franklin standing near the window waiting for him.

"Close the door," Franklin said, "and let's have it."

Mercier closed the door and stood with his back to it.

"Well?" Franklin demanded. "What happened? You almost killed a boy out there. Haven't you anything to say?"

Mercier didn't answer.

"I'm talking to you, Mercier!" Franklin said angrily. "When I left you in charge out there, I thought you had brains. You haven't. You're as thick as the bloody wall and you don't give a damn for anyone but yourself. Now – I don't know whether Rogers informed on those boys or not. It makes no difference. But, I'll tell you this – Rogers is one of the most frightened and pathetic creatures I have ever met. His parents are dead. He has no friends. And if he survives at all, it will be no thanks to you."

He paused. "What, in God's name, did you hope to achieve by beating a boy like that? Does it mean you feel tough? Are you a man now? Is that the measure of it?"

Mercier stared at him, but still refused to answer.

"Talk to me, Mercier! I came here to help – but I can't do it on my own. I need your help – all of you – and by God you need mine. Because without it you're going to walk out of here with a gravestone round your necks. Do you understand what I'm saying?"

"I don't need you," Mercier said coldly. "I don't need anyone."

"Why not? Do you think that you can survive alone? You can't. No one can. I learned that a long time ago. I learned it in Spain. Why do you think we were defeated over there? We needed help – and there was no help. You may think you've got it rough in here, Mercier. But you don't know what roughness is.

"All over Europe now, men are being hunted down, tortured, burned out, shoved up against prison walls and shot to death. And they're the lucky ones, Mercier – because they're out of it. There's worse to come. And sooner or later we're all going to be involved. And do you know why? Because we're all part of each other. There's no other way, Mercier. We can't survive alone. Not any more."

"Can I go now?"

"Is that all you have to say to me, Mercier?"

"Yes."

Franklin looked at him, puzzled and disappointed by what he saw. He had expected more from Mercier. Defiance, an explanation – understanding, maybe – or a single word of regret. But Mercier offered nothing. He stood with his hands in his pockets and his back against the door and, to Franklin, the expression on his face was one of complete indifference. He turned away.

"All right," he said sadly. "Get the hell out of here."

Mercier opened the door, hesitated for a moment, then looked back at Franklin.

"Mr Franklin."

"Yes – what is it?"

"That book of Spanish poems you lent me."

"What about it?"

"Brother John took it from me."

"So?"

Mercier shrugged his shoulders. "Nothing," he said. "I just thought I'd tell you, that's all."

He departed from the room, without closing the door, and walked silently along the stone corridor.

*

Dear Mannie —

I would have liked to have told you of a bird that died in the garden — and the madness of crowds …

Seventeen

"You were saying, Brother John?"

Father Damian was kneeling on the floor in his office with the bellows in his hands, endeavouring to coax the dying embers of the fire back to life.

Standing in the centre of the room, Brother John was growing more and more irritated. Father Damian had already interrupted him twice with this ridiculous nonsense about the fire, and now here he was again, on his knees this time, puffing and blowing at the embers.

"I was saying, Superior – if you will only put that bellows away for a moment – that Mercier will be punished. He will be flogged and then placed on bread and water for one week."

"That seems rather severe, doesn't it, Brother John?"

"Would you rather that I ignored the matter?"

"Of course not. It was a dreadful business. Most distressing."

He placed a log of wood on the fire and watched the flame rising slowly around it. He was cold, his back ached and the last thing he desired was a confrontation with Brother John.

Struggling to his feet, he stood warming his back at the growing fire.

"How is Rogers?" he asked.

"I have no idea," Brother John replied. "That is Brother Tom's department. May we now discuss more important matters?"

"By all means. And I'm sorry about the fire – but since you are not a frequent visitor to this room, you may not be aware of how cold it can become. It is essential to keep the fire going."

"I believe that you have other means at your disposal for dealing with that problem," Brother John said sarcastically, "but be that as it may. You are aware, no doubt, that Mr Franklin is a corrupting influence in this reformatory?"

"I am not."

"Then let me inform you. The man is a Communist. He fought in the International Brigades."

"Many people fought in the International Brigades," Father Damian said wearily. "They're were not all Communists."

"They were an anti-Christian force, Superior. They fought against General Franco. That is sufficient. Mr Franklin will have to leave this reformatory."

"That is for me to decide," Father Damian said firmly.

"You refuse to dismiss him?"

"Yes. Mr Franklin is an excellent teacher. I have no cause for complaint."

"I beg to differ," said Brother John, with barely controlled anger. "I have but recently confiscated a collection of poems which he lent to Mercier. They were Communist propaganda. And there was one particular poem which attacked, in the most obscene and unholy manner, the person of General Franco."

Father Damian smiled. "I must read it," he said, and placed another log of wood on the fire.

"That will not be possible," Brother John declared. "I have already destroyed it."

Father Damian looked at him. "You know, Brother John, there are times when I wonder how this Church of ours has survived the actions of men like you."

"It has survived," Brother John said with conviction, "through the power of Christ. And not, if you'll forgive me for saying so, through the apathy and weakness of muddle-headed priests like yourself. Now, I am asking you for the last time. Will you dismiss Mr Franklin from his post in this reformatory?"

"No, Brother John. I will not."

"Then you leave me no alternative. I shall take the matter to a higher authority."

"Without my permission?"

"With or without it, Superior. I am a Brother in Christ. And I have been placed in this reformatory to correct, guide and protect the young from the corruption of this world. I see much of that corruption embodied in the philosophies of men like Mr Franklin. With God's help, they were defeated in Spain. I do not intend that they shall be given the opportunity to resurrect themselves here."

Father Damian sighed. "You realise, of course, that I can remove you as Prefect?"

"You have that authority. But it will not prevent me from taking the matter further. I would be failing in my Christian duty if I did not do so – and I will not be accused of that."

There was a knock at the door and Father Damian waited for a moment before answering it. Brother Tom entered the room.

"Oh, I'm sorry, Father," he said. "I didn't realise you were busy."

"That's quite all right, Brother Tom. Brother John was just leaving."

Brother John glared at both of them. "We have not yet finished discussing this matter!" he said.

"I think we have, Brother John," Father Damian stated calmly, and turned towards the fire. "Good-day to you."

Brother John stared at him for a moment – then

marched from the room, slamming the door behind him.

The sound startled Brother Tom. "Good Heavens! I seem to have arrived at the wrong moment, Father. Is there anything I can do?"

Father Damian warmed his hands at the fire. "I'm afraid not, Brother Tom. How is Rogers?"

"Not too bad. I had a long talk with Doctor O'Brien from the village. He says that, with a little care and attention, Rogers should be on his feet again in a couple of weeks."

"Thank God for that," Father Damian intoned – and looked at Brother Tom. "Would you care for a drink? I certainly would. You'll find the bottle in the bottom drawer of my desk."

Brother Tom opened the drawer of the desk, removed the bottle of whiskey and poured out two drinks. Father Damian sat in the chair, close to the fire, and Brother Tom handed him a glass.

Father Damian nodded his thanks. "I could have done without that altercation," he said. "I don't feel well today. Must have a cold coming on."

"The whiskey will do you good, Father."

Father Damian sipped his drink. "How, in God's name, did Brother John find out that Mr Franklin was in the International Brigades?"

"There was a dedication to Mr Franklin in that book he lent to Mercier," Brother Tom replied. "It was quite explicit. And, no doubt, Brother John made further enquiries."

"You can be sure he did!" Father Damian exclaimed. "It was very foolish of Mr Franklin. I thought he had more sense. Drink up. You don't look all that well yourself."

"I'm just tired, Father," Brother Tom sighed – and without realising what he was saying, he added – "And I could do with a new pair of shoes."

"Shoes?" Father Damian queried.

Brother Tom had been thinking about shoes all night. His feet ached, he had the beginnings of a blister on his left heel and there was a hole in the sole of the right shoe. He was determined to bring the matter to the attention of Father Damian, but when he entered the room and saw Brother John, in obvious confrontation with the Superior, he had decided against it. It wasn't the time. Father Damian had more important things on his mind and could not be expected to deal with such things as aching feet and worn-out shoes. But, having raised the issue now, there seemed no point in not continuing with the matter.

"Yes, Father. I'm sorry to bring it up at this moment, but I'm badly in need of a new pair of shoes."

"Then go and get them," Father Damian said simply.

"I have been trying to get them for the past three months," Brother Tom stated – "but Brother John is of the opinion that I don't need them."

Father Damian looked at Brother Tom's shoes. "Take them off," he said, "and let me look at them."

Brother Tom removed his shoes and handed them to Father Damian. He felt embarrassed standing there in his stockinged feet. He was conscious of the hole in one of his socks – and was beginning to regret having entered the room at all.

Father Damian examined the shoes. "How long have you been going about in these atrocities?" he asked.

"Oh, for quite some time now, Father."

"You should have mentioned this to me sooner," he said angrily – and cast both shoes into the fire.

The suddenness of Father Damian's action staggered Brother Tom – and he almost knocked over the bottle of whiskey standing on the desk.

"You can wear a pair of mine for the moment," Father

Damian continued. "They're about your size. And tomorrow you will go into the village and get yourself a new pair of shoes. Brother John will provide the money."

"Yes, Father."

"Now, pour me another drink. And learn to take care of yourself a little more. It would never do to have you out of action."

"I'm sorry, Father."

He filled Father Damian's glass and set the bottle of whiskey down on the floor, close to Father Damian's chair.

"You won't have one yourself?"

"No, Father. Thank you all the same. The one will do me."

"You'll find the shoes among that chaos in the corner over there. Help yourself."

Brother Tom rummaged through the piles of old shoes, books and folders, in the corner of the room and finally managed to find a pair of shoes that suited him. As he tried them on, he noted that they could do with a good polish – but he would see to that as soon as he returned to his room.

"All right, Brother Tom?"

"Yes, Father. These will do fine."

"Then off you go, like a good man. Let me open the door for you."

He rose to his feet and moved towards the door. And as Brother Tom was leaving, he said: "Have you ever punished a boy, Brother Tom?"

"No, Father."

"But you could if you felt it was necessary?"

Brother Tom shook his head. "I don't think so, Father. Being young is punishment enough."

"Take care, Brother Tom."

Brother Tom left the room, wearing Father Damian's shoes. Father Damian watched him as he hurried towards his own room, where he would sit and polish them with a soft cloth, until they shone like new. Father Damian then closed the door.

The room was warmer now and he resumed his seat near the fire and nursed his drink. He had thought, for a moment there, that if he were to remove Brother John from his post as Prefect, he might replace him with Brother Tom, in spite of what the Bishop would say, but he knew now that that was impossible. Brother Tom was too old and only barely managing to keep up with his present duties. The business with the shoes was extraordinary, and he couldn't understand why Brother Tom had put up with such indignity. But then, there were many things he might have fought for himself, had he not lacked the courage or the will to do so.

There were others, of course – dispersed in various workshops throughout the school grounds, but most of them were noviciates or tradesmen, and the only time he encountered them was at Mass or Benediction. And there were two more – Brother Mac and Brother Whelan – but they were more suited to the confines of a psychiatric ward.

Father Damian swallowed his drink, lay back in his chair – and heard the first sound of Brother John flogging Mercier.

He closed his eyes and counted each fall of the leather strap onto Mercier's back. He could almost feel the pain. When there was silence again, he reached for the whiskey bottle and refilled his glass.

*

In the Public Library in Cork, a man sat in the Reading Room every day reading The Life Story of Saint Theresa of Avila. *He read nothing else. When he entered the Reading Room he removed his shoes and stockings and sat in his bare feet close to the radiator. I spoke to him once and he said he was in love with Saint Theresa, and that one day he would walk to Avila in his bare feet and kiss the ground she'd walked on. The last time I saw him he was eighty years old, and he was still reading the same book. He died in Cork and never kissed the ground of Avila.*

"Franco did," my mother said. "The curse o' God on him. They'll have to wash the place out when he dies."

When my mother died, I promised to tend to her grave. Who tends to you now?

Eighteen

We stood in the refectory and thanked God for what we were about to receive. Brother John clapped his hands and then we sat down.

In the centre aisle of the refectory, Mercier knelt on the stone floor. His head had been shaved. And, on the chair in front of him, lay two slices of bread on a plate and a cup full of water.

Brother John clapped his hands again, but we did not eat. We sat in silence.

At the door of the refectory, Brother Mac stood nervously watching us. He had his rosary beads in his hands, and we could still see traces of the hair which he had recently cut from Mercier's head along the edges of his soutane.

Brother John ordered us to eat – but we did not move. He struck the boy nearest him with the back of his hand, and the boy's eyes smarted with tears – but he did not eat.

Brother Mac crossed himself, lowered his head and backed repentantly out of the refectory.

We began tapping the tables with our cups. The noise spread from one table to another, growing louder and louder as it circled the refectory. We used knives and forks in rhythm on our plates. We stamped our feet – and the sound reached a crescendo of noise that could be heard clearly, far from the refectory.

Brother John waved his strap, threateningly, in the air. "You will stop this noise at once!" he shouted.

"Continue with your meal – or I will flog every boy in this refectory!"

The noise continued – and we sang:

I want to go home
I want to go home
I don't want to live
In this rat-house no more
I don't want to eat
Like a pig on the floor
Take me over the sea …

Father Damian entered the refectory. "Boys! Boys! For Heaven's sake," he pleaded. "What's happening here, Brother John?"

"They are refusing to eat," Brother John said. "They say they will not do so until Mercier is taken off bread and water."

We all cheered – and Father Damian appealed to us again. "Please! Stop this nonsense immediately. Silence, I say!"

We stopped cheering. The banging and the noise gradually subsided. And there was silence in the refectory.

Father Damian waited for a moment and then approached Mercier.

"Get up off your knees," he said gently, "and go and sit at the table with the other boys."

"No."

"Let me deal with him!" Brother John demanded – and moved swiftly towards Mercier. He raised his strap and was about to strike Mercier across the head, when Father Damian stood in his way.

"Leave this to me," he said quietly. "Move back." And when Brother John hesitated, Father Damian shouted "Now!"

Brother John stepped back, and Father Damian turned to Mercier again.

"Listen to me, Mercier. You have nothing to gain by this behaviour. I want you to sit at the table. I want this entire incident forgotten. There will be no recriminations. No further punishments. Do you understand what I'm saying?"

"You have no right to make such promises!" Brother John protested.

"That will do, Brother John! Now – on your feet, Mercier, and go and sit at the table."

Mercier rose to his feet and had almost reached the table when Brother John rushed forward, shouting: "I will not tolerate this! Come here, you disgusting object …"

Mercier grabbed a knife from the table and pointed it directly at Brother John's stomach.

"Touch me again," he screamed, "and I'll run this knife through your guts!"

Brother John paused, then said menacingly – "You will regret this, Mercier. You will regret it to your dying day."

Father Damian placed a restraining hand on Brother John's arm and tried to pull him away. "Please, Brother John. No more of this. Leave the refectory."

Brother John looked at him with astonishment. "At once!" Father Damian added. "I am the Superior here. Get out!"

Brother John stammered in disbelief. Then, unable to contain his anger any longer, he pushed Father Damian aside and stormed out of the refectory.

We cheered. And we were still cheering when Franklin entered the refectory a moment later.

"Cut that!" he shouted. "What the hell is going on here?" – as Father Damian pointed to Mercier, who was still standing near the table, with the knife in his hand.

227

We stopped cheering – and watched Franklin as he held his hand out to Mercier.

"All right," he said. "The knife, Mercier. Hand it over."

"Why? You said you were on our side. Why?"

"I am on your side, Mercier. But this is not the way. Hand it over."

"No! You're a creep! You're like all the others. A creep!"

Franklin moved closer. "Trust me," he said. "That's all I'm asking. Trust me."

"Oh, Christ!" Mercier sobbed. "Oh, Jesus Christ. Trust me!"

He burst into tears and the knife fell from his hand and landed at his feet. Franklin picked it up and placed a protective arm around Mercier's shoulders.

"All right, Mercier," he said. "It's all right. Come with me."

Mercier wept – and Franklin led him along the centre aisle and out of the refectory.

We sat in silence. Father Damian clapped his hands and we rose to our feet. He asked us to pray – and we thanked God for the bounty of His gifts.

*

Upon an autumn day, Connors and I sat on the quay wall and watched the Innisfallen *leave its berth and move out past Blackrock Castle to Roche's Point. We talked of England then, or maybe America, and Connors said that if he was emigrating at all, he would not take the* Innisfallen, *but would walk from Cork in his bare feet.*

I thought of the man in the Cork Public Library then and Connors and I talked about Spain. "It's a long walk from Cork to Avila," he said, and shook his head.

It was late in the afternoon and we sat there for a long time, watching the Innisfallen *disappearing slowly over a grey horizon.*

Nineteen

Father Damian sat on the bench beside Franklin in the garden of Saint Jude's. He knew that the following morning Franklin would be leaving Saint Jude's and he would never see him again. It was the hour before Benediction.

"I suppose it's no good my asking you to stay on, Mr Franklin?" he asked.

"I'm afraid not, Superior."

"What will you do?"

"I'm going to England."

"To join the army?"

"Yes."

Father Damian sighed deeply.

"I thought that's what you might do – now that England has declared war on Germany. At the same time, Mr Franklin, I do feel that you would be more useful here."

"With Brother John?"

"There are wars and wars," Father Damian said. "I can deal with Brother John. And with Brother Mac too, for that matter. I have already got the boys working on the removal of that dividing wall. And I have every intention of removing Brother John from his post as Prefect, as soon as I can find a suitable replacement. Brother Tom, unfortunately, is a little too old for the post – and he hasn't been at all well these past few days."

"I'm sorry about that."

"So am I. But we shall manage, Mr Franklin. We always have."

"In spite of your mistakes?"

"Yes, Mr Franklin. And, if you'll forgive me for saying so, I think you've made one or two mistakes yourself – but we won't go into that now. I would still like you to stay. It's not easy being a priest. And it's not easy being the Superior of a school like this. I need help."

"It wouldn't do any good, Superior. And besides …"

"And besides – you've got a war to fight. So have I, Mr Franklin. You told me once that what these boys needed was love and affection. Someone they could trust. You appear to have changed your mind on that score. A pity. Enjoy your war, Mr Franklin. It's almost time for Benediction now. I must go. Good luck."

"And to you, Superior."

Father Damian rose to his feet and stretched out his hand to Franklin.

"I've left a medal of Saint Jude in your room," he said. "He's the patron saint of lost causes, you know. Take him with you. He might come in useful some time."

Franklin smiled and shook Father Damian's hand.

"I'll do that," he said. "Thanks for the thought."

Father Damian nodded.

"Good luck," he said again – and turned towards the garden gate. He opened the gate and stood looking back, for a moment, at Franklin, who was now standing near the wall. He closed the gate and walked quickly in the direction of the chapel.

Franklin heard the gate closing – and, presently, he heard the bell ringing for Benediction. He looked at the wall, and at the names and the numbers scratched there over the years by the boys of Saint Jude's. He recognised many of the names and wondered if he would always remember them – or if they would remember him.

*

Letter from my father. Penned by Mrs Cotter.

"When you come home again, I will meet you at the station. I have papered the walls and painted the front door. Your friend Connors helped me. Mrs Barrett is dead. She had a good funeral and Connors and myself followed the hearse to the graveside. You would have been proud of Connors – though I think he has a screw loose somewhere. All the windows of his house are boarded up and he has a notice in his window advertising free love to atheist widows. I tapped the news of Mrs Barrett's death to your man next door, but he never answered me – though he did stop ripping up the floorboards for a week which, I suppose, is his way of showing respect.

"I don't know what you'll do when you come home. There's no work and everyone in the street seems to be emigrating to England. I hope you won't have to do the same. It's lonely here and I could do with a bit of company.

"Yesterday I was walking along Frenches Quay and I saw Paddy Kilroy's boat still rotting away near the South Gate Bridge. The sky above it was clouded with seagulls. He left the boat to you, but God knows what you could do with it. Some people say that it's haunted and that Paddy has changed back into a seagull again and comes back at night to make sure it's all right. If I was you, I'd sink the bloody thing – but it's up to you. I'll see you soon."

Epilogue

On the morning of my release, Father Damian called me into his office and said he was sorry to see me go. He said I looked well in my new suit and my new pair of shoes and that there was many a one outside who'd pay a fortune for an outfit like that, if they had a fortune, which nobody had these days on account of the war.

He said the war had the country in tatters. There was no coal. The cars were running on gas. You had to have coupons to buy a suit, the tea was rationed to a half-ounce a week, the coffee was made of dandelion roots and the flour was so bad that it had to be sieved daily, to take the rubbish out of it, so that people could have a decent loaf of white bread on the table before they expired altogether from malnutrition.

I was beginning to feel sorry for Ireland – but Father Damian hadn't finished yet.

He said that the country was surrounded by U-Boats, the fishermen hadn't had a catch in years, the roads were deserted, the newspapers were censored, there was nothing on the wireless and Dublin was full of German spies – and British ones, too, only they wouldn't admit it because England was a free country and they didn't go in for such underhand tactics.

For a brief moment I wondered whether I should remain at Saint Jude's – but Father Damian had already signed the release form and was now in the process of providing me with the means to return to Cork.

He handed me a rail ticket and a packet of sandwiches. He pressed a shilling into my hand. He said he would walk with me as far as the main gate and that I could catch a bus from there which would take me to the local railway station.

"It's not far," he said, "but you might as well take the bus and it will only cost you a penny."

I placed the shilling in my pocket and carried the packet of sandwiches under my arm. Father Damian patted me on the head and walked beside me as we left the Office and headed towards the main gate.

He opened the gate.

"Now mind yourself," he said, "and keep out of trouble."

I promised I would – and Father Damian closed the gate and returned to his Office.

I stood outside. I removed my shoes and threw them over the wall. I put my socks in my pockets – and walked, barefoot, towards the local railway station.

SONG FOR A FLY BOY

To Diana and María

Prologue

I had never met Adolf Hitler, but my mother heard him speaking on the radio one night and said that the one good thing to be said for him was that he was now at war with the British. The fact that he had also supported General Franco during the Spanish Civil War, and sent the Condor Legion to Spain to blitzkrieg Guernica and the Spanish Republicans into submission, did present her with some difficulties, but my mother was like that. When in doubt – bomb the Brits.

My father, on the other hand, was not in favour of bombing anyone and, though sympathetic to the British, spent most of his time praying for Eamon de Valera and the remainder of his time offering up novenae for the conversion of Russia to the Catholic faith.

Adolf Hitler was also rather keen on the idea of converting the Russians and sent his Panzer Divisions to Moscow with orders to deliver the message. But the snow got in the way of the Panzers, who had to make a hasty retreat to Berlin, with nothing to show for their efforts but a postcard from the Red Army saying – "Don't call us. We'll call you."

In Ireland, however, no one was calling anyone because the telephones were tapped. De Valera said we were neutral. The ports were closed to the British and the Germans. The newspapers were censored, and when a well-known Irishman was killed in a naval battle in the Atlantic, his death was reported as an unfortunate boating accident.

Occasionally, some news did filter through – but the British appeared to be forever on the retreat, and the Russians had an extraordinary tendency to advance backwards, even when they were halfway to Berlin with snow on their boots.

William Joyce, in the guise of Lord Haw-Haw, confirmed the news. From Galway, he spoke on Radio Berlin every night to comfort the British in their hour of need. He also believed in miracles and said that the war would be over by Christmas, the Germans would be dining in Moscow, and Hitler was already preparing a banquet in Buckingham Palace, to which all were invited – provided they had blond hair, blue eyes, and were not degenerates. He also, incidentally, believed in acupuncture and kept a needle by his bed every night to keep the Reds away.

In Cork, of course, nobody believed in anything that wasn't written on the back of a five pound note. And in Margaret Street we were more concerned with the horrors of rationing than with anything happening in Europe. Seán McEntee introduced us to the weekly half-ounce of tea and when that failed to please us, we were subjected to a concoction called "Coffee O' Eire" – made from sawdust and dandelion roots – which did more to increase the mortality rate than anything since the Famine.

In desperation, many people joined the Local Defence Force – where extra rations were provided for those who could see and rosary beads for those who could not. Created by de Valera to defend us against invasion by the British or the Germans, the LDF blossomed in areas more renowned for their addiction to martyrdom than for anything to do with common sense. Rifles at the ready and rosary beads pointing west, the LDF stood guard over our coastline and dared anyone who was mad enough to come and invade us – as occasionally, someone did. A group of German parachutists were reported to have landed somewhere in the

Midlands, but they got lost in the Bog of Allen – and when they finally managed to dig their way out, they were too exhausted to do anything but surrender to the Gardaí. Some time later, another German parachutist arrived in Wicklow enquiring for the address of the local Commander of the IRA. When he was informed that the latest incumbent was presently incarcerated in the Curragh, he went into a decline and had to have medical treatment.

The British, of course, didn't have to invade. They occupied six counties in Northern Ireland and when they, accidentally, strayed into the Republic, to view our defences, they were promptly returned to the North. The Germans, on the other hand, were interned because no one could think of a way of shipping them back to Germany without a Safe Conduct Pass from the British. The British weren't issuing Safe Conduct Passes that year, being more interested in sinking anything that could float and wasn't one of their own. So the Germans stayed put and waited for Hitler to rescue them from oblivion.

In Cork, we were used to waiting. We waited in dole queues to be rescued from poverty. We waited in schools for a revelation in learning. We waited in church for a guarantee of eternal salvation, while the LDF waited for an invasion under neutral lights, which shone brightly and could be seen clearly across the water. In Margaret Street, however, the lights were going out and we were down on our knees seven days a week, praying to be invaded by anyone who could provide us with a cup of tea or a bag of coal to light the fire. We waited a long time and then some of us moved out.

One

"None can remain neutral. Everyone must show through his deeds where he stands – whether against us and freedom, or by our side in the great army of the world of the future."

–Sir Stafford Cripps

The Recruiting Sergeant in Belfast looked like Richard Greene advertising Brylcreem and said he was glad to see me. He shook my hand, motioned me towards his desk and offered me biscuits and tea. I declined the offer and sat close to the desk. I expected him to sit facing me, but he remained standing, back to the wall, trousers pressed to a knife edge, his Royal Air Force jacket bedecked with campaign ribbons.

"Distinguished Service," he said and touched the ribbons. "Battle of Britain", he declared and touched them again. I waited for more, but he lit a cigarette and turned to the wall. "The rest is history," he sighed – "and Hedy Lamarr."

I looked at Hedy Lamarr. Her portrait hung upon the wall beside a large map of Occupied Europe and her lips spooned "Kiss me. I'm all yours." The Sergeant kissed her and the smoke from his cigarette encircled her head and clouded her face.

"Does that surprise you?" he asked.

"Not at all," I replied. "She's a beautiful woman."

"I'm glad you think so," he said. "I saw her in a film some years ago. She was running naked through the woods and I've never forgotten her."

Benito Mussolini hadn't forgotten her either. He had also seen *Ecstasy* and became so obsessed with Hedy's naked body that he screened the film nightly to remind himself of what he was missing by allying himself with Adolf Hitler.

The Sergeant, however, didn't appear to be missing anything. His imagination worked wonders, and the light of ecstasy, radiating from his face, was enough to blind a regiment. I coughed twice and cried "Excuse me! Anyone there?"

"Frightfully sorry," he mumbled. "Do forgive me. Where was I?"

I could guess, but my religious upbringing prevented me from saying so.

"I've come to join the Air Force," I said. "Is this the place?"

"It is," he replied. "His Majesty welcomes you."

"Is he about?"

"Not at the moment, I'm afraid. He's rather busy. The war, you know. But I'm his representative. You may speak freely."

"I saw this advertisement in a magazine. It had Betty Grable on the cover. 'Come Fly with Me,' she said. That's why I'm here."

"Wrong Air Force, Old Boy. Are you sure it's the Royal Air Force you want to join?"

"Well, I'm here now. I'll take anything that's going."

"Indeed! Are you fit? We're not like the Americans, you know. They appear to accept anything that moves and has a vocabulary of three words in English. The Royal Air Force, on the other hand, does require a somewhat higher standard. How old are you?"

"Nineteen," I lied – at which Hedy Lamarr blushed and hid behind the bushes. I was sixteen and much too young for her.

"You don't look nineteen," the Sergeant said. "You don't look anything like it. Have you a disease?"

"No, Sergeant. It's just that I'm small for my age. It runs in the family."

"No offence, but you'll have to be medically examined. I was about to say, by a doctor. But, from the look of you, an undertaker might be more appropriate. Is there a next of kin?"

"Certainly. My parents."

"And the address?"

I gave him an address and waited for him to write it down, but he remained standing, back to the wall, his hair brushing Hedy Lamarr's breasts.

"If you pass the medical examination," he declared, "you will be required to sign the Official Secrets Act. Do you know what that is?"

"Tell me."

"The Official Secrets Act is binding for life. And that means that anything you see, hear or do during your service with His Majesty's Forces is Top Secret and may not be disclosed, spoken of, or even whispered to anyone, including yourself. The penalty for such disclosure in wartime can be most severe."

"Could I be shot?"

"That is possible. We are fighting a ruthless enemy and the enemy has ears. He may be standing beside you in a pub. He could be sitting beside you on the No 9 bus. He may even be lying beside you in bed …"

I raised an eyebrow at that, but he ignored me and continued: "The object of the exercise is to make you aware at all times of the presence of the enemy. A careless word, a momentary lapse of thought, a comment on the state of the weather in a letter or on the telephone, may result in the loss of many lives."

I glanced at Hedy Lamarr. She was listening intently –
and she was not alone. Displayed on the wall behind me
were posters of other Mata Haris urging the nation to buy
Liberty Bonds and defeat the Hun. But Lana Turner's
sweater wasn't fooling anyone – and the Disney-painted
torso of Rita Hayworth, stretched along the fuselage of a B-
29 bomber, was guaranteed to keep anyone's mouth shut for
life. I promised eternal vigilance and Hitler choked.

The Sergeant nodded. The posters were an American
import. "Not quite the thing, you know – but one has to
humour an ally."

Hedy was different. Painted in oils, she had class written
all over her. So had the real Mata Hari, but I saw no point
in mentioning that. The walls were listening.

Stacked on the desk in front of me was a neat pile of
Enlistment papers. The Sergeant asked me to fill one in and
I listed my cousin's name, his superior education, his total
lack of contagious diseases, and his ardent desire to fight for
freedom anywhere in the world. I signed his name with a
flourish and sat back, impressed. The Sergeant was not.

"Can you see?" he asked.

"I beg your pardon?"

"I ask, merely, because you have filled in the wrong form.
The Enlistment form for airmen is on your right. The one
you have filled in is an application to join the WAAF. But
no matter. Neither is valid until you have been passed
medically fit by the MO."

"What happens after that?"

"You will be required to take the Oath of Allegiance to
His Majesty. It is a most solemn moment."

I lowered my head and prepared to be canonised.

When the Medical Officer arrived, I was ushered into an
adjoining room and advised to strip. I undressed, furtively,
behind a bamboo screen and reappeared later with both

hands covering my extremity. The Medical Officer emerged from behind his desk and closed his eyes.

"Is one permitted to view?" he quipped. "Or do I take it we're closed for the winter?"

I raised my hands and thought about Lady Hamilton.

The Medical Officer stared at me, speaking as if he were about to take flight.

"Pox!" he cried. "Have you ever had pox?"

"I don't think so."

"Crabs? Gonorrhoea? Syphilis?"

"No," I replied – and the insignia of rank, pinned to the shoulders of his battle-dress uniform, wilted with disappointment.

"A pity," he sighed. "I was so looking forward."

He opened my mouth, knocked on my teeth and peered down my gullet. He said I had soft skin.

I said I loved him too and wondered whether to call the Fire Brigade.

He examined my eyes, looked inside my ears, drummed on my chest with his well-manicured fingernails, then asked me to cough. I coughed.

"Your Dick is not moving!" he screamed. "It should jump when you cough!"

I coughed louder and Dick went into convulsions.

"That's better. You should have done that before. We can't have people in the Royal Air Force with paralysed Dicks, you know."

He returned to his desk and sat facing me. "You can get dressed now," he said. "I've seen all I want to."

I dressed hurriedly and inched towards the door.

"By the way," he called. "Who put the notion into your head to join the Air Force – Vera Lynn?"

"Betty Grable."

He smiled. "The legs, of course. Used to be a leg man

myself once. Gave that up. I'm a breast man now – all the way."

"I don't think I've reached that stage yet," I said.

"Oh, you will, Dear Boy, you will. There's something particularly riveting about a pair of well-developed mammary glands."

I retreated from the room – *virgo intacta*.

In the outer office, the Recruiting Sergeant was still standing with his back to the wall.

"Can I have a glass of water?" I asked, but there was no reply.

"Hedy Lamarr drinks water," I winced. "She drinks nothing else!"

The Sergeant looked at me. "Have you passed your medical examination?" he enquired.

"I think so."

He moved towards his desk and, for the first time, I could see that he limped.

"Nothing serious," he said. "Just a little flak."

He sat down – under the seductive gaze of Hedy Lamarr.

Two

Having sworn allegiance to His Majesty, his heirs and successors, I was transported to Newtownards in Northern Ireland to be kitted out, and from there to Padgate in England for the basic training as Airman Second-Class. I had expected a somewhat higher rank to begin with, but was informed by the Recruiting Sergeant, with regret, that everyone had to start at the bottom. Betty Grable, of course, had made no mention of that.

On a damp morning in November, I was introduced to Corporal Hines. He stood, ramrod stiff, on the Parade Ground in Padgate and said he was going to be my mother. He informed the other forty recruits standing beside me that he was going to be a mother to them too, but I was special. I was the worst recruit he had seen in his entire life. I apologised profusely and said the ground was wet.

Corporal Hines was from London and believed that anything north of the Wash should be encircled with barbed wire and anyone found inside shot while trying to escape. He was now stationed in Padgate and spent most of his evenings playing with a hand grenade and debating whether to pull the pin. Being a good Samaritan myself, I encouraged him to do so.

When the war started, Corporal Hines was stationed in Egypt and though he enjoyed the company of Egyptian laundry boys, no one could persuade him that some earlier Egyptians had built the pyramids.

"Couldn't build a shithouse, Mate! Never mind a pyramid."

Sometimes, when in his cups, the Corporal would invite us to what he described as an evening of art and music. The art consisted of a series of faded postcards depicting the amorous adventures of an Egyptian Mummy and an arthritic donkey – while the music consisted of a number of bawdy songs, listing the sexual activities of Adolf Hitler and King Farouk and the astonishing variations they managed to achieve together with the aid of a fiddle and a bicycle pump.

But on this November morning, the Corporal was inviting us to stand at ease and call him Mother. We did both and the Corporal yelled: "You're a shower! An absolute shower! What are you?"

"An absolute shower!"

Looking pained, the Corporal informed us that, on present showing, we had no hope of defeating the enemy. We would be trampled to death, blown to bits, machine gunned, blasted, crushed under foot, and generally disposed of before we had time to say bollox. The Corporal was very fond of the word bollox and repeated it to himself several times a day, whenever he saw anyone crossing the Parade Ground with their hands in their pockets or their caps askew.

He repeated it now and told us to pay attention.

"My job," he announced, "is to instruct you in the art of survival. A bollox of a waste of time, in my opinion, because I can't see any of you surviving beyond the first obstacle course. However, I obey orders – and that's what you're going to do. You will march, jump, crawl, stand on your heads, roll in the mud, shoot straight and bollox to the man who can't. Clear?"

We stood in the rain and shouted "Clear!"

"Attention!"

We did our best. Corporal Hines paused, lowered his head in disbelief, and said his bleeding Granny could do better and she was dead.

"By the left – *LEFT*, ye bollox! – Quick march!"

We marched. And for the next six weeks we continued to march. We climbed mountains, hung precariously over fast-flowing rivers, dangled from training parachutes in hangars and from trees, and learned to kill the enemy with rope, knife, broken glass, bayonet and machete. We learned to strangle him with wire, blind him with pepper, break his legs, deafen him and cut his throat – silently and with speed. Corporal Hines said we were useless.

"If you are going to bayonet a man, don't tickle him. Ram the bayonet into his guts – and then twist. That lets the air in and makes it easier to pull the damn thing out again. If the bayonet does get stuck, squeeze the trigger and blast it out! You are not playing pocket billiards."

I removed my hands from my pockets and promised to do better next time. Corporal Hines yelled bollox and said it was now time for us to become acquainted with the hand grenade.

He produced one and stood before us, his back protected by a stone wall.

"The hand grenade," he waxed lyrically, "looks like a small pineapple and is, as you can see, a very beautiful object. Note the outer shell. It is made up of forty-eight equal squares of metal, not including the top and bottom. Imagine that you are sitting comfortable in a well-organised brothel, and feel it – touch it."

We felt it. We touched it – and what I imagined almost gave me a heart attack.

"When this little darling is lobbed into a confined space," he continued, "it is guaranteed to clear that space of all enemy personnel. We are not in a confined space. We are standing beside this here wall. And the object of the exercise is to throw the grenade over the wall and hit the deck before it explodes. Clear?"

"Clear!"

"Then I will demonstrate. The grenade is held in the right hand. Pause. Remove the pin with your left hand – making sure to hold on tightly to the spring. Pause. Release the spring – throw the grenade over the wall – and you have three seconds to... *HIT THE DECK!!!*" We dived to the ground. A moment later the grenade exploded on the other side of the wall, and I came to the instant conclusion that Corporal Hines was a lunatic.

Corporal Hines waxed even more lyrical a few days later, when describing the endless attractions of the Browning Machine Gun. This time we were asked to imagine we were sitting in a Turkish bath, surrounded by a bevy of well-disposed nuns. Actually we were standing in three feet of mud, at the safe end of the firing range, while Corporal Hines sat on a box of live ammunition, caressing the machine gun.

"Beautiful," he cooed. "Stroke the barrel. See how it shines."

The machine gun purred. It lay on his lap and smiled up at him.

Corporal Hines waxed on. "You are looking at a sweetheart," he said. "It has a firing rate of eleven-hundred-and-fifty rounds a minute. The magazines hold three hundred rounds – enough for bursts of fire of up to four seconds – and the Hurricane and the Spitfire carry eight of these, firing simultaneously. The effect is devastating."

He rose to his feet, eyes gleaming with happiness and, like a priest offering the gift of Holy Communion, presented us with the machine gun.

We held it in our hands. We stroked it gently. And I decided to join the WAAF and surrender to the first German paratrooper who landed in Padgate.

Corporal Hines, however, was not going to surrender to anyone. He set the machine gun on a tripod, loaded the magazine, and faced the target area.

"Observe the enemy!" he cried.

We looked hard – and saw Hitler grinning at the destruction of Warsaw, Mussolini pouring poison gas over the villages of Abyssinia, and Hirohito proclaiming his divinity over all things, including Pearl Harbour.

Corporal Hines squeezed the trigger of the Browning Machine Gun and three hundred rounds of .303-inch ammunition ripped through the Axis in four seconds flat. Corporal Hines was ecstatic. He reloaded the machine gun and fired again.

"Bollox!" he yelled. "And bollox to that!"

We stood in the mud and the air reeked of cordite and *Lebensraum*.

When Corporal Hines had finished demolishing the power of the Axis, he announced we had now reached the stage in our training when a spot of leave was in order. We would be provided with a Weekend Pass. We could spend the time in Warrington. We could sample the delights of the camp cinema, or we could do what he was going to do – lie on his bed and play with a hand grenade.

Playing with a hand grenade didn't appeal to me at all. The camp cinema had been taken over by Eric Portman, Mervyn Johns, Leslie Howard and Anton Walbrook – and I firmly believed that had I to sit through *Dangerous Moonlight, The First of the Few, Squadron Leader X, The Next of Kin* or *The 49th Parallel* again, I would end up in a mental home. Where was Ann Sheridan? I cried. Jean Arthur – Sylvia Sydney – Ida Lupino – Bette Davis? "Oh, Jerry, don't let's ask for the moon. We have the stars."

I opted for Warrington and found it occupied by the Americans. They filled the bars, rode in jeeps through the streets, lay in heaps on the pavements, waved nylons at the girls and swore they were all single, lived in Hollywood, and were looking for a Limey wife.

They listened to Glenn Miller and the Andrews Sisters in the American Forces Canteen, smoked Camels and Lucky Strikes, ate hamburgers and ice cream, and lamented the passing of the American Dream. At night, they haunted the railway station platforms. They slept on mailbags and kitbags, waiting for trains that were late or never arrived at all. They wandered the countryside, waving the American flag, unable to find their way because all the signposts had been removed, or turned the wrong way round, to confuse the Germans, who were still threatening to invade.

Lost in the blackout, they ended up asking an equally lost Irishman the way to the American Embassy in Warrington. Together we found the American Forces Canteen and Glenn Miller welcomed them home.

The following morning, I woke up dead. I was convinced I was dead because I had no head and my feet refused to carry me to the nearest hospital. An American 'Snowdrop' told me I was still drunk. It was my first time and I blamed Glenn Miller, the Andrews Sisters, and the American Forces of Liberation.

On my way back to Padgate, I shared a taxi with a woman who wept on my shoulder. She had just been to the station to say goodbye to her Canadian boyfriend, who was passing through Warrington, on his way to 'Somewhere Over There'. She'd missed the train. She longed for his touch. She had a parcel in her hand, intended as a parting gift. She offered it to me.

"It's what he would have liked," she said. "Having missed

him, at least I gave it to another Canadian."

I accepted the gift. She kissed my cheek. It rained heavily. Oh, *Waterloo Road* and Vivien Leigh! Romantic movies were never a miss.

The last two weeks of our training in Padgate were devoted to less romantic activities. Corporal Hines said we were fighting a war. We sat in hangars staring at silhouettes of approaching aircraft and learned to tell the difference between theirs and ours – "So that you don't make a bollox of it and shoot down one of our own!" We stood in the bomb-dump on rainy afternoons, listening to Corporal Hines on the gentle art of handling high explosives – "without blowing your bleeding knackers off!"

The bombs were laid out in rows along the perimeter of the bomb-dump. Corporal Hines sat on a general-purpose bomb and listed its destructive capabilities, while we stood as far back as possible, hoping he would forget himself and strike a match.

He said the Incendiary Bomb had great potential when dropped in clusters on houses and factories, but was even better when accompanied by the 250-lb medium-capacity bomb, dropped in batches of eight from a Wellington Bomber. He praised the 500-lb bomb and the 1,000-lb bomb and the 4,000-lb bomb, which exploded a few feet above the ground, causing a lateral blast. He praised the 8,000-lb bomb, painted green so that the enemy couldn't see it from the air, before turning his attention to the magnetic mine.

The magnetic mine weighed only 2,000 lbs, but was lethal to shipping. Dropped from the air by parachute, it rested silently on the sea bed, until activated by metal from the hulls of vessels passing overhead. The vessels, Corporal Hines declared with a grin, were blown to shagging bits.

"We are fighting a war," he repeated. "We are not playing pocket billiards."

And that was that. Corporal Hines said that we had now completed our basic training and were ready to face the Hun. He expressed little hope of our surviving the encounter, but there was nothing more he could do. "See you in Hell!" he cried, looking, for one moment, like John Wayne about to lead a cavalry charge. I kept my hands in my pockets, and the following day we were Passed Out for war.

Three

Rejected for Air Crew, but considered adequate for Ground Duties, I was posted, along with a Conscript named Bill Harrison, to a Bomber Command station in the Midlands for further training as Armourers. Harrison claimed that he had been chosen for this particular trade on grounds of diminished responsibility, while I was selected because the Assessment Officer – a man of mesmerising stupidity – was convinced that all Irishmen were born with a silver gun in their mouths. "Never met a Paddy yet who wasn't good with a gun," he flowered. "Quite extraordinary!"

Betty Grable had a lot to answer for.

Bill Harrison had never been seduced by Betty Grable. He was a Conscript from London. Destined for the Army, but given a choice, he opted for the Royal Air Force. He was a tall, lanky, dark-haired twenty-four-year-old who couldn't stand still. During breaks in the NAFFI canteen, he would philosophise about the war, wave his arms about and knock the cups off the table. He said that was what war was all about – knocking things off tables and smashing them. Corporal Hines christened him 'Windmill' and the name stuck.

When we arrived at our new station, Windmill said that we were now entering the War Zone. The gates were manned by airmen with machine guns. The runways were crowded with Lancaster Bombers. Giant searchlights lined the perimeters. Ack-Ack gunners scanned the skies for approaching enemy aircraft, and the air smelled of gasoline and apple blossom.

"Shit!" Windmill said. "This bloody place looks dangerous. Have you ever thought of emigrating to Australia?" I hadn't. But it was too late now.

Entering the War Zone, we were greeted by Warrant Officer Payne and his two Alsatian dogs. Payne, with a pair of .38 revolvers strapped to his waist, was convinced he was a second General Patton. The dogs agreed with him. They stood by his side, mouths open, and saluted him with their teeth.

"Late!" he bellowed. "Goddamn late! It won't do." We apologised, without prejudice, and said we'd been caught in an air raid.

"No excuse. Use your initiative. Grab a taxi. If the driver refuses – shoot the bastard!"

The dogs barked their approval and Warrant Officer Payne patted their heads.

"Sense!" he cried. "They've got sense. Nobody else has. How are we expected to win this goddamn war?"

He marched away and the dogs followed him. We followed the dogs.

When Payne joined the Air Force at the beginning of the 1920s, he wanted to be another James McCudden, the pilot who engaged "The Red Baron" in aerial combat during World War I and was credited with the destruction of fifty-seven German aircraft. The powers-that-be, however, decided otherwise. The War To End Wars was over and there was nothing to do now but wait for another one to begin.

Payne was confined to the armoury and remained there, reading adventure stories of the heroes of yesteryear and wondering when he'd be called upon to defend the Empire against another band of flying Huns. The call never came. When World War II broke out, Payne was still in the armoury, charged with teaching younger men how to service machine guns and load bombs into the bomb bays of Wellington and Lancaster Bombers. The aircraft were new. Payne was getting on. Only his dogs understood him.

"Do you know General Patton?" he asked.

"Not personally," I replied.

"That man is a genius. Knows what he wants. Goes after it. Grabs it and moves on. That's the way to win wars. If he wanted to fly, they'd let him. Bloody well have to! There's no stopping the man."

Warrant Officer Payne had forgotten James McCudden and was reading now *The Exploits of General Patton*. "Genius," he repeated. "Absolute bloody genius! If I'd joined the American Army when I was young, I could have been up there now, standing beside him, Christ!"

The dogs agreed. They too could have been standing beside General Payne. Windmill Harrison, on the other hand, had no desire to stand beside any of them. He hated dogs and believed all Generals were psychopathic morons, with square heads, and cordite for brains.

How many bodies make a star?
How many stars make a General?
In Flanders Fields the poppies blow,
Ask them, my child –
They know.

Windmill Harrison didn't have to ask. His father had been killed in the trenches during World War I, and he knew the answer.

"Ever heard of the Valkyries?" he asked. "They are the war maidens who hover over the battlefields of the world, and carry the fallen warriors of their choice to Valhalla. But there is no Valhalla for Privates. It's Officers only – and Private soldiers are left in the mud, to be buried in heaps. My Old Man was a Private soldier."

In Padgate, Windmill and I had been branded together

as "the two airmen least likely to achieve officer status". I didn't know then about the Valkyries. The knowledge strickened me. We'd be left in the mud, with no hope of an afterlife with General Patton.

In the armoury, Windmill and I listened to Warrant Officer Payne's translation of the Articles of War. "Harass the enemy. Blast him into submission. Give no quarter – and winner take all."

The dogs sat at his feet and sharpened their teeth.

"There is no joy in losing a war," he proclaimed. "You have to win – whatever the cost. Our job is to hit the enemy from the air and it is your job, as armourers, to make sure that the equipment required to do that job properly is in top-class condition at all times. It's no good depending on the bloody air crew wallahs to check. Most of them haven't a clue. "Sorry, Skipper – me Browning won't work" and – "Oh, dear – the bomb doors won't open." And they end up coming back here with their knickers in a blitz. It's up to you. The guns fire, the bombs fall and the enemy gets hit. Understood?"

"Understood."

"Sometimes these kites come back from a raid in a right bloody mess. Rear turret blown apart – undercarriage shot to pieces – guns jammed – engines crapped, and Christ knows what else. They've got to be moved – cleared off the runway – ripped apart – repaired pronto – and put back in the air again. No shit. No messing. Is that understood? Don't echo me! Nod your heads."

We nodded our heads. The dogs growled. And we could hear the Lancasters moving slowly towards the runway, preparing for take-off.

During the weeks that followed, Warrant Officer Payne stood over us as we stripped and reassembled machine guns, bombed up aircraft, loaded magazines with endless belts of ammunition, worked beside fitters and electricians, firemen and medics, and waited on runways for aircraft returning from bombing missions over Germany. We listed the missing, assessed the damage to man and machine, helped to clear the runways and prepare the bombers for another raid over enemy territory.

In the evenings, we listened to Vera Lynn on the radio singing 'We'll Meet Again' and "There'll be Bluebirds over the white cliffs of Dover/ Tomorrow, just you wait and see ..."

We waited for the morrow and heard Joe Loss and His Orchestra, 'Workers' Playtime' from a factory in Birmingham and Carol Levis asking us to tune in next week – same spot on the dial. Max Miller joked, Flanagan and Allen sang 'Underneath the Arches', Bing Crosby dreamed of a White Christmas, and The Ink Spots looked at the dreaming of America and cried – 'This is Worth Fighting For'.

Didn't I build that cabin?
Didn't I plant that corn?
Didn't my folks before me
Fight for this country
Before I was born ...?

On the One O'Clock BBC news, the announcer declared that in last night's raid on the city of Berlin, eight hundred heavy bombers were employed. The enemy was hit. There were no losses. "All our aircraft have returned safely to base." You could sing that if you had an air to it.

One night, I was standing guard outside the armoury. Four hours on, four hours off. Warrant Officer Payne had ordered me to shoot on sight anything that moved. Nothing moved. The enemy had gone to bed. I stood with my back to the wall and thought about the wonders of Australia.

In the Sergeants' Mess, the Air Crews were celebrating another day of survival in the air. And in the Officers' Mess, they were promising to pay their Mess Bills tomorrow, next week or whenever, if they happened to be here.

The blinds were drawn. The searchlights were dimmed. The Lancasters rested on the runways – giant shadows reaching for the moon.

"It's a Bomber's Moon," the Flight Sergeant said.

Standing at the door of the Sergeants' Mess, he held a glass in his hand. "Would you like a drink? You must be freezing standing there."

"No, thanks, Flight. Not permitted."

"Payne? A fantasy artist. He should have been bombed out years ago. My name is Benson, by the way. What's yours?"

I told him. He sat on the steps to the Sergeants' Mess and sipped his drink, slowly and with ease.

"I'm a little drunk," he said. "Not much, but a little. I'll be sober tomorrow."

In the Sergeants' Mess, someone was singing a bawdy version of the George Formby song 'It's in the Air'. The Flight Sergeant winced.

"Not my style," he said, "but they have to let off steam. They're good kids." He spoke as if he were an old man, and the kids were playing on the living room floor. They were wrecking the furniture – but they were good kids. He was twenty-nine years of age – the oldest member of a Lancaster Bomber Crew.

"You flying tomorrow?" I asked.

"Probably. Don't know why we're not flying tonight. The moon is right."

"Is everybody on 'Stand-Down'?"

"Shouldn't think so. Other stations. Other squadrons. They're up there somewhere. Heading for Hamburg, I expect – or Berlin again. There's no let-up."

"Have you been flying long?"

"It seems like a lifetime," he said. "I came in at the tail-end of the Spanish Civil War. How long ago was that? A hundred years?"

"Not that long. I knew a few people who were involved in that."

"On the Republican side, I trust!"

"Yes."

"Then you were privileged. They were the real first of 'The Few' – but Churchill forgot to mention that. But then, he would, wouldn't he!"

He rose to his feet and looked at the sky. "Some of those lads up there won't be coming back," he said, and shrugged. "But that's how it goes. Good night, Kid."

He swallowed his drink and walked into the darkness. And, a moment later, I heard the sound of breaking glass.

In the early morning, a glistening frost covered the ground. Four hours on, four hours off. It was Windmill's turn now to stand guard outside the armoury. He would stamp his feet, fling his arms about, march up and down, alert the enemy, and ask why the hell Bomber Harris or the Wing Commanders or Warrant Officer Payne didn't stand guard, as usual – instead of lying in their beds hugging their electric blankets. Shit! The arms waving. Feet stamping. The frost darkening and churning to mud. Shit!

I lay in my bunk and listened to the radio. Field-Marshal Goering had promised the German people that no bombs would fall on German territory. Now Bomber Command and the US Eighth Air Force were bombing the Ruhr and the Rhineland, Cologne, Dusseldorf and Hamburg. Last night's news. Tomorrow's news. Bombs falling on Essen and Berlin. No let-up.

No let-up in the weather either. Continuing frost. Some rain. Dense fog in low-lying areas. The Luftwaffe had attacked a number of airfields north of London during the night, but no serious damage was done. Twelve German aircraft had been shot down. Ed Morrow remembered the beginning. Churchill forecast the end. A whirlwind of fire. The burning of clouds. A holocaust.

The frosted windows and the sound of winter. Big Ben on the Home Service. The 'V For Victory' signal on foreign news broadcasts. "Courage, my friends! Together, we'll beat the Boche!" No let-up.

I listened to the music. Music for day workers. Music for night workers. "Give us the tools and we'll finish the job." Listen, my friends, to the Victory sound. Listen to the voices of our boys serving overseas. Listen to the Ink Spots:

I know there are oceans we must cross
And mountains that we must climb
I know every grain must have its loss
Until we are free
Please wait for me
'Till then,
My darling, please wait for me.

I listened to the news:

DIRECTIVE: "The objective here is the morale of the enemy civilian population, in particular the industrial workers." TARGET: Rostock. Visibility excellent. Approximately seventy per cent of centre destroyed. CASUALTIES: Heavy. 100,000 people evacuated. Rough estimate. Losses unconfirmed.
TARGET: Cologne. 1,000 Bomber Raid. Buildings destroyed: 18,000. Badly damaged: 9,500. CASUALTIES: Civilians killed: 500. Civilians injured: 5,000. Civilians made homeless: 59,000. TIME: Ninety minutes. Firestorm visible for 150 miles.
TARGET: Hamburg. Houses destroyed: Sixty-one per cent. CASUALTIES: Civilians killed: 41,000. Civilians

injured: 38,000. Firestorm.
LOSSES ON COLOGNE AND HAMBURG RAIDS:
Not for release at this time. See Berlin and Nuremberg
figures. Compare.

I slept fitfully and dreamed of a whirlwind and the burning of clouds. A holocaust.

Four

Warrant Officer Payne stood beside a 4,000-lb bomb and said we were doing an excellent job. He was surprised, he had to admit, but credit where it's due. We were doing all right. Without us – the bombs wouldn't fall. Right?

"Right."

We'd primed them, loaded them into the bomb racks of the Lancasters, and all the Bomb Aimer had to do was drop the bloody things. Right?

"Right."

"Right. With a few thousand 'Cookies' like this, we could end this goddamn war in a month."

He handed Windmill a camera and said he wanted to be photographed standing beside the 'Cookie'. Twenty years from now, people would look at it and say – "This man helped to win the war with a Cookie."

The dogs lay at his feet. They wanted to be remembered, too.

Windmill belched. He had joined the Air Force because he hated the Army, and now he was helping to bomb civilians? The dogs barked. The Warrant Officer reached for the two revolvers, strapped to his waist, and fired into the air.

"You're a twit, Harrison! An absolute twit! What's the matter with you?"

"I think he's worried about the civilian population," I said.

"Civilians? What civilians? Are you dense?"

"Frightfully sorry," replied Windmill. "Would you care to pose again?"

Warrant Officer Payne paused. The dogs showed their teeth.

"You're not with it, Harrison. Not with it at all. You don't win wars piss-balling about and worrying about the civilian population. If I had my way, I'd bomb every goddamn one of them!"

"I'm sure you would!" Windmill muttered – but Warrant Officer Payne wasn't listening.

"Bomb and blast them to hell," he continued. "That's how you win wars. Do you think General Patton worries about civilians? Like hell he does! The civilian is as much a part of this war as anyone else. General Patton knows that. I know it – and so does everyone else. The only one who doesn't know it is you."

"I do apologise," Windmill said, with a smirk. "But I was brought up in a convent. You know what that's like."

"I do not! And I think you're a goddamn poofter, Harrison. I've always suspected that – and the Royal Air Force is no place for poofters. You should have joined the Navy. They appreciate poofters."

"Well, I did think about it … "

"Crap! And don't try to be funny with me. I'm your Superior Officer. And I have a damn good mind to put you on a charge. A few weeks on jankers might knock some sense into you."

Windmill smiled. The Warrant Officer glared. The dogs smelled poofters.

"Now, listen to me, Harrison. There is such a thing as dumb insolence. That's good enough for six months in the glasshouse. Do I make myself clear?"

"Quite clear, Sir."

"Then catch yourself on. We're fighting a war here. A

264

war to the death. It is not funny and we are not playing games. Take a lesson from General Patton – the greatest General the American Army has ever produced. Kill the bastards. Incinerate them. Burn them out – and keep moving. There's no other way, Harrison. None!"

The dogs agreed. They stood up on their hind legs and pawed the air. The Warrant Officer patted them on the head.

"First class. Now take the photograph."

Windmill prepared to photograph them. "Say Cookie," he said without expression. The Warrant Officer blenched. The dogs growled. Only the Cookie smiled. Warsaw – Rotterdam – London. Tit for Tat.

Around the runways, the Lancaster Bombers were lining up, manoeuvring for take-off. The engines roared. The bomb racks were loaded. The machine guns were oiled and ready for firing. Along the perimeter of the main runway, the fire tenders waited on Emergency Stand By.

We watched the Lancasters take to the air – a hundred bombers on combined operations with hundreds more from other Bomber Command stations. They would meet over Dover and follow the Pathfinders heading for Germany.

Protected by fighters from attacks by enemy aircraft, the Lancasters would battle their way through searchlights and flak and some would be hit and never reach their projected target.

They would drop their bombs in the sea. They would bale out over enemy territory. They would die in the cockpit, or the rear turret, and the aircraft would crash in flames on some crowded village or isolated patch of Occupied Europe that was never recorded on the navigator's map.

The survivors would move on, bomb-heavy and fuselage

littered with spent cartridge shells, until they reached their target and released their bombs on a city lit to a phosphorescent glow by markers and flares dropped by the Pathfinders. Blinded by searchlights and under heavy attack, some of the crews would drop their bombs short of the target and turn for home. But as the bombs fell, the camera installed near the undercarriage of the aircraft would record the 'creep-back' and the sortie would not count among the thirty prescribed for an operational tour.

On the return journey, the Lancasters would encounter more flak and more attacks from enemy aircraft. The leaders would survive, the stragglers would fail, never to reach their home base. We waited for the survivors. In small groups, we stood along the perimeter of the main runway and watched them land.

Some landed safely. Others, with engines on fire and undercarriages jammed, overshot the runway and ended up in a nearby field. The fire tenders raced to the rescue and the medics followed in the ambulance.

We cleared the runway. We towed the crippled aircraft into hangars, and waited for one Lancaster, listed as badly damaged, but still heading for home. We heard the drone of the engines as it approached the station. We could see the smoke and the flames as the pilot lowered the undercarriage and struggled to pinpoint the oil-splattered runway.

He came in slowly, two engines in flames and smoke issuing from the bullet-riddled fuselage. He landed with a crash, the aircraft skidding off the runway and spinning to a halt, close to the Operations Room. We waited for the explosion, but the fires blew themselves out and the Lancaster lay, a twisted heap of metal, still smoking and strangely silent.

There were no survivors. The bodies were removed from the cockpit and the fuselage. The rear-gunner was prised from the tomb of his turret. Only his blood remained and particles of flesh. We hosed it down.

A few days later, I went to visit the Flight Sergeant. Wounded in the raid, he was now recovering at Base Hospital. He greeted me with surprise and I stood by his bed.

"I didn't think they allowed Other Ranks in here," he said. "How did you manage it?"

"Influence," I replied. "I lit Churchill's cigar one time. I felt he owed me a favour. How are you?"

"Not bad, Kid. Just a few scratches. I'll be out of here in a few weeks. What are you up to? Still lumbered with General Payne?"

"And his Alsatians."

"There ought to be a law against those. Payne is bonked, you know. Should have been strapped to a Cookie years ago and dropped from a height."

"I'll tell him."

"Do that. The war has certainly produced more than its fair share of lunatics – on both sides of the divide. Unfortunately, they're the ones who'll survive."

"You think so?"

"They always do – ready for the next one. It's the story of the human race. Lunatics win, Foot-Sloggers lose."

"Maybe it'll be different this time."

"I doubt that. Millions died in the last war. Cannon fodder for the lunatics. Twenty years on, the lunatics are at it again. One goes on fighting them, of course. I seem to have spent my life fighting them, but they always win. It would be nice if, just this once, they actually lost. Christ! That would be something, wouldn't it?"

"Well, my mother always believed the Foot-Sloggers were bound to win sometime."

"Let's hope she's right, Kid. It's long overdue."

"Is this the end of your tour of Ops?"

"No. Two more to go – if I managed to avoid the five per cent."

"What's that?"

"The rate of losses. We lose five per cent on every mission. Last time out, it was twenty-one per cent. Didn't General Payne tell you that?"

"I don't think he's into losses."

"Of course. Win, whatever the cost. That's the Patton philosophy. Hitler's, too, I've no doubt. But when you're up there, dodging flak and releasing bomb-loads on people you can't see, you begin to wonder about things like that."

"Would it make any difference if you could see them?"

"I don't know, but I think about it a lot. It's a strange kind of war when you can't see the enemy. You wonder what's down there. What's burning in the dark. Who dies when you drop the bomb-load? You turn away – because all you can see are the fires burning and the flames reaching for the bomber in the sky. Sometimes, you imagine you can feel the heat. It's nonsense, of course. You're a million miles away and it's freezing cold."

He paused. "Payne is right about one thing, Kid. It's a war to the death, maybe none of us will survive – apart from the lunatics of course."

"You will."

"So everyone keeps telling me. Fly with Benson and you'll always come back. It's crazy. Like something out of a movie – and not a very good one at that."

"I've seen a few of those – and they're usually British. Sorry!"

"Don't be. The Irish always had difficulty appreciating the genius of the Brit. Sometimes we can be so bad, we're brilliant."

"I'll take your word for it. Is there anything you need?"

"No, but thanks for coming to see me. You'd better go now, before someone comes in and starts quoting King's Regulations. They're inclined to do that around here."

"The genius of the Brit? Good luck, Flight. I hope you're better soon. Take care."

"You, too. And watch out for those Alsatians. They're German, you know. Hitler's pets."

I waited for him to smile, but he spoke without expression and lay back in his bed. I moved towards the door.

"See you, Flight."

He made no answer. He was staring at the ceiling and the only sound was that of the electric heater, switched on, to keep an even temperature in an otherwise chilly room.

Flight Sergeant Benson did not survive the war. He died when his plane was shot down on a bombing mission over Germany. It was his twenty-ninth sortie. One more to go, before finishing his tour. Lunatics win, Foot-Sloggers lose. Over and out.

Five

In the NAFFI canteen, Windmill and I sat in a corner and drank lager and jungle juice in memory of Flight Sergeant Benson. No shroud or bier. No sounding brass. No poems like 'Johnny, head in air, he sleeps as sound as Johnny underground'. Nothing to show but a listed number among the five per cent loss rate. Even the Valkyries were missing. They were looking for the Generals.

When a WAAF named Linda Warwick walked in, she said we were both drunk – and didn't we know there was a war on? Windmill told her to get to a nunnery. We were trying to hold a wake, I said, but couldn't find the corpse. Linda said we were mindless.

Linda believed that parachutes were invented by God and anyone could be saved if they really wanted to be. I couldn't see the connection myself, but Windmill said she was probably a religious maniac and the best thing to do was ignore her. I tried hard, but the flesh was weak.

After three bottles of lager, she looked like Linda Darnell. Two more, and she looked remarkably like Ann Sheridan. I said I believed in God. I said I was only pretending to be an atheist. I asked her to sit on my lap and I'd play with her uniform. She poured a glass of jungle juice over my head and threatened to report me for blasphemy.

In another corner of the NAFFI, two members of the RAF Regiment were mourning the loss of their Alsatian. I said nothing, but suspected that Windmill had poisoned it. Linda sat beside them. They sang 'All Good Doggies Go to

Heaven' and 'Jesus Lives Beside the Thames'. Windmill said he was welcome to it and drank a toast to the Unknown Soldier.

We drank to Sergeant Benson. We drank to all who were buried in heaps on the battlefields of the world. We drank to the Foot-Sloggers – and then we fell on the floor. Windmill was sick.

He sang 'Jesus Wants Me for a Sunbeam' – and passed out. I joined him and woke up in the guard-room.

"Suffering, are we?" Warrant Officer Payne enquired, with dubious concern.

"A little," I replied, from the grave.

"It will get worse," he smiled. "Much worse. You are both on a charge. Drunkenness, disorderly conduct, blasphemy and offensive and lewd behaviour towards a member of the WAAF. Need I go on?"

"Only if you have to," Windmill groaned. "I'm feeling extremely fragile this morning."

"Mouth like a sand-pit?"

"I'm afraid so."

"Oh, dear! The Commanding Officer was so looking forward to hearing you sing 'Jesus Wants Me for a Sunbeam'.

He paused. The smile faded into oblivion and, with devastating suddenness, he roared – "Piss Artists! Absolute Bloody Piss Artists! I've never seen anything like it!"

"Frightfully sorry … "

"Shut up! You're a disgrace to His Majesty. If I had my way, you'd be taken out and shot!"

We stood awkwardly to attention and I wondered whether he'd already arranged for the firing squad. Would I be permitted to write a last letter home? Would I die quickly or would Warrant Officer Payne have to deliver the *coup de grâce*? My heart sank. I would insist on a blindfold.

"Quick march!" he yelled.

We marched from the guardroom. "On the double!" he shouted and we doubled. "Halt!" he cried and we halted. Then he repeated himself. He was like that. Better to be heard twice than never to be heard at all.

"Feeling better?" he asked – and started again.

We marched round the parade ground and doubled along the runways. We climbed walls and fell in the mud. We crawled under barbed wire and dug holes in the sand and then filled them up again. I said Hitler was a saint and a friend to the downtrodden, and I prayed for the Germans to invade – but the Warrant Officer wasn't listening. He was fighting a war.

Paraded before the Station Commander and the Station Adjutant, we looked as if we had just been dug up for an autopsy. The Commanding Officer ordered us to stand-at-ease and motioned Warrant Officer Payne to leave the room. The Adjutant stood beside the Commander's desk and read out the charges.

"Celebrating?" asked the Commanding Officer.

"Holding a wake, Sir," I replied.

"I beg your pardon?"

"It's one of those peculiar Irish customs," the Adjutant explained. "They have this dead body lying on the bed and everyone stands around getting drunk."

"Good grief!"

"I'm afraid. It's quite primitive, but still something of an addiction among the Irish."

"And what about you, Harrison? You're not Irish, are you?"

"No, Sir."

"So what on earth were you doing engaging in this ridiculous nonsense?"

"Paying tribute to Flight Sergeant Benson, Sir."

"Getting drunk?"

"Well, we did have a few, Sir."

"I take it that the Flight Sergeant wasn't present during these activities?"

"No, Sir."

"Well, that's a relief. For a moment I thought you'd actually gone out and dug him up! Now, look here, Harrison – primitive rituals of this sort are not permitted in the NAFFI. Good grief, man – it hardly bears thinking about."

"May I explain, Sir?" I asked.

"No, you may not. The Adjutant has explained it sufficiently well. Dead bodies lying about. Piss-ups and that sort of thing. It won't do, Airman. Won't do at all."

"But it's the custom in Ireland, Sir."

"No doubt. And it may very well be the custom in Borneo and the African jungle, but it will not do here."

"Yes, Sir."

"Quite uncivilised. You are also charged with making lewd remarks to a member of the WAAF and singing blasphemous songs. Is that part of the ritual?"

"No, Sir."

"I'm relieved to hear it. Personally, I have no objection whatever to blasphemous songs. One has to be a true believer to engage in that – and I doubt if either of you two believe in anything. But I will not permit a member of the Royal Air Force to make lewd remarks to a member of the WAAF. That kind of behaviour may be acceptable in the Army, but it will not be tolerated here."

"Yes, Sir."

"One must, at least, strive to be a gentleman. You will be confined to barracks for ten days and, during that time, you will carry out extra duties as directed by Warrant Officer Payne. Any questions?"

"May I be excused Church Parade?" Windmill asked.

"Church Parade? What the devil are you talking about, Harrison?"

"Well, as a non-believer, Sir – I would prefer not to take part in the primitive rituals of the Church of England."

The Commanding Officer paused and turned to the Adjutant. The Adjutant coughed. "He's listed as C of E," he said.

"An error of judgement," Windmill countered. "I had flu at the time."

"Now listen to me, Harrison. I think I have been extremely lenient with both of you. Do not try to provoke me. The only people who can be excused Church Parade are Jews and Roman Catholics. Other denominations as and when. You are listed as C of E. Request refused. Dismiss."

We stood to attention, saluted manfully and marched from the room. We were now Janker Wallahs.

In the bomb-dump, Warrant Officer Payne sat on his favourite Cookie and enumerated the extra duties to be performed. We would paint the larger bombs green and the smaller ones black. The two Alsatians sat at his feet and nodded their heads. They would inspect the finished works of art and provide critical appraisal. The remaining extra duties made no demands upon our artistic talents. They consisted of cutting the grass outside the Officers' Mess – for which a pair of scissors was provided – and scrubbing the NAFFI floor with a toothbrush, which had obviously been designed for a midget with no teeth. The man who devised this particular form of torture was clearly related to Vlad the Impaler and I fervently hoped that he had blown himself up with a megabomb.

A week later, we were still cutting grass outside the Officers' Mess, when the air raid siren sounded. I discarded the scissors and followed Windmill, in a heap, as he raced towards the air raid shelter. When the first planes appeared above me, I tried to dig a hole in the ground – with my head – and failed miserably. Windmill dived under a nearby lorry and shouted – "Shit! I've twisted my ankle!" Meanwhile Warrant Officer Payne stood, heroically, on the parade ground, firing his two revolvers in the air and missing everything except the weather balloon.

"Advance!" he screamed. "Kill the bastards! Keep moving!" I had no idea who he was screaming at. I couldn't move an inch and Windmill was still lying crippled under the lorry.

The aircraft came in low. Bullets ripped through the walls of the Officers' Mess, and columns of earth and smoke rose from the ground in front of me. I saw one man falling, blood streaming from a wound in his head, and another cast like a doll in the air when a bomb hit, exploding behind him. I tried to reach Windmill, but couldn't see the lorry because the area around it was covered with debris and clouds of acrid smoke. I managed to reach a bomb crater to my left, and rolled in on top of someone, who appeared to be dead, but was merely unconscious from a blow to the head.

Everywhere was smoke. The sound of bombs falling and exploding, fire tenders and the ambulance rushing to the scene, and the smell of oil and gas escaping from burst pipes.

"Put that cigarette out, you stupid git!"

I recognised the voice. It was Warrant Officer Payne, still standing on the parade ground, guns smoking, and shaking with rage at the departing enemy.

When the smoke cleared, I saw Windmill sitting on the ground with his back against a rear wheel of the lorry, which had miraculously escaped being blown to bits during the attack.

"Are you all right?" I asked him.

"Shit! Are you kidding? If I'd any sense, I'd be in Australia. I told you this shagging place was dangerous. Knew it the minute I saw it. Shit! Are *you* OK?"

"I think so. There's a couple of bodies lying back there, but the guy in the crater seems to be all right. Just a gash in the head."

"He'll get his ticket so. Lucky bastard. Give me a hand."

I helped him to his feet and we stood together surveying a scene of almost total disaster. Two Lancasters were burning on the runway. Three more were badly damaged and lying on their sides near the perimeter. Flames issued from the guardroom, the orderly room, the NAFFI and the airmen's quarters. The windows in the Officers' Mess had been blown out and the armoury had been reduced to rubble. A number of bodies were scattered in various directions and there were bomb craters everywhere. By the time Warrant Officer Payne appeared, sporting his now empty revolvers, I was halfway to a monastery in Tibet.

"Have you seen my dogs?" he demanded. "Can't find them anywhere."

"Maybe they've deserted," Windmill replied through his teeth. "Or died in action. Have you checked the casualty list?"

The Warrant Officer turned pale. "Not funny, Harrison. Not funny at all. Move away from there and help clear up this mess. You can begin by filling in those bomb craters."

"What about the bodies?" I asked.

"Forget the bodies. Let the Medics take care of that. Move!"

"I've twisted my ankle," Windmill pleaded.

"You can limp, can't you? What's the matter with you? We're fighting a war here – not nursing a shower of goddamn dodgers. Get moving."

We moved. Windmill limped towards the nearest bomb

crater and we started to fill it in. In the distance, we could see the Medics loading the bodies on to the back of a lorry and helping the wounded into the ambulance. Fires still raged throughout a number of buildings and the Fire Crew struggled, with punctured hoses, to douse the flames. I looked towards the main runway, where the two Lancasters continued to burn. No one attempted to save them.

Two days later, Warrant Officer Payne discovered that his two Alsatians had been killed during the raid. The Medics had dumped the bodies into a bomb crater. Warrant Officer Payne ordered us to dig them out again. They would be buried properly, placed in a casket draped with the Union Jack, and the Warrant Officer would read the eulogy.

He read slowly, with tears in his eyes, and fired two shots over the grave, as we lowered the casket into the ground.

"Lay it down gently," he said, "and cover it with grass. They were good dogs." Then he walked away.

"Pass me the bucket," Windmill groaned. "I think I'm going to be sick."

I looked at Warrant Officer Payne. He was standing at the edge of the runway, staring at the horizon. He stood there until the light faded and then moved on.

Six

Orders came for sailing,
Somewhere over there,
All confined to barracks
'Twas more than I could bear
I heard your footsteps in the street
And I was sad I could not meet
With you, Lily Marlene,
My own Lily Marlene.

The overseas posting for Windmill and myself arrived without warning. Our two weeks' Embarkation Leave was cancelled, but we were given a Weekend Pass to "settle our affairs", after which we would take the train to Blackpool, to be fitted out with tropical kit, before being posted to parts unknown.

We settled our affairs by visiting London and ending up in a police station in Paddington with two Polish anarchists, who insisted that all wars were the by-product of Capitalism, and the only answer was to shoot everyone who mentioned the word Government without spitting, and then throw a bomb. Being a gentle soul myself, I was inclined to agree with them, but the policeman who arrested us in the Edgware Road said we were obviously foreigners and invited the four of us to Paddington Green police station for afternoon tea, while he checked our credentials.

The two Polish anarchists were released the following morning, and a Sergeant in the CID drove Windmill and myself back to the railway station, where we boarded a train for Blackpool. Windmill thanked the Sergeant. I said English policemen were wonderful, and the Sergeant said he was glad to be rid of us, but wished us luck on our journey overseas.

At the Blackpool transit camp we were inoculated against yellow fever and fitted out with tropical kit, but the rumour was that we were going to Russia and would be issued with snow boots as soon as we boarded the boat. I was convinced we were going to India, but Windmill said he didn't give a hang where we were going as long as it was close enough to Australia, where he intended to jump ship and live with the Aborigines.

We stayed ten days in Blackpool, waiting for the boat, and spent most of our time visiting the local cinema and searching the promenade for the Golden Mile. We managed to find a café in one of the side streets, but the only food on the menu was Spam, carrots and chips. Carrots were recommended for improving the eyesight and, for those who smoked, there was 'Passing Cloud' – a blend of grass roots and floor sweepings – guaranteed to cause blindness, impotence and sterility in anyone foolish enough to inhale it.

We retreated to a nearby pub, known locally as 'The Arsehole of The Empire'. The landlord was an ex-Sergeant Major in the Army, who recited Kipling's 'Danny Deever' when drunk and 'Onward, Christian Soldiers' when sober. Drinks were rationed, but you could get two if you charmed the landlord and ten if you charmed his wife.

The Americans, on the other hand, didn't have to charm anyone. They could drink as much as they liked and, when in doubt, brought their own in wooden cases marked *PX* and *Mae West For Queen!* Windmill fell in love with Mae West, but couldn't quite see her as Royalty. "Beulah, peel me a grape!"

Having sampled the delights of wartime Blackpool, we were finally transported to Liverpool, where we boarded a troopship bound for Somewhere Over There. No one else on the boat seemed to know where we were going either, but I still favoured India. The Officers occupied the first-class cabins on B-deck, the Non-Coms were allocated the mid-section, and the Foot-Sloggers were relegated to the lower depths. It was hot and nauseous, there was little ventilation, and the whole place reeked of sick, sweat and engine oil.

Here, we were divided again. Army Privates to the left – Airmen to the right. Windmill said he disapproved of the caste system, but where the Army was concerned he was prepared to make an exception. "Even Socialism has its limits!" We stored our gear and climbed the hatchway to E-deck.

The boat was crowded. A P & O liner, now converted to wartime use, her decks and cabins were now clear of all pretensions to pleasure cruises in the East. Holds filled with munitions and spare parts. Bofors guns fore and aft. Tanks, jeeps and cannons lashed firmly to the upper decks. Hundreds of airmen and Army personnel occupying all other available space. We pulled away from the pier, moved slowly down the Mersey, past the Royal Liver Building, and out into the Atlantic.

"Depressing," said Windmill. "Very depressing."

"What do you mean?"

"The Royal Liver Building. It seems to suggest that if you haven't insured yourself by now, it's too shagging late."

We were about to return to the lower depths when the Captain addressed us over the tannoy.

"Attention, everybody! This is the Captain speaking. We will shortly be joining a convoy of merchant vessels and destroyer escorts in the Atlantic. We will remain with these vessels until further orders. During the voyage, all enlisted men – repeat all enlisted men – will be under the command of the Army. Good luck – and God speed."

"OK!" the Army Sergeant shouted at once. "Get in line and face me. Brylcreem Boys to the front. That's right, I look like Errol Flynn, but I shoot straight and he can't. From now on, you take your orders from me – and get your finger out, understood?

"Yes, Sergeant."

"Right. Any of you RAF wallahs been overseas before?"

"No, Sergeant."

"Right. In a few days from now we'll be entering The Danger Zone. No smoking on deck. No one permitted on deck after dark. Stay in your hammocks and observe the blackout. If you feel sick, puke in a bucket and wait for the "All Clear" before dumping it down the bog hole. Do not dump it over the side. Nothing goes over the side – except you, if you foul up. Got the message?"

"Loud and clear, Sergeant."

"The Mess is on F-deck. It stinks, so you'll have no difficulty in finding it. Just follow your nose. Any questions?"

"Yes, Sergeant. I thought only merchant ships carried munitions?"

"You thought wrong. Any more questions?"

"How do we know when we've reached The Danger Zone?"

"When I tell you. Now, one more thing: there are over five hundred troops on board this ship. Most of them are Army bods. They're experienced and know what it's about. If you have any more stupid questions, ask them."

"Is there a bar on board?" Windmill asked.

"A-deck. Officers only. If you need a drink, there's a canteen of sorts. It serves warm beer, and you'll have to queue for an hour. But you can pass the time looking through the window at the officers being served gin and tonics by monkeys in white coats."

"With ice, I presume?"

"Watch yourself, lad! Now, are there any armourers among you?"

"Well, we're supposed to be," I replied.

"What does that mean? Either you are or you're not. Out with it, lad!"

"We've just graduated," Windmill said. "We're not quite *au fait* with the finer points yet."

"Jesus Christ! You've been trained, haven't you?"

"More or less."

"Well, for all our sakes, let's hope it's more. You'll man the Bofors guns. Four hours on, four hours off. And keep your eyes skinned."

"Are we looking for anything in particular, Sergeant?"

The blood drained from the Sergeant's face. "No," he replied. "But if you happen to spot a German U-boat, or something that resembles an aeroplane about to drop a bomb on us, you might let me know."

"Yes, Sergeant."

"Now, get moving – both of you – and be quick about it!"

We marched away in no particular direction.

Strapped to the Bofors gun in the forward turret, I felt like I'd escaped from a Hollywood B movie. Knee-deep in sea water, I scanned the skies for enemy aircraft, and the broad Atlantic for anything resembling a German U-boat.

We had now entered The Danger Zone, wherever the Hell that was. I saw nothing but waves during the day, while at night, in the total blackout, I could barely see my hand in front of me. If we were attacked, I suspected the first thing we'd know about it was when the boat sank.

During my fours-off duty, I marked out the position of the lifeboats. Windmill threatened to jump overboard because he couldn't stand the Army, and when the Sergeant told us that there weren't enough lifeboats to go round anyway, I was tempted to hang myself, but hadn't the courage.

Sometimes Windmill and I managed to scrounge a break together, and when the weather was warm, we'd lie out on deck, or lean over the rails and watch the other boats in the convoy and their destroyer escorts. Painted ships upon a painted ocean, going nowhere. When darkness fell, they vanished, and nothing remained but a sky full of stars.

Leaning over the rail one day, Windmill said – "If there's a U-boat out there, I'll bet it's got my name on a torpedo."

"Scared?"

"Shit! Aren't you?"

"I'll tell you when the war is over."

"If we live that long. I sometimes wonder why you joined this lot. Ireland is neutral, isn't it? It's crazy. I wouldn't join my hands, let alone the Armed Forces. I had to be conscripted."

"And you chose the RAF?"

"Only because I wanted to avoid the Army. Now, here I am, in the middle of the Atlantic, lumbered with the bastards."

"It won't be for long. We're just hitching a ride with this mob. How are you getting on with the Bofors gun?"

"Like yourself, I suspect. First time I've ever seen one. But it's not that difficult. Just point and press the trigger. You won't hit anything, but it will make a hell of a lot of noise."

He paused for a moment and stared out to sea. "How old are you?" he asked.

"Mind your own shagging business," I said.

"Fair enough. I just wanted to say, I'm much older than you. And before I joined this lot, I don't think I had a friend in the world. A few girlfriends, maybe – and my mother. But no one I could really talk to. You know what I mean?"

"No."

"Well, it doesn't matter. All I really wanted to say was – I'm glad we're mates. OK?"

He lit a cigarette, inhaled once, then cast it aside. It was growing dark and the boat moved steadily over a calm sea.

The weather was becoming much warmer now and the Sergeant ordered us to change into tropical kit – shorts, shirts with sleeves rolled up, and bush hats.

"You look like the risen dead," he said, when we paraded before him – " but it won't take you long to get your knees brown."

"Any idea where we're going, Sarge?"

"None. I'm sure the Officers know by now, but they haven't seen fit to inform me. But, if my guess is right, we'll be stopping off at Freetown to refuel shortly. So, if any of you want to write letters home, now is the time to do it. You can post them there."

"No thanks," said Windmill.

"You're not writing home?"

"No."

"Why not? No loving mother? No crumpet left behind with a bundle in her arms? You worry me, lad. You don't function right."

"He's just sensitive," I said.

"Sensitive? You should have joined the Army, lad. Put some lead in your pencil."

He turned away, shaking his head, and muttering to himself – "Sensitive! Jesus Christ …"

Windmill waited until the Sergeant was out of sight. "I am, too!" he said. "Very sensitive. Can you imagine some gin-sodden Army Captain censoring your letters? 'Frightfully sorry, Old Chap. Embarrassing, really – but that line will have to go.' The mind boggles!"

He waved his arms about and swept my newly acquired bush hat over the side.

"Shit!"

I agreed – and decided to wait until we reached dry land before writing to anyone.

We arrived in Freetown, West Africa a few days later, somewhat short of India. No one was permitted to leave the ship, but members of the Royal Air Force were instructed to pack their kit and stand by for further orders. We waited on E-deck, leaned over the rails, and listened to the African fruit-sellers struggling to sell their wares from bumboats in the harbour. Some of the men threw pennies into the water, and others shouted – "Jiggy-Jig!" – "Grab hold of this!" and "How much your sister?"

Western culture. Going cheap. How much your mother?

When orders came for members of the RAF to disembark, Windmill grabbed hold of his kitbag, tripped, and almost broke a leg in his eagerness to escape from the Army.

"Leaving us?" the Sergeant enquired, with what passed for a smile.

"*Force majeure!*" Windmill replied, and fled towards the gangway.

The Sergeant said we were lucky. He still didn't know where the Army was going. I wished him luck. He nodded, and walked silently away.

A few days later, Windmill and I stood on the edge of the pier and watched the troop-ship leave the harbour. Hundreds of troops lined the rails and there was no sound as they waved goodbye to no one in particular.

"I wonder where they're going?" I asked – and Windmill shook his head.

"No picnic ground," he replied. "Not with all that gear on board."

He turned away and we both headed towards the market place in Freetown.

The air around the market reeked of rotting fish, dried manure and over-ripe mangoes. But Windmill said it was Paradise. He knelt on the ground, scooped up handfuls of brown earth and let it fall gently between his outstretched fingers.

Snowflakes of the mind. Forget the humidity, the sweat oozing through unwashed bush jackets, snakes, sleeping-sickness, yellow fever, flies, mosquitoes and malaria. It wasn't Australia, but Windmill didn't care. He was free of the Army, free of the sea, his feet planted firmly on dry land.

"Africa!" he cried to a group of astonished Africans – "I love you!"

I wasn't so sure. I had seen Johnny Weissmuller in *Tarzan the Ape Man*. I had suffered through *Sanders of the River* with Paul Robeson and Leslie Banks and I knew what Spencer Tracy had to go through in his efforts to find Dr Livingstone – who turned out to be Cedric Hardwicke in the end, which surprised no one but his elocution teacher. I knew all about Africa. I had seen it in the movies and had been blessed by an African Missionary.

Father Doney was a little man with a sunburned face and an obsession with black babies. He had spent ten years in Darkest Africa telling the natives that God was a Corkman and a personal friend of an Italian Pope. When the natives got tired of listening to this revelation of Divine Truth and tried to roast him over a slow fire, he returned to Cork with a limp and spent his remaining days collecting money for the black babies. He didn't seem too keen on the larger Africans, which was understandable after the business of the fire, but he had great faith in the little ones. "I limp for

286

Jesus!" he cried to a startled congregation in the South Chapel. "Support the African Missions and the babies will see God."

On weekdays, Father Doney visited the local tenements, dispensing Plenary Indulgences to those who contributed a shilling and promising Hell and Damnation to those who contributed less. My mother refused to contribute anything, on the grounds that the Africans had suffered enough at the hands of the white man, and she accused Father Doney of having fathered more black babies himself than anyone could count. The good man denied this unholy accusation. His face turned an extraordinary shade of pink and he fled from the door, panting at the knees.

When I met him in the street a day or two later, he said that my mother was a raving Communist and handed me a holy medal to place under her pillow, the moment she went to sleep. "It will help her to see the light," he intoned. "Africa calls!" Then he blessed me.

Being a polite child, I thanked him for the blessing and gave the medal to my father. He was a great believer in the miraculous powers of holy medals and whispered – "Do you know what's wrong with the Africans? They've never washed themselves in the Ganges." It was a most profound observation and I've never forgotten it.

Yet when I told Windmill this, he wanted to know where my father had obtained his PhD in Geography, and I had to restrain myself from kicking him.

"What are you going to do when the war is over?" he asked.

"Be a Missionary," I replied. "I've always wanted to know how the collections are spent."

"Do you know what I'm going to do? Live here on a plantation."

"I thought you were going to live in Australia?"

"I've changed my mind. Africa calls! I can feel it in the air."

The only thing I could feel was an itch, but I saw no point in disillusioning him.

We stayed in a transit camp for ten days where the humidity was killing me, but Windmill blossomed. He either lay in the sun, hoping he'd turn black, or explored the beyonds of Freetown, looking for a possible site for his plantation.

"You have money enough to buy it, of course?" I enquired.

"Money? When one has a vision, dear boy – who needs money!"

I was beginning to wonder about Windmill. People who have visions worry me. They either end up in bacon factories or mad-out in lunatic asylums. I retired to bed and hid behind a mosquito net.

When a few weeks later we were ordered to leave Freetown and move north to Bathurst, I protested loudly. I had never heard of Bathurst. It had never featured in any movie I'd seen and, apart from that, I was paralytic with the heat and couldn't breathe. Windmill, on the other hand, was falling over himself at the thought of it.

"There might be better possibilities for a plantation up there!" he gushed. "It's great growing land."

"Who said?"

"A guy I met in the market. He said you could grow mangoes up there without leaving your bed."

I resolved to kill Windmill and bury him in a mango swamp.

We were flown to Bathurst in what was loosely described as a Sunderland Flying Boat. It had four engines, two of which spluttered when you looked at them sideways, while the other two screamed whenever they saw water. Windmill and I sat on the floor, and when she finally managed to take to the air, I was convinced that the bottom was going to fall out.

"Is this thing safe?" I asked the pilot.

"Not to worry," he grinned. "Marcella's a bit short of breath, but she can still fly."

"Yeah! But in what direction?" Windmill muttered.

"I've been nursing her for two years and she hasn't let me down yet. You just have to talk to her, that's all. Tell her how beautiful she is. She's dropped a few depth charges in her time and never missed a U-boat. Now, all she does is carry freight – and the odd collection of bods in transit. It's a bit of a come-down, you know."

"She should be scrapped," Windmill said.

"No fear! People like you have no feelings for aircraft. Marcella is a lady. A bit battered and bruised now, but still class. You can't beat that."

The pilot smiled, patted the instrument panel with his hand and cooed – "That's my baby!" "She's at home in the air. It's just the take-off and lands that make her cough."

When we reached Bathurst, Marcella hesitated before landing. As soon as she could see the water, her engines spluttered and coughed and everything inside her rattled and complained.

"Take it easy, Baby," the pilot whispered, "Nice and easy. You know what to do."

Marcella knew exactly what to do. She screamed loudly, then hit the water like a dead whale falling from a height.

"Are you guys all right?" the pilot yelled from the cockpit.

Windmill looked at me, through a heap of broken crockery and overturned ammunition boxes.

"Is he stupid?" he cried.

I made no answer. My heart had stopped and my stomach was still in the air and darkening over Bathurst.

289

Seven

Situated on the Gambia River in Senegal, on a sandy peninsula close to the Atlantic, Bathurst was founded by the British in 1816 as a port and a base for suppressing the slave trade. I read that in a book.

When Windmill and I arrived in Bathurst, the only person who wanted to talk about the slave trade was Flying Officer Clare and, as far as he was concerned, the abolition of the slave trade was a grave error on the part of the British Government. "We have here," he declared during our first meeting on the Parade Ground in Bathurst, "a very sad collection of miscellaneous wogs. They live in mud huts, mouth a form of pidgin-English and have no understanding whatever of the modern world. When you speak to them, as unfortunately one must, speak slowly and in words of one syllable. Anything more results in inextricable confusion."

He paused, removed a royal blue handkerchief from his breast pocket, and wiped the sweat from his face.

"You may think," he continued, "that I am being a trifle harsh. But I can assure you, I am not. You have no idea how the Black Man functions. Most of the time he doesn't function at all – and the notion that you can treat these people as equals is utterly ridiculous."

"I take it we'll be provided with whips?" Windmill quipped. But the Flying Officer ignored him. "Treat them firmly, but fairly," he continued. "You are here to do a job. Do it. But always remember that you are in command.

Don't be too friendly. Don't mingle. Keep your distance and they will respect you all the more."

Sighing deeply, he wiped the sweat from the back of his neck.

"Now – one more thing. You are a long way from home and there are certain needs and desires which we are all prone to. I will refrain from going into details – but there is, at least, one establishment in town which caters for this sort of thing. You will learn soon enough where it is. It is relatively free of disease. It is examined at regular intervals by our own Medical Officer and the services offered are many and varied. You may visit this establishment in your own time. However, all such visits must be reported immediately to the Medical Officer in charge. This is still a pox-ridden country, in spite of our efforts to keep it clean."

"I don't think I'll bother," I said.

"That is entirely a matter for yourself. I am merely providing information. Further information is available in a series of Ministry of Information leaflets, which you are advised to read, and there is also a Ministry of Information film which all ranks are required to attend."

He paused again, wiped his hands with the handkerchief, then continued: "Now, tomorrow morning at eight sharp, both of you will parade outside the main gate where a lorry will be waiting to convey you to the bomb-dump. Also waiting at the main gate will be a group of six wogs. You will escort them to the bomb-dump where you will meet Sergeant Humphries who will instruct you in your duties. The Sergeant, I may add, is not quite with it these days and you may find him a little strange, but no matter. He knows his job. Are there any more questions?"

"Do the natives speak English?"

"I have already informed you. They speak a form of pidgin-English. Personally I find the whole thing totally incomprehensible, but you may not find it so. In any case, if you encounter any difficulties, consult the driver. He seems to understand these people more than I, and will know what to do."

"Yes, Sir."

He wiped his hands again, looked at his handkerchief, sighed and shook his head. "It's like living in a grave," he said. "Everything rots." He cast the handkerchief aside and produced a second one from his side pocket.

"On the matter of relaxation," he droned – "you will find the usual entertainment in the NAFFI canteen – drag acts and the like, and the Salvation Army provides tea and buns at the Sally Ann down the road. There is also an open-air cinema – if you can stand the wogs hanging from the trees outside the fence to watch a free movie – and there is a hovel, not far from here, where you can purchase palm wine and jungle juice."

"No ENSA Shows?" Windmill asked – and the Pilot Officer looked at him.

"I think that will be all," he said. "You may stand easy. Dismiss."

We saluted Flying Officer Clare. He returned the salute, wiped the sweat from his brow and wandered off to the Officers' Quarters.

"Did you get the message?" Windmill asked after he'd gone.

"What message?"

"He doesn't appreciate Africa."

"I don't think he appreciates ENSA shows either."

"He's do-lally. It happens to some guys out here. The humidity gets in to their brain. Reading too much Conrad, I expect."

"Never heard of him."

"You haven't missed much. Depressing bastard. He'd

have you suicidal in a week."

"You've read him of course."

"That was during my blue period. I'm into my red period now. Labour wins. Bring back Ouida."

"I think I'll stick to Ann Sheridan."

"Does that mean we'll be attending the cinema tonight?"

"Well, I'm not sitting through some bloody drag act in the NAFFI – that's for sure."

"Fair enough. Afterwards we can sample the palm wine."

Encircled by trees, the open-air cinema was situated at the rear of the camp and fenced off to prevent people entering without paying.

"We should have joined the natives," Windmill said, as we sat on a wooden bench close to the screen. "They've got brains."

We waited for the film which was listed on a poster outside the gate as a *World Première – with thanks to our American Allies.*

"It'll be some bloody musical, or a war film with Errol Flynn," Windmill moaned. "That's all they're making nowadays."

"As long as it's not *We Dive At Dawn* again, I don't care."

We had seen that world première on the troopship coming over, and the thought of hearing John Mills crying "Up periscope" and "Down periscope" again was not comforting.

"The Yanks wouldn't do that to us, would they?"

"I hope not," Windmill replied. "I'm beginning to feel sick already."

I held my breath as we sat through the Gaumont British News, a James Fitzpatrick travelogue bidding farewell to yet another 'panorama of loveliness', and a trailer of *Blood and Sand* starring Tyrone Power and Rita Hayworth.

There was a pause before we were introduced to the

World Première and the words appearing on the screen did not inspire confidence: "For those who believe in God, no explanation is necessary. For those who do not believe in God, no explanation is possible." My heart sank. The film was *The Song of Bernadette* with Jennifer Jones kneeling in a rubbish dump and claiming Linda Darnell was the Virgin Mary. I was ready to jump into the Gambia – when Charles Bickford yelled "Wake up, Bernadette! You are playing with fire!" and Windmill fell off the bench.

"Abandon ship!" he cried. "Head for the hovel!"

We headed for the hovel and got drunk on palm wine. War is hell.

The following morning Windmill reported sick, and I stood alone at the main gate waiting for the lorry that was to take us to the bomb-dump. The lorry arrived at eight but the driver, LAC Wiggins was obviously suffering from pre-menstrual tension.

"Have the bloody wogs arrived yet?" he screamed.

"Doesn't look like it."

"Bloody typical! Where's your mate?"

"Sick."

"What's the matter with you?"

"Nothing."

"You were pissed last night. I saw you – and that crappy mate of yours. No wonder he's sick. Fucking palm wine. You want to watch yourself with that."

"I didn't have much."

"Muck. The wogs piss in it. Can't trust the bastards."

"I don't believe that."

"Believe it! Wogs' Revenge, they call it. Christ knows why. They'd still be climbing the bloody trees if we hadn't come along."

"Flying Officer Clare said you knew how to talk to them."

"Clare? Fucking lunatic! Doesn't know his arse from his

elbow. Nobody knows how to talk to them. They're wogs. You shout and point – that's all."

"Has he been here long?"

"Years, for all I know. He appears for five minutes, when some new bod comes along – and then he disappears again. He's like a bloody apparition. Nobody knows what he does."

"Does he fly?"

"Not in no bloody aircraft, he doesn't. He has *The Times* delivered once a week. Maybe he flies through that."

"You're a great help."

"Forget him. You won't see him for another six months anyway. Not till another intake comes along. Then he'll appear from the bushes again – and be gone before you know where you are."

"Thanks!"

"Don't thank me, mate. I don't give a bollox anymore. I'm out of here tomorrow. Eighteen months I've been here. Another six months and I'd be floating through windows and climbing lavatory walls. You haven't got your knees brown yet. Is that your crappy mate? I thought he was sick."

Windmill looked sick. He was feeling his way slowly towards the main gate with both eyes closed.

"Palm wine!" shouted Wiggins. "Bloody palm wine!"

"Am I here?" Windmill managed to croak as he reached the main gate.

"Wogs' Revenge!" shouted Wiggins. "What did I tell you?"

Windmill held fast to the gate and lowered his head. "Speak softly," he moaned. "You tread on my dreams."

"Jesus! Get into the lorry, for Christ's sake. You look like death."

"Are the natives here yet?"

"They're coming now. Ambling along as bloody usual.

Take half-an-hour to cross the street."

"Are you OK?" I asked Windmill. "I thought you were going to see the MO?"

"Couldn't face it, mate. I'll be all right. Just help me on to the lorry."

I helped Windmill onto the back of the lorry while Wiggins screamed at the six approaching Africans. "Get your bloody finger out, you lazy bastards! We haven't got all day, you know."

The Africans nodded – and one of them smiled. "Yes, Massa. We's a coming."

It was my first meeting with Sewa. He lowered his head and climbed, slow and easy, onto the back of the lorry.

Eight

Known as 'The Rain Man', Sewa was regarded by his neighbours as the only man in Africa who could create a flood by spitting on a palm leaf. He had removed his own teeth to facilitate the process, and now wore them around his neck as a dedication to the art of rain-making and flood providing.

Sewa said that in a former life he had been a prince of the Soninke people in Kambi Saleh, and was killed by the Muslim Sanhaja Berbers when they overran his kingdom in 1076. He had lived several lives since then, none of which he considered to be of any importance, until the morning he woke up in the Sewa river in a basket filled with palm leaves. The woman who adopted him said she had been expecting him for years and christened him Sewa after the river.

Sewa's first experience of flood-making occurred when his mother offered him a palm leaf for breakfast. Sewa spat on the palm leaf, the river Sewa rose ten feet in the air, his mother was drowned, and the entire village almost destroyed. Sewa was encouraged to leave the village after that and moved to Bathurst – and it was here that he had decided to extract his teeth.

He was standing near the Atlantic Ocean one day, when the thought occurred to him that there might come a time when he would be asked to repel invaders. Sewa was always dreaming about invaders, convinced that one day they would arrive in Bathurst with swords in their hands. He had no idea who these invaders might be, nor was he too sure that a mere flood would be enough to repel them. But if he could raise the Atlantic, that would be a different matter. Sewa bought himself a pair of pliers and removed his teeth.

On Sundays Sewa sat at the edge of the Atlantic, wearing his traditional Soninke costume, but on weekdays he worked in the bomb-dump, sporting a set of false teeth, provided by the RAF, and a pair of shorts, courtesy of the Salvation Army.

"I am a prince in reduced circumstances," he intoned, shortly after our first meeting.

"You speak very good English," I said.

"I speak many languages and am familiar with over a hundred dialects. I am not a savage."

"I didn't say you were."

"You implied it. Of course, there are savages in Africa, but they are strictly of the amateur variety. The European, on the other hand, has developed savagery to a fine art. He is a professional savage."

"What happened to your teeth?"

"That is no concern of yours."

"I'm curious."

"Curiosity? The White Man's excuse for raping Africa."

"Well, don't blame me! I've just arrived."

"I trust that you have a return ticket?"

"I beg your pardon?"

"Forgive me. I do not speak personally. I do not know you. When I do, I will tell you what I think. In the meantime, I suggest that we get on with our work. I am, after all, being paid by His Majesty and I would not have it said that I obtained money under false pretences. That is the prerogative of the European."

"You know, Sewa – I think I could get very tired of you."

"That is your privilege. The African has been tired of the White Man for many years. Shall we proceed with the work in hand?"

The work in hand consisted of moving 500-lb bombs and depth charges from one part of the bomb-dump to another, taking into account the heat and the angle of the sun. Too much heat and the bombs became too hot to handle and the depth charges were likely to explode. You could feel the heat and you could see it shimmering low across the bomb-dump.

While two men manoeuvred a bomb or a depth charge out of its position in the sand, two more stood by with sticks to beat the snakes that often lay hidden from the heat beneath them. When a snake was discovered, it was beaten to death and then skinned.

"Massa like snake-belt?" Sewa smiled – and I thought of ten ways of killing him. He was organised, he worked hard, he didn't sweat and he smiled incessantly.

"Tomorrow I will make rain," he said. "It will ease your burden." I had the distinct feeling that I was being knifed slowly. The following day, it rained.

One day, during a break for tiffin, as Windmill struggled to make a fire with elephant grass and I sat in the shade still sweating, Sergeant Humphries emerged from his office, wearing nothing but a bush hat and a tie around his neck. It was the second time we'd seen him.

On the day of our arrival he had greeted us warmly, instructed us regarding our duties, and then retired to his office at the far end of the bomb-dump. The office door was locked, the curtains drawn and a 'Do Not Disturb' notice pinned to the door.

What Sergeant Humphries was doing in what must have been like the inside of an oven, nobody knew. But he appeared now, looking cool, calm and refreshed. "Excuse the body," he said. "But I do like to get close to nature. Are we getting on well?"

I wasn't getting on at all well, but Windmill rose to his feet and replied: "Fine, Sergeant. Did you enjoy your holiday?"

Sergeant Humphries grinned, and carried his body into the shade. "I have been here a long time," he said – "and I have learned three things. Keep out of the sun – avoid cold water – and drink plenty of hot tea."

"That's what I'm trying to do," Windmill said – "but I can't get this fire to light."

"You will never do it like that," Sergeant Humphries declared. "Outside my office, you will find an empty petrol tin with some holes in it. Fill it with sand, pour some petrol over it and then light it. The fire will last for hours."

"Are you sure?"

"Quite sure. You can fry bacon, boil a kettle, or cook a chicken. You're wasting your time doing it any other way."

Windmill wasn't convinced. But he collected the drum, filled it with sand and poured petrol over it. Ten minutes later, we were drinking African tea, laced with petrol.

"You will never taste anything better," the Sergeant said. "I drink it all the time."

"I hope you don't mind my asking," Windmill enquired. "But what do you do in your office all the time? The heat must be desperate in there."

The Sergeant paused. "As a matter of fact," he said, "I lie flat on a marble slab. It's ice cold – a gift from my predecessor. I never met him, of course, but I gather he left here untanned, untouched, as white as the day he arrived He's dead now."

"Pneumonia, I presume?"

"In a way, yes. The troopship he was sailing on was sunk on the way home."

"That's war," Windmill sighed.

"Is it? I try not to think about the war. I think of all those people one meets for an hour, or a day, or a week, or maybe a month – whom one never gets to know. Who are they? How do you measure them? They pass by with a nod of the head, and sometimes they're called Tich or Lofty or Sparks, or the guy with the hammer who is sometimes called Chippy and sometimes nothing at all. I must have seen thousands of those people pass through here in the last six months and I couldn't tell you a damn thing about any one of them. Mind if I sit down?"

"Go ahead."

The Sergeant scooped out a hole in the sand and sat into it. "It's cooler lower down," he said and folded his arms.

"Are you comfortable like that?" I asked.

"You mean naked? Of course. It's the only way to live. But if it embarrasses you, say so."

"No! I was just … You were saying?"

"Was I? Sometimes I forget."

Windmill coughed and poured himself another cup of tea. "What about the Africans?" he asked. "Have you learned anything about them?"

"Of course. The African doesn't move. He stays where he is. We're the ones who move about. And every time we do, we create chaos. Look at the African. He's the beginning of the world. The first foot through an open door. We're just the tail-end. We come here with what we call the gift of civilisation, but civilised societies have existed here for a million years. We're just the blink of an eye to the African. Passing through, so to speak, and the African will be here long after we've gone."

"It's nothing like I expected," I said, "apart from the heat."

"You'll get used to that. But if it becomes too difficult,

you can always share the marble slab with me. In the meantime, I suggest that you study the African. See how he works. Slow and easy. People come here and think the African is lazy. He's not. He knows the land. He knows how to breathe. He doesn't burn himself out. What do we know? We come here with a Bible in one hand and a sword in the other, and the only thing we learn is the name of the brothel down the road. We're a foolish people."

"Sewa certainly seems to think so, He's getting on my nerves."

"He's a very intelligent man. Proud of his country and with every right to be so. I'm going back to my office now. Thank you for the tea. The slab is there, if you need it. Enjoy your day."

He stood up, straightened his tie and tightened the strap of his bush hat under his chin.

"Excuse the body," he said again – and marched off in the direction of his office.

"Good afternoon," he called to Sewa as he marched past.

"And to you, Mr Humphries!" Sewa replied. "A very pleasant day."

The Sergeant entered his office and the door closed behind him.

Nine

One of the duties that Windmill and I were assigned to during our stay in Bathurst was to instruct a group of African recruits in the use of firearms. The firearms provided were the .303 Lee Enfield rifle and the Sten-gun, and the recruits were being trained to fight in Burma because "They're dead-used to the jungle and can't be seen in the dark." Most of the Recruits had no idea what the war in Burma was all about, and many of them were destined never to return to Bathurst.

"They're like the Sten-gun," Windmill groaned. "A throwaway weapon."

The Sten-gun was a throwaway weapon. Based on a German design, it was selected for mass production because it was cheap to make, light in action and used non-standard 9mm ammunition. It was also a disaster. Fired from the hip, it over-heated and frequently jammed. There was also no finger-guard when the breach-block shot forward. Someone did design a finger-guard later, but only after they'd counted the missing fingers and wondered what the hell was happening out there.

The rifle, on the other hand, was more reliable – provided you loaded the magazine with the correct ammunition, pointed it in the right direction and not towards your foot. It was also necessary to clean it – particularly the inside of the barrel; otherwise, when you pressed the trigger, the rifle had a tendency to explode in your face.

When I tried to explain these little problems to the group of Recruits I was supposed to be training, most of them decided to return to their beds while the remainder sat on the ground, shaking their heads and hoping I'd blow myself up.

"The rifle is your best friend," I assured them. "All you have to do is to look after it properly – especially in the jungle."

"Massa been to Burma?"

"No."

"Massa go to Burma – shoot rifle – shoot Sten-gun – come back and tell us"

"What's the point of that?"

"Point is – Massa know nothing about Burma – nothing about rifle – nothing about fighting in jungle – and fuck all about Sten-gun."

"I'm doing my best, for Christ's sake!"

"Best not good enough. Massa go to Burma – shoot rifle – shoot Sten-gun – and if he come back alive, we listen."

Education and common sense, I decided, was a curse and had no place in the colonies.

Windmill, on the other hand, fared a little better. He told his recruits that the rifles were worse than useless, the Sten-gun was a danger to life and limb, and only a fool would want to go to Burma anyway when he could stay at home and eat mangoes. He then asked them to keep an eye open for a suitable plantation site for himself, after which they all got drunk on palm wine and played music on the lids of empty petrol drums.

Two days later, our teaching careers came to an end. We were instructed to remove ourselves from the firing-range, avoid familiarity with the natives and return to the bomb-dump.

"Cannon fodder!" Windmill exclaimed. "Bloody

cannon fodder. That's all they're being used for."

I was learning something about Africa and it had nothing to do with the movies.

Every day, along the main road and in the marketplace in Bathurst, old men and young boys set up their stalls and clamoured to sell bananas and mangoes, palm wine and dirty postcards to passing troops. Diseased beggars whined for money, naked children were ruthlessly pushed aside, and the old and the young offered their wives, daughters and sisters to the troops, for two shillings, five shillings, or for anything they could get.

The Army grinned, the Air Force felt superior and the passing troops cried "Monkeys! A lot of bleeding monkeys!"

Everywhere you looked, there was poverty and disease, hunger and malnutrition. But in the Royal Air Force camp we sat comfortably at clean tables, dressed in neatly pressed uniforms, fed on well-cooked food, much of which was dumped in the garbage cans outside the gate, to be fought over by hordes of children with flies breeding on their eyelids and in their hair.

"Monkey, mMate! A lot of bleeding monkeys."

On Fridays, in addition to our pay, we were provided with tins of cigarettes and bars of chocolate, vitamin B and Mepaquin pills. We were medically examined, lectured on the dangers of consorting with the natives and catching syphilis or gonorrhoea from the women who haunted the streets or sat with their legs open on the side of the road.

We were shown films about venereal disease, films about the dangers of drinking water outside the camp, films about yellow fever and malaria, elephantiasis and leprosy, hygiene and the lack of it everywhere in Africa. We were told we were fighting a war. We were told that victory was ours and Africa was ours and India was ours and that all things were possible when the enemy was defeated and the Empire was safe. We felt superior to the monkeys and were advised to behave accordingly.

Sometimes, during our off-duty weekends, Windmill and I went to visit Sewa at his home in Bathurst. He had invited us to visit him, but the invitation was more like a Royal Command, to be declined on pain of death and, at first, I was tempted to refuse. Windmill, however, was obsessed with getting to know the Africans in their homes and persuaded me to accept the invitation.

Sewa greeted us at the door of what looked like an enormous beehive. After entering, we had to sit on the floor, while portraits of his ancestors stared at us, accusingly, from the mud walls. Sewa wore his traditional Soninke costume, and having removed his teeth, neither of us could understand a single word he said.

"He's testing us," Windmill said afterwards.

"He's what?"

"That's why he invited us. He wants you to look at his ancestors, consider their traditions and see him for what he is – a prince of his people. He was watching your reactions."

"He could, at least, have put his flaming teeth in!"

"Why should he? He's in his own home, with his own history. He owes nothing to us."

Our second visit was more successful. Sewa still wore his traditional costume, his ancestors continued to stare at us from mud walls, but Sewa had put in his false teeth and spoke benignly of our previous visit.

"It was very kind of you to come," he smiled, "I did not expect you to accept my invitation."

"I thought I'd be shot if I didn't," I said.

"This is not the custom here," Sewa replied. "In your country, perhaps?"

I didn't know whether to kick him or have a hair-cut, so I said nothing.

"Now you are here on a second visit," he continued. "I'm glad. You are welcome at any time."

"We were advised not to come," I said.

"Of course. Would you care for some wine? I make it myself. It will not give you a headache."

We accept the offer. Sewa produced a bottle of wine, filled three cups and sat beside us on the mud floor.

"It is not pleasant," he sighed, "what you see in the streets."

"Do you blame us for that?" I asked.

Sewa didn't reply. "I made the cups too," he said. "Your continued good health."

We drank the wine, under the watchful eyes of his ancestors. "What do you think of them?" he enquired.

"Formidable," Windmill replied. "I wouldn't like to get on the wrong side of them."

"They were a friendly people," Sewa said. "And they were not prepared for the savagery and greed of strangers."

"You mean the White Man?"

"Among others. The White Man has merely perfected the art."

"I think you said that before," I said.

"Did I? It is worth repeating. But you are here on a social visit. You are not, I presume, seeking a lesson in history?"

"I don't know the history," I replied. "But every time we meet, I get the distinct feeling that I'm being got at in some way."

"Folk memory," he smiled. "Perhaps, one day, we may talk about it – but not today. Would you care for some more wine?"

"Yes!"

He refilled the cups. The room became a palace and the ancestors refrained from sticking a knife in our backs.

"Is it true that you can produce rain by spitting on a palm leaf?" Windmill asked.

"A slight exaggeration. But I have managed to do so on occasions. I have also created floods – but not for many years. It is a gift from the Gods and requires a great deal of concentration."

He sipped his drink and looked at both of us. "You do not believe me, of course. There is no reason why you should. It is not your culture."

"Sometimes I wonder if we ever had a culture!" Windmill muttered drunkenly.

"I will not argue with you there," Sewa replied and turned towards his ancestors. "A very friendly and trusting people," he sighed and raised his cup. The ancestors stared at him and the afternoon sun filled the room with an extraordinary light.

In the months that followed, Windmill and I continued to visit Sewa in his home and in the brothel where he met with his friends. The brothel was medically examined by a Medical Officer from the RAF and passed as reasonably free from venereal disease – but Sewa and his friends never availed of the services on offer. They sat in a corner, drank palm wine, played cards and watched the White Man, as he climbed the stairs and returned, ten minutes later, with a grin on his face.

"I don't know why you come to a place like this," I said on one occasion when Windmill was away searching for a site for his plantation. "Isn't there a decent pub or café anywhere about?"

"They serve good food," Sewa said. "The wine is palatable and it is also cheap. It is not necessary to climb the stairs."

"Tell that to the troops! They're going up and down there like bleeding yo-yos."

"If you feel like going yourself …?"

"No thanks!"

308

"Then no one will bother you. I come here when His Majesty condescends to pay me for the work I do in the bomb-dump. I sit with my friends. We play cards and drink wine. It is not as good as the wine I make myself, but as you can see it is drinkable."

"Where are your friends today?"

"At home with their wives and children."

"Are you married?"

"No. My wife died some years ago."

"I'm sorry."

"Thank you. We should be used to death here. Children die every day. Men and women years before their time. It was not always so. At least, not in the way we die now from diseases that were unknown in Africa before the White Man came."

"You're getting at me again."

"I assure you, I am not. You are a young man. Much younger that you pretend, I imagine – but no matter. I am simply stating a fact. You know very little about Africa, its history or its culture. You see what you are meant to see – the misery and the poverty and the degradation of our people. You are not meant to see anything else. We have a history longer than anywhere else in the world. We were standing up when the rest of the world was still crawling in the mud. Our bones have been found in deserts and in caves – and our art has been discovered in areas where no art was ever thought possible. What you see is a brothel."

"Well, we are sitting in one."

"So we are. But a greater and more lethal brothel exists in the streets. Created by the White Man for his pleasure and profit. Here, at least, they do provide good food and drinkable wine. Though perhaps that, too, is another form of slavery."

"You never give up."

"One day the White Man will leave Africa. He will not be coming back."

"Others may come."

"We are a rich country and greed is not confined to those who are white. This is obvious."

"I'll drink to that."

We drank and continued to drink until late in the evening, when the troops had departed in search of pleasures elsewhere and a young girl appeared from behind the bar to clean the tables and sweep the floor. Smiling at Sewa, she made no sound as she moved from table to table, before directing us to the front door. I staggered towards her and Sewa steadied me.

"Will you be all right?" he asked.

"Just point me in the right direction."

"I'll walk with you," he said – and kept his hand on my shoulder until we reached the main gate of the camp, where the airman on guard duty let me through without comment.

"Good night!" Sewa called as I made my way slowly towards the Nissen hut. "See you tomorrow."

"Tomorrow," I said as I entered the room. "Tomorrow and tomorrow."

The room was dark. The air reeked of stale wine and sickening tobacco smoke. I slept in the uniform I was wearing and dreamed of slavery.

Ten

During what German U-boat Commanders called 'The Happy Time', German U-boats sank over 4,500,000 tons of Allied shipping in the North Atlantic, the Bay of Biscay and along the West Coast of Africa. Now The Happy Time was drawing to an end. The *Bismarck* and the *Scharnhorst* had been sent to the bottom by the Royal Navy, the *Prinz Eugen* had been torpedoed by a British submarine and saw no more service, the *Gneisenau* had been badly damaged in a dawn attack by a solitary Beaufort, the pocket battleship *Lutzow* was damaged off the coast of Norway by another Beaufort, and the Wolf Packs had been recalled to German waters by Adolf Hitler, to prepare for an invasion of Norway by the Allies which Hitler said had been foretold to him in a dream.

The British, of course, were more than happy to encourage Adolf in his dreamings, especially as Allied shipping losses had dropped dramatically to an average 125,000 tons a month, and so sent him a postcard saying they were coming, but hadn't made up their minds on the exact date. Meanwhile, along the West Coast of Africa, the Beauforts, based near Freetown, and the Sunderlands, based in Bathurst, continued to patrol the coastline in search of the few remaining U-boats reported to be still lurking there. The Sunderland, armed with six machine guns and eight depth charges, patrolled the coast for eight hours at a stretch, but the Beaufort, armed with a 1,610-lb torpedo and fitted with extra fuel tanks, could remain in the air for much longer. No one asked the air crews what they thought and no one asked the A/C Plonks. It was eight hours on and eight hours off and, once again, no let-up.

In Bathurst, Windmill and I, with the help of Sewa and his friends, loaded the depth-charges and ammunition boxes on to a lorry, drove to the slipway, transferred the depth charges and ammo-boxes on to a barge and were driven out to the waiting Sunderlands where we bombed-up. The barge moved up and down in the water, the Sunderlands swayed dangerously from side to side, and Windmill got sick as we struggled to hook the depth charges securely under the wings. It was a relief when we climbed on board the Sunderlands to store the ammunition and test-fire the machine guns.

Sometimes Windmill and I were required to take to the air and test the machine guns and bomb-release equipment over the Atlantic. I fired at everything but U-boats, and Windmill dropped his depth charges on nothing but salt water.

While in the air, however, we were promoted to the rank of Acting Sergeants, in case we were shot down and had to spend our time in a German prison camp. But the moment we landed back in Bathurst, we were relegated to the A/C Plonk brigade and had to eat in the cookhouse with the rest of the unfortunates.

For much of our time in the air, Windmill tried to look like the experienced Bomb-Aimer that he wasn't, while I sat in the rear turret, strapped to a machine gun, reading Agatha Christie and Dorothy L Sayers. The only other reading material available were a few battered copies of *Penguin New Writing*, which the Second Pilot held on to as if they were gold nuggets, and a collection of poems by Siegfried Sassoon, from which he quoted whenever he raised his head.

"There are no war poets like Sassoon now," he said. "Or

Wilfred Owen for that matter. They were the real war poets."

"What about Rupert Brooke?" Windmill asked. "Don't you include him?"

"The 'Honey Boy'?" he asked sarcastically. "When that clock struck three, it should have knocked him on the head. War is not about home and beauty. It's about dirt and living in dirt and dying in dirt. Sassoon knew that and so did Owen. It is also boring – very boring – and there's madness in that."

"It's certainly boring sitting up here for hours," I said.

"Then educate yourself. Get something out of this war. There was a guy in the squadron last year who'd been flying this run for nine months. He got so bored that he ditched his kite in the drink. Killed everyone on board. They gave him a medal for that. Pinned it to his widow."

"Well, don't look at me," said the First Pilot. "I'm educated."

I was relieved to hear it and spent the next two hours glued to Agatha Christie.

There's something very comforting about Agatha Christie, especially when you are strapped to a machine gun in the rear turret of a Sunderland Flying Boat. She softens your brain, murders you with class and buries you with ease in an English garden. The Second Pilot said she was a twit and Windmill dropped his first depth charge. I turned to Dorothy L Sayers, but the Second Pilot didn't like her either.

"All right before she got the religious bug," he said. "She had style. But there's no style in Christianity. It's just a Crucifixion – whichever way you look at it. Dorothy should have stuck to Peter Wimsey. He hadn't much going for him as a character, but he did have a modicum of style."

The Nine Tailors had style. The sea had style and waited for us to embrace it.

Lying on the floor, wondering when to drop his next depth charge, Windmill did not have style. He shook his head and waved his arms about, his long legs reaching across the galley to where the remaining crew members were struggling to make tea, play cards and smoke endless cigarettes.

"Not a bloody U-boat in sight!" he moaned. "Not even a floating target. Nothing but sea and more flaming sea. They must have known we were coming."

The sea was calm, not a ripple in sight. A lone cargo ship passed slowly beneath us, on the port side, and the First Pilot changed course and circled over it. The Second Pilot signalled to it with his Aldis lamp and the ship responded with a series of quick flashes of light.

"She's heading for Dakar," he said.

"Vichy?"

"French anyway. Should we follow it?"

"No. Let the Yanks take care of it. Just flash it through and give Dakar the nod. She looks harmless enough."

The Second Pilot signalled with his Aldis lamp again and the First Pilot resumed course.

"I could have dropped one right down her funnel," Windmill said.

The First Pilot shook his head. "Just drop it in the drink and let's get out of here," he ordered. "We're not touting for medals today."

Windmill looked disappointed and dropped his second depth charge into the Atlantic.

"Nothing but sea," he complained. "Nothing but shagging sea."

The Second Pilot nodded and picked up a copy of *Penguin New Writing*. "There's a poem in here by WH Auden," he said. "It's all about boredom. Anyone want to read it?"

314

There was no response. Windmill stretched his legs further into the galley, where the remainder of the crew cursed the length of him, yet continued to play cards, drink tea and smoke. You could feel the air and taste the boredom, as the cigarette smoke circled the gun turrets and clouded the gallery.

"Not long now," the First Pilot announced. "We'll make one more sweep and then break for home."

"What about the remaining depth charges?" Windmill asked. "Are you going to try to land with those on board?"

"No way! You can drop them a few miles out. You might even hit something."

We continued the search, the engines groaning as the shadow of the Sunderland appeared dark and menacing upon the surface of the sea. It followed us everywhere, and nothing else appeared directly beneath us.

"Sorry for the lack of U-boats," the First Pilot grinned, as we turned and headed back towards Bathurst. "Maybe next time round."

"Can I drop them now, Skipper?"

"OK, Harrison. Go ahead."

"Bombs away!"

Windmill released the remaining depth charges in one stick, as the Sunderland, relieved of its burden, drop-lashed high in the air.

Agatha Christie screamed, the Second Pilot instantly converted to Christianity, and the remaining crew members fell over themselves in an effort to reach Windmill and strangle him.

"You stupid bollox!" yelled the First Pilot. "One at a time, for Christ's sake. Not six!"

"Frightfully sorry," Windmill spluttered. "I wasn't expecting that."

"It's a good job we're outside the limit. Jesus Christ!"

As we approached the limit, I had visions of Bathurst writhing in flames and Windmill being hanged as a War Criminal.

"Oil, dirt and boredom," the Second Pilot said as the Sunderland ripped through the water, creating fountains of spray, before coming to a screaming halt yards from the slipway. "Oil, dirt and boredom. Did I say that?"

Returning to the camp, Windmill and I resumed our place within the ranks of the A/C Plonks.

The following morning, Windmill rose from his bunk with a pain in his head, saying he had spent the entire night dreaming of U-boats. "They were coming at me like sharks. Bloody great sharks with teeth like headstones. What about you?"

"I slept with Agatha Christie," I replied. "You should try it sometime."

Windmill winced. "Being Acting Sergeant for a day has addled your brain, mate. I couldn't wait to get rid of those stripes."

"You seemed happy enough dropping those depth charges. You almost obliterated Bathurst."

"A mistake. I just couldn't wait to get rid of those things. Anything to relieve the boredom. I don't know how those guys stand it."

Neither did I. But I wasn't depressed and I didn't have a headache. I was thinking of the Second Pilot sitting in the cockpit of the Sunderland and quoting from Siegfried Sassoon whenever he raised his head.

He would be there again today, patrolling the coast, reading poetry and talking about the boredom of war. Tomorrow would be the same. No change. No break in the routine until, one day in the future, when he would be posted to another station farther down the coast. Same crew. Same task –searching for U-boats along a similar stretch of coast.

I wondered who he was and where he came from. We never exchanged names. He was a Second Pilot who quoted from Siegfried Sassoon, and carried *Penguin New Writing* with him everywhere he went.

In the bomb-dump, Windmill and I, along with Sewa and his friends, continued with our routine – moving depth charges from one area to another and killing the snakes that lay hidden beneath. Windmill made tea, Sergeant Humphries appeared from time to time, wearing nothing but a bush hat and a tie around his neck, while Sewa talked about the lack of civilisation in Europe and beyond.

Sometimes we listened to the radio. We heard that General Eisenhower had been moved from his post in the Mediterranean and appointed Supreme Commander of something called 'Overlord', that the Russians had broken out of Leningrad, that Stalin was calling for a Second Front, and that an earthquake had occurred in Argentina. We heard that Allied Forces had reached Cassino, that the Americans had bombed Hanoi and the Burma Road, that Tokyo Rose would be shot when captured by the Allies – and that an Irishman, John P O'Reilly, known as the Irish Lord Haw-Haw, had landed by parachute in Ireland and was now having breakfast in Mountjoy Prison in Dublin, where the British hoped he would choke to death on his bacon and eggs.

Sergeant Humphries never listened to the radio. He lay on his marble slab during the day, emerging from his office only when he smelled tea and wanted a five-minute chat in the shade. He occasionally changed his tie to a different colour, but the bush hat remained fixed to his head like a wet rag stuck on a thorn bush.

"It's an odd kind of war," I said to him one day as we sat in the shade, while Windmill lay on his back, sipping tea through a straw. "Everything seems to be happening a million miles away."

"Would you prefer to be fighting in Burma, or dropping bombs on cities in Germany?"

"I don't know. We almost dropped a stick of them on Bathurst a few days ago."

"It doesn't surprise me. Nothing does anymore. That's why I never listen to the radio. Every time we advance, people die, every time we retreat, more people die. People die when bombs fall on Germany or London or in the Far East. They die when a U-boat fires a torpedo or when a battleship drops a depth charge. And every time the announcer opens his mouth on the radio, you can be sure it's to tell us that somebody else has died or will die by the time he's stopped talking. I'm sick of it. The world is choking to death on dead bodies and I don't want to know any more. I just want this whole obscene ritual to end."

"It's got a long way to go yet, from the sound of it."

"I know that – and that's why I don't read newspapers any more or look at a newsreel in the cinema. I've seen enough pictures of burning cities, enough newsreels of mangled bodies lying on the road and refugees fleeing from advancing armies. What's the point? Every day someone invents a new weapon, a bigger and more destructive bomb, a gun that will kill more people faster and with less trouble to ourselves. Am I supposed to be proud of these things? Am I expected to stand up and cheer the genius who invented them? Pat him on the back and pin a medal to his chest? I don't have any medals. I don't wear a uniform, except to greet newcomers like yourselves. Otherwise, I walk around naked."

"It's a good way to get your ticket," Windmill said between sips.

"What ticket? They don't give tickets to naked men. They send them to Africa, hide them away in the bomb-dump and forget about them. The MO comes here once a month to see whether or not we're still alive, and guys like you turn up every six months to shift bombs and brew tea. The only one who remains is Sewa. He's permanent."

"What do you think of him?"

"I've told you before. He's a very intelligent man. He is also a gentleman. There are very few of us left."

"Thanks!"

"No offence. Take that uniform off. Bury it in the sand and you'll feel better."

He finished his tea, thanked us for the chat and returned to his office.

"He may be cracked," Windmill said, after the office door had closed behind Sergeant Humphries and the blinds were drawn – "but he's cracked in the right way."

"You think so? Well, I'm not walking around naked, I can tell you that!"

Windmill smiled. "A pity," he said, rising to his feet. "A great pity."

And the following day, he removed his clothes and ran around the bomb-dump, wearing nothing but a bush hat. It was not an attractive sight.

"Are you going to carry on like that every day?" I asked.

"Certainly!"

"You look ridiculous. What's the matter with you?"

"Freedom," he replied – as if he had just discovered the wheel. "Absolute freedom! And I feel beautiful!"

"You don't look it," I said. "Not with that thing waving about."

He turned his back and addressed Sewa and his friends. "Do I look beautiful?" he cried. "Do I look beautiful?"

"You look extremely beautiful," Sewa replied – and his friends applauded. Windmill bowed and spent the next three days running around the bomb-dump with his extremities falling about.

Sewa smiled, his friends continued to applaud, and a week later, we were both ordered to report to the Orderly Room and await further orders.

"Bomb-dump?" the clerk enquired as we entered the room.

"Bomb-dump," we replied.

He shook his head. "Pack your kit. You've been posted to another station."

"Any idea where?"

"Burma, for all I know. Report to the slipway at six tomorrow morning. A Sunderland will pick you up."

"Shit!"

We packed our kit and Windmill said he was going to kill himself. I offered him a Sten-gun. He was not happy.

We said goodbye to Sergeant Humphries, who changed his tie for the occasion, and spent our last evening in Bathurst, drinking palm wine with Sewa and his friends, and denouncing all those who sat in little brown offices, wearing shabby brown uniforms, moving numbers and names from one part of the world to another, just to occupy their time. We promised to write to each other. We promised to return when the war was over; Windmill would set up his plantation, and we could all work together and live together in an African commune. Windmill wept. He said he hated the war, he hated uniforms and wanted to be like Sergeant Humphries and walk around naked. Sewa sympathised and said he showed great spirit.

As we sat on the slipway the following morning, waiting for the Sunderland to pick us up, Windmill was still weeping. He did not want to go to Burma. Neither did I – all I could think of was strangling Betty Grable and dying in the jungle with a bayonet stuck in my ribs.

Eleven

It was not Burma. It was not India either. Rather we were standing on the edge of the Spanish Sahara, in the middle of a sand storm, and not a jungle in sight. Nothing but sand and wind and a Foreign Legion that had come straight out of *Beau Geste*. The sand swirled and surged and swept across the desert, stinging our hands and faces and bare knees. It matted our hair, lined our clothes, entered our nostrils and mouths, and stuck like glue to the warmest parts of our bodies. We tried to protect ourselves by wrapping our shirts around our heads. We tried digging holes in the sand to shelter from the storm, but the holes filled up again, faster than we could dig them out.

Windmill yelled at the sand. He said he hated the sight of it, had never sat on a beach in his life and anyone who did was a raving lunatic. He denounced Blackpool, Brighton, the Costa del Sol, the South of France, Greece – anywhere that wasn't filled with solid rock and clouded with rain twelve months of the year. He tried to hide under his kitbag, but the sand followed him and clung to him and stuck to him and burned his face and his eyes and penetrated his skin. He felt possessed by sand, devoured by sand, lashed and skinned by sand and, in the end, buried under mountains of it.

I tried hard not to listen to him. I lay face down in the sand and let the wind sweep over me, as he continued to rave and was raving still when the storm abated and the desert lay stretched before us, silent and still, in a solitude that was immense.

In the Foreign Legion fort, nothing appeared to move either. The gates were closed, the guard-house stood empty and the only thing missing was the smoke rising from a Viking funeral, à la *Beau Geste*, and the dead bodies of Legionnaires manning the parapets.

"If Sergeant Markoff appears now," I said, "I'll scream."

But no one appeared. We struggled to brush the sand from our clothes and bodies, and waited, miserably, for someone to come to collect us.

Windmill cursed. "Where the fuck are we?" he bellowed. "Where the fuck are we?"

"Fort Zinderneuf," I said. "It has to be."

"Lunatics!" he exclaimed. "Bloody lunatics!"

"Calm down. You'll burst a blood vessel."

"I think I've burst one already," he said. "Nobody tells you where you're going, nobody tells you what to do when you get there – and you end up in the middle of a desert being ravaged to death by wind and sand. It's crazy!"

"I asked the pilot where we were going. He said it was 'Top Secret'."

"Another nutcase! What the hell is so secret about this place? There's nothing here but sand. And even Rommel couldn't stand that. He couldn't wait to get home and leave it to Montgomery."

"Nice place for a plantation though."

"Shit!"

We sat on our kitbags and tried to wash the remaining sand from our mouths with water from our canteens. The water was hot and Windmill started again. He cursed the desert, the sky, the sun, the heat, and the Foreign Legion fort, and said he was going to blow his brains out with a Sten-gun.

"Not again!"

"Again!"

I waited, hopefully, but his Sten-gun was still full of sand and so was mine.

"You'll have to organise it better next time." I said – but Windmill wasn't amused. He lapsed into silence and we sat there in the blazing heat waiting to be rescued.

When Corporal Whyles arrived in a jeep, he said we looked like vulture-meat. He wore a bush hat and khaki shorts and was armed with two rifles, a Vickers Machine Gun mounted on the jeep and a .38 revolver tucked under his belt.

"Sorry I'm late," he grinned. "Had to wait for that bleeding sandstorm to end. Are you guys all right?"

"Oh, sure!" Windmill replied. "What's the arsenal for? Shooting up sand?"

"Hyenas, mate. You'll see plenty of them here – and they haunt the place at night."

"Christ – that's all we need! Hyenas, yet!"

"Pile in."

We loaded our own kitbags into the rear of the jeep and sat in the front seat beside Corporal Whyles.

"Mind telling us where we are?" I asked.

"You mean you don't know?"

I refused to answer and Windmill looked at his Sten-gun again.

"Well," Corporal Whyles announced as we moved off into nowhere, "you are now driving through the Spanish Sahara – or Rio de Oro – whichever turns you on. This little oasis is called Port Etienne. On your right is the Atlantic Ocean, either side of you is Mauritania and Morocco and somewhere over there is Algeria. The French occupy the fort, we occupy the tents behind it, and what the fuck anyone's doing here I haven't the faintest notion."

"Well, that's a comfort."

"The important thing to remember is that, for now anyway, the French are in charge – though what the hell they're supposed to be in charge of, apart from the Legion, nobody knows. Most of them are not French at all. They're deserters from the German Army, ex-convicts, muggers and drunks who'd cut your throat for a Pernod or a piss-up on French brandy. There are also a few Spaniards knocking about, but the only thing they seem to do is play guitars and lay claim to the desert. The French occasionally invite us to the fort for a drinking session – but, for the most part, they spend their time charging backwards and forwards across the desert, shooting at sand dunes and carrying bloody great packs on their backs."

"Keep going, Corp," Windmill groaned. "Your gift for inspiring confidence is awesome."

"Then there's Captain Monet. He's O/C Fort, wears full-dress uniform, carries a cane under his arm and is covered in gold braid. He comes to inspect us once a week because he's convinced that we're some weird branch of the French Foreign Legion. We keep telling him that we're just attached to the bloody thing on a temporary basis, but he doesn't seem to understand a word of English and stands there shouting '*Mon Dieu*!' You'll meet him tomorrow."

"Any other good news?"

"I'll save it. This is where you'll kip for the next six months. And, as you can see, it has every mod-con."

As we drove round to the rear of the fort, I expected to see the usual array of Nissen huts, a NAFFI and a cook-house, but there were none – just a sprawling collection of tents, at least half of which had collapsed during the recent sandstorm, and a number of lorries and jeeps parked higgledy-piggledy right across the camp. Corporal Whyles pulled up outside the largest of the tents.

"This is the armoury," he said. "You can stow your gear

in there while I go and check the duty roster."

"Where do we sleep?"

"In tents. You'll find a stack of them back of the armoury there. Grab a couple and set them up."

We removed our kitbags from the rear of the jeep and, as Corporal Whyles drove off in a cloud of sand and dust, Windmill said: "I don't believe this. I do not believe it!" I didn't believe it either, but having seen Claudette Colbert in *Under Two Flags* three times, I felt there was always a chance she might turn up as a camp follower and organise the cooking.

In the armoury, the over-greased rifles and machine-guns were chained and locked in gun-racks; broken ammunition boxes lay scattered over the ground, belts of ammunition hung from the centre poles, and tents lay in corners under sandbags and piles of old newspapers.

We managed to extract two, dragged them outside, and set about erecting them as best we could. Windmill had never been close to a tent in his life and what I knew about tent life wouldn't cover the back of a postage stamp. But we did manage to erect something that looked like a tepee before Corporal Whyles returned with more good news.

"Locusts," he said. "I forgot to tell you about those."

After we'd picked Windmill up from the ground, the Corporal explained. "Dead ones. You'll find them lying on the top of the tent some mornings. Millions of the bastards. Just sweep them off and burn them."

"Where do they come from?"

"The wind carries them from the north, I think. They're all over the place. Dig a hole, sweep them in and pour petrol over them. No sweat. You're OK for a few days – I've checked the duty roster. No guard duties. Just sort yourselves out in the armoury and clean the place up. The last guys made a shambles of the place. Drunk most of the time and one of them went off his head."

325

Windmill raised his eyes. "Surprise me!" he said.

"A few things to remember: make sure those ground sheets are securely fastened to the ground and lay some planks along the edges. It gets very cold here at night and you get all sorts of crawlies creeping in under the ground sheets. Hang your gear up, don't leave it lying on the ground and shake your boots and socks out every morning before you put them on. If you see a couple of Arabs knocking about flogging fruit – don't touch it. It's crap. You'll find plenty of fruit in the fort – it's flown in once a week; just wash it carefully and cut the ends off the bananas. That's where the insects get in. One more thing – crumpet. You won't find much of that around here, but if you're crawling about on all fives there's a couple of Arab bints living in one of the tents over there and they'll provide the necessary. Otherwise, you'll have to wait till your leave comes up and you can go to Dakar. OK?"

"Food?"

"No shortage of that the cookhouse is at the far end of the camp. You can't miss it. And the MO's tent is one with the cross painted on the roof. One more thing – if you need a crap, you'll find a trench about a hundred yards to your left. The Janker Wallahs dig one every morning, fill it with lime every night and cover it. Next day, they dig another one. You'll soon get used to it."

"I doubt it!"

"Can't think of anything else. I'll leave you to settle in for now. Just relax and take it easy. If you need me, just follow the jeep. It's parked right outside my tent."

He wandered off as Windmill and I set about securing our ground sheets and pegging the guy ropes more firmly into the ground. We found the water-wagon in the centre of the camp and carried buckets of water back to our tents to wash and brush up. Everyone around the camp seemed to be busy, clearing up after the storm, and no one took the slightest notice of us as we passed backwards and forwards to the water wagon and the latrine.

In the cookhouse, the A/C Cook, who looked nothing like Claudette Colbert, shouted "Come and get it!" and ladled out soup, sausages and mash, meat and veg, and fish and chips, all from what appeared to be the same enormous tureen. The only other visible container sat on a table in the centre of the cookhouse, filled with peanut butter, which Windmill plastered onto his bread as if he were weather-proofing a house, saying he had never tasted anything better. I have never been able to look at peanut butter since and remain convinced that it addled his brain.

Later, in the evening, Corporal Whyles invited us to join him for a drinking session at the fort, but Windmill was too exhausted to do anything but sleep and I was in no humour for drinking, preferring to lie in my tent and read a book. So Corporal Whyles provided me with the only two books he had in his possession – *Memoirs of a Woman of Pleasure* by John Cleland and *Riders of the Purple Sage* by Zane Grey. Reading the memoirs of a woman of pleasure almost gave me a complex, while I refrained from reading Zane Grey because of the title.

With nothing else to read and unable to sleep, I stood outside my tent in the growing dark and cold night air. Windmill appeared to be sleeping soundly and I could hear him breathing through the canvas walls of his tent. I felt both lonely and alone, but strangely content under a sky filled with stars. In the camp nothing moved, everything clean and shining brightly in the darkness of the earth.

Twelve

The following morning, Windmill and I stood outside the armoury, waiting to be inspected by the gold-braided Captain Monet. The Captain was a little man with broad shoulders and close-shaven head. He also walked sideways. When he arrived in a jeep, accompanied by the Gorilla, his driver, he shouted "*Mon Dieu!*" for no apparent reason at all, looked us up and down, repeated himself twice, then moved sideways into the armoury, followed by the Gorilla.

A moment later, he screamed something totally incomprehensible, marched out, fell to his knees and began beating the sand with his cane. The Gorilla nodded his head, the Captain cried "*Mon Dieu!*" again, climbed into his jeep, and the Gorilla drove off.

"That was interesting," I said. "What did he say?"

"My French is a bit rusty," Windmill replied. "But I think he said something about firing squads and shooting people in the balls. I hope he wasn't referring to us?"

"I wouldn't bet on it! I should keep your clothes on, if I were you."

Windmill kept his clothes on and we wandered over to the cookhouse, where the A/C Cook had prepared a breakfast of fried eggs that tasted of rubber, kippers and jam that were simply indescribable, and tea that had obviously been boiling for hours, then boiled again to give it character.

The A/C Cook, however, convinced of his culinary expertise, stood there waiting to be congratulated by Windmill and myself. I was incapable of speech, but

Windmill, more diplomatic, said something like – "Most unusual … Never tasted anything quite like it before … Did you prepare the kippers yourself?"

The A/C Cook beamed a broad smile, saying he had indeed, and was obliged to Windmill for the compliment.

"People don't appreciate good food here, Harrison," he said. "I give them the best, but they don't appreciate it."

"Artists are never appreciated in their lifetime," Windmill intoned. "And the greater they are, the less so."

The A/C Cook nodded his head. "How true," he sighed. "How very true. I must remember that. Do you cook yourself?"

"I'm afraid not. I am not an artist."

The A/C Cook almost fell over himself with delight and I had visions of having to suffer kippers and jam in Port Etienne for the next six months.

"Thank you," he said. "Thank you very much."

"Not at all. My pleasure."

"You didn't have to go that far," I said to Windmill as we were returning to the armoury. "That eegit couldn't boil water."

Windmill paused. "You know," he said – "When I looked at the food that man prepared I was almost sick to my stomach. I felt the same last night and the only thing I enjoyed was the peanut butter. But when I looked at him today, I saw a man who really thought he was a great cook. He'd put everything he had into it. He was trying to create something, to give pleasure. You can't pass a man like that without congratulating him."

"I could."

"Not if you think about it. A bad artist works just as hard to create a work of art as a good one. Sometimes, more so. The difference is – one has talent and the other one hasn't."

"Spare me!"

"Fair enough. Let's say I've done my good deed for today. And now I'm about to be sick."

"The latrine is in that direction."

"Excuse me."

Windmill rushed quickly towards it as I returned to the armoury.

During the weeks that followed, Windmill and I spent most of our time cleaning up the armoury, wondering what was so Top Secret about a handful of tents and a Foreign Legion fort stuck on the edge of the Sahara desert. There was nothing to see, no bomb-dump, no secret underground passages, and the only aircraft available was a Sunderland that was used for carrying airmen and supplies from Freetown to camps dotted along the West African coast.

My imagination ran wild when our weekly cargo of supplies arrived, containing the latest world première from Hollywood – *Five Graves to Cairo*. The film was shown on a make-shift screen in the open air, where Windmill and I sat on the back of a lorry and watched Erich von Stroheim swatting flies, Akim Tamiroff sweating, Anne Baxter struggling to make a living, and Franchot Tone pretending to be a spy as he limped around tables, looking for the secret of the five graves.

The graves turned out to be Rommel's supply dumps, buried in the desert before the war, when Germany was studying Egyptology and the British were having afternoon tea. But were they? Or were we now sitting on Montgomery's secret supply dump, buried under Port Etienne? And was Captain Monet a limping German agent, pretending to be French? Are movies bad for your health? I promised to give them up.

"We've got them on the run now," Mr Tone said at the end of the film. "We're after them!"

The only thing we were after were the flies in the

armoury and the dead locusts on the roof of the tent. We sprayed the flies and burned the locusts, burying them deep under sand dunes and in trenches. After which we struggled to remove sand and grease from everything in sight.

We found live ammunition scattered over the ground, hand grenades and flares lying under tents and old newspapers, a petrol drum filled with oily rags. Had anyone dropped a lighted match anywhere inside the armoury, the whole place would have gone up in flames and Windmill and I would have been listed among the missing.

"Fought heroically, Ma'am – but killed in action, defending the Empire."

By the time Windmill and I had put the armoury back in shape, we were ready to defend Rommel.

One morning when Captain Monet arrived, accompanied by the Gorilla, he did not shake his head. He did not mutter or shout "*Mon Dieu!*" either, and when he entered the armoury he did not scream.

"I think he's going to give us a medal," Windmill whispered – but Captain Monet must have been short of medals that day, since the only thing he did was to climb back into his jeep, nod to the Gorilla, and drive off.

A few days later, however, the Gorilla arrived, without Captain Monet, and invited us to visit the fort. "Drink. Much drink. You come."

"Can we refuse?"

The Gorilla shook his head, so Windmill and I washed the grease from our hands and joined the Foreign Legion.

When we arrived at the Fort, late in the evening, we were greeted by J Carrol Naish. The hyena in *Beau Geste*, he was now pretending to be on guard duty outside the gate. I refused to recognise him, but he let us through anyway, after I told him that we had been invited by Captain Monet.

"The Captain will not drink with enlisted men," he said.

"You will drink with Legionnaire Maroc and Jesus."

"I beg your pardon?"

He gestured towards a door at the far end of the parade ground where the Gorilla was waiting.

"Maroc," the Gorilla said, by the way of introducing himself. "Maroc!"

"Thank God for that!" Windmill exclaimed. "I thought for a moment you might have been Jesus."

"Aha?"

The Gorilla was not French, neither was he German, yet when I asked him what nationality he was, he just nodded and said – "Yes."

"He speaks English anyway," Windmill whispered as we entered what appeared to be the Records Office. "I had no idea he could speak at all."

The Gorilla could speak and when he couldn't or wouldn't – he pointed. Now he pointed to a bench and said "Sit!", then pointed to drink and said "Drink!"

I was tempted to say "Me Tarzan", but thought better of it when I looked at his hands, which were large enough to strangle an elephant. The Gorilla was no joker. He stood well over six-feet tall, with shoulders on him like an ox, and when he walked across the room or stamped his foot on the ground, you could almost hear the walls crumbling.

"Do you come here often?" Windmill asked, as the Gorilla poured Pernod into something that looked more like a bucket than a glass. The Gorilla didn't answer.

"Drink!" he roared. "Drink!"

We drank. The Gorilla drank, and when our glasses were empty, he filled them up again and repeated himself.

"Drink!" he roared. "Drink!"

"Take it easy," Windmill said. "The night is young."

"Aha?"

We drank. The Gorilla sat at his desk and stared at us.

332

He smelled of insects. The room smelled of insects, and the folders and papers stacked along the shelves and tied with ribbon smelled of insects. Centipedes and cockroaches crawled across the floor, insects burrowed through the records on the shelves and the moths crashed, suicidally, into the oil lamp hanging from the ceiling. The Gorilla ignored them.

"Is this where you work?" I asked.

"Work?"

"Forget it."

It was a relief when, a few minutes later, the door was pushed open and J Carrol Naish entered with Jesus. J Carrol looked exactly like he did in the movies, but Jesus, in spite of his crucified appearance, looked half-French and nothing like Cecil B DeMille.

"He's most disappointing," I said.

I was hoping for a remake of *King of Kings* – but there was no response. J Carrol Naish sat on the bench beside me while Jesus sat in the corner opposite and removed his shirt.

"Lice," he said – and proceeded to examine the seams of the shirt, looking for lice.

"Drink," shouted the Gorilla. "Drink!"

Jesus lit a candle, placed it on the ground in front of him, and as he found the lice, dropped them, one by one, onto the burning candle. "Burn!" he cried. "Burn, you devils!"

The lice sizzled, the Gorilla yelled "Drink!" and I was ready for a bed in a lunatic asylum.

"Have you seen *Beau Geste*?" I asked. "It's a movie," I said. "Gary Cooper?"

The Gorilla looked at J Carrol Naish. J Carroll Naish looked at Jesus – and Windmill said: "He likes movie. He's addicted."

Naish paused, Jesus paused, and the Gorilla paused, for a moment, before shouting – "More drink!"

Windmill was by now beginning to slide, ungraciously, under the desk, but the Gorilla and J Carrol Naish continued pouring Pernod into any receptacle that looked empty.

"I take it that Jesus doesn't drink Pernod?" Windmill said, as he slid closer towards the ground.

"Only wine," Naish replied. "Only wine."

"That's logical," Windmill muttered – and disappeared under the desk.

Jesus raised his head. "Your friend has no stomach," he said. "He should kill lice."

"Is that all you do?" I asked. Jesus didn't answer and continued burning lice.

"He fasts," Naish said. "And every night he walks in the desert. He thinks God is out there. God is not out there. There is nothing out there but sand, wind and lice. Some night, an Arab will cut his throat – and then he may see God. Who knows?"

Jesus smiled. "You do not know the desert," he said. "I have seen what is there. God reigns. He suffers. It is his testing ground."

"Madman," said Naish. "One day you will die in the desert. You will be eaten by insects. They will crawl all over you."

"And you," said Jesus. "It is the fate of mankind."

The Gorilla tried to stand up and knocked over his glass. "More drink," he slobbered, before sinking back into his chair. "More drink … "

"You've had enough," Naish said.

The Gorilla paused, raised his hand, then with a roar you could hear across the Sahara, swept the remaining glasses and bottles from the desk in front of him. Broken glass cascaded around the room, as Naish and I fell over each other in our efforts to shelter from the storm. Jesus, however, did not rush for shelter. Shielding the candle flame

334

with both hands, he sat perfectly still and waited until the Gorilla had calmed down.

"You are better now," he said quietly. "Go and lie down."

"Assassin!" Naish yelled. "Bloody ape!"

The Gorilla looked at him. "I will not die in the desert," he moaned. "I will not die in the desert."

"Ape!"

The Gorilla lowered his head until it rested on his desk. "I will not die in the desert," he wept. "Not in the desert … "

He slept soundly and Naish and I regained our seats and listened to him snore.

"Maroc is an ape," Naish said. "Always an ape. When he fought in Morocco, he was an ape. When he fought in Tunisia, he was an ape. Always an ape."

"Not always," Jesus said. "Sometimes he can be very gentle."

"Like you?"

"Not like me."

"You are desert mad. You see God in the sand. There is no God in the sand. It is sand. Stinking sand, crawling with lice. The lice own the desert."

"The Arabs think it belongs to them."

"I piss on the Arabs!"

"Then the Spanish come and the Germans and the French and the English. They all think they own the desert. But they are wrong. The desert belongs to God. It reaches out to heaven and, though it be filled with lice, it still belongs to God. I burn the lice. They are devils."

"Is Jesus your real name?" I asked.

"When you see God, ask him."

J Carrol Naish reached into a drawer in the desk and produced another bottle of Pernod.

"Madman," he said. "Burn the lice. Burn the desert, too. Madman."

He drank from the bottle, then offered it to me. I shook my head. I had had enough and could barely stand up.

It was not like the movies.

"I'm going," I said. "I must go."

"What about your friend?"

"Him, too."

Jesus rose to his feet and doused the candle. "I will help you," he said. "I have finished with the lice. Tomorrow, I will kill some more."

"You'd better put your shirt on first," Naish said. "You'll freeze out there."

Ignoring him, Jesus knelt close to the desk under which Windmill lay curled up, the Gorilla's feet planted firmly across his back. Pushing them aside, Jesus dragged Windmill into the centre of the room. The Gorilla moaned, but did not wake up.

"He has passed out," Jesus said. "I will carry him."

"You will need to," Naish sneered. "He's a woman. He drinks like a woman."

"Fuck off!" I said. "Go back to Hollywood." And I helped Jesus draw Windmill to his feet and raise him onto his shoulders.

"He thinks he's carrying a cross now!" Naish laughed. "A bloody cross!"

I opened the door and followed Jesus out into the night air.

We crossed the parade ground, Jesus carrying Windmill, out through the main gate and around the side wall of the fort towards the armoury tent. Naish followed us for part of the way, before making his way to a tent at the far end of the camp.

"Where is he going?" I asked Jesus.

"To the brothel," he replied.

Jesus looked exhausted by the time we reached the

armoury, but he did not complain. I opened the flap of Windmill's tent and, between us, we managed to carry him inside and put him to bed. Jesus covered him with a blanket and said, "Let him drink plenty of water and he'll be fine tomorrow. I guarantee it."

"You do?"

"Yes. But your friend should not drink Pernod. It is not for him. Let him drink wine instead."

"I'll remember that. And – thanks for your help."

Jesus shrugged his shoulders and stood there for a moment looking at the stars.

"Goodnight," he said – and walked slowly away from the camp, into a cold and silent desert.

Thirteen

Albert Pierrepoint, the English Public Hangman, flew from London to Gibraltar to hang two young Spaniards accused of spying for Germany. He said the journey was difficult, that he had never gone that far before to hang anyone, but this was war and one was obliged to do one's duty whatever the cost. The Spaniards didn't complain, there being nothing to complain about in the circumstances, and he hanged them with speed and efficiency. Albert was pleased with that; he took pride in his work, and after a hearty breakfast, he returned to London to await further requests for his service.

The sound of gunfire and a voice shouting something that was not English awakened me suddenly the following morning at dawn. Dressing as quickly as I could, I grabbed a Sten-gun and rushed outside, ready to defend the sand dunes against all hostile invaders. Corporal Whyles was standing there, shaking his head.

"They're at it again," he said. "Shooting up the Sahara."

"Who, for Christ's sakes?"

"The bloody Legion. Look at the bastards!"

A platoon of Legionnaires, in full battle dress, were charging backwards and forwards across the desert. Every now and then they would fall flat on their faces, cock their rifles and fire into the nearest sand dune.

"I thought we were being attacked," I said. "What's the matter with them? Are they training for something?"

"Aye. The invasion of Europe. It's amazing the number of sand dunes you'd find in Paris! Where's your mate?"

"Sleeping it off, I think."

"With all that racket going on? He must have had a packet."

"He passed out."

"Lucky bleeder!"

The Legionnaires continued their training for the invasion of Europe. The Sergeant in charge shouted orders at them in French, the Corporal standing beside him shouted orders in German, and the Legionnaires shouted "Hup! Hup!" as they charged backwards and forwards across the desert, full packs on their backs.

"Nutters!" Corporal Whyles said. "Bloody nutters!"

"How long does this go on for?"

"Could be hours, mate. It's a long war."

My head ached and I thought of Rommel, now sitting at home, nursing a nose infection and wondering how he was going to defend Europe against the coming Allied invasion.

The Gorilla was leading the pack in the desert. J Carrol Naish ran sweating behind him and Jesus trailed at the rear, as if the last place he wanted to invade was a sand dune in Europe.

Corporal Whyles and I watched them for a while, until presently Windmill appeared, looking like Lazarus emerging from his tomb.

"What's happening?" he groaned. "Has the Afrika Korps made a come-back?"

"If they had, you wouldn't be of much use," Corporal Whyles said. "You look as if you'd already copped it."

Windmill said he thought he had, then sat in the sand, covering his ears with his hands. "Pernod," he grieved. "Never again."

"How many times have I heard that! I suppose you had crumpet as well?"

When Windmill didn't answer, Corporal Whyles stood beside him and looked into his face. "You look wanked out, mate. Have you puked?"

"No."

"You will."

"It's just a hangover, Corp. Too much Pernod."

"Pernod, me bollox! It's malaria, you twit! Go back to bed and I'll see if I can get the MO to have a look at you."

"Are you sure?"

"I'm sure. I've been in Africa long enough to know malaria when I see it."

Helping Windmill to his feet, he guided him back inside his tent. I waited outside and when Corporal Whyles returned he said: "He's flat out. How the hell did he get back to camp last night?"

"Jesus carried him."

"You mean the lofty creep who wanders about the desert at night?"

"That's him."

"You know what they say about him, don't you? He killed his old lady in Germany. That's right. Chopped her up with an axe and then dumped the bits in the river. He was sentenced to death, but managed to escape somehow and joined the Army."

"I don't believe that."

"Believe it! I do. He was with Rommel's mob out there for a while, but he deserted when Jerry was clobbered in Tunisia. That's why he's in the Legion. They don't give a fuck. No questions. Sign on, under any name you like, and that's it."

"I still don't believe it. How does anyone know what he did, if they don't ask questions and he doesn't answer them? It doesn't make sense."

"People have ways of finding out, mate. But as long as

you do what you're told in the Legion and don't make trouble, they'll stand by you. That's the rule. I've talked to guys in there and I can tell you, there's not one of them that hasn't got a record of some kind."

"I take people as they come, Corp. The only thing he did last night was to burn lice over a candle – and then carry Windmill all the way back here. I liked him."

"His old lady probably adored him, too – and look what happened to her! Take my advice and avoid him. I'd better go see now can I get the MO for your mate. I think those lunatics are just about ready to pack it in."

I stood there for a moment after he'd walked away, watching the Legionnaires fall into line before being ordered back to the fort. They marched on-the-double, shouting "Hup! Hup!" with every step.

When the MO arrived, he said that Windmill indeed had malaria. He said some people had good systems and some people had bad systems. Windmill had no system. There were a few people in this world who were like that, he said, and Windmill was one of them. If there were a flu epidemic in Australia, Windmill would catch it in Africa. Even if there had been no mosquitoes in Port Etienne, Windmill would catch malaria anyway.

The MO had met people like that before – and had hoped never to meet one of them again. He'd been happy in Port Etienne. He'd been here six months and no one had caught malaria. Even the mosquitoes were free of it. You could pick them up with your hand and let them crawl all over you. You could even eat the little bastards – and would you catch malaria? No, Sir! Not in a million years. But this guy comes along and he's got malaria. He's riddled with malaria. And why, you may ask? I'll tell you why. Because he's got no fucking system, that's why!

People without systems worried the MO. He couldn't

341

sleep at night thinking about them. They gave him nightmares. They hid in dark corners, waiting to pounce on him. He could see them peering at him through his surgery window. People like that shouldn't be allowed into the armed forces. They shouldn't be allowed in anywhere, for Christsakes! They should be locked up in concrete rooms with hoods over their heads. Rooms painted with blood and booby-trapped with land mines. But was that decent? Was it democratic? Wasn't this a People's War? And weren't people without systems entitled to join in? Of course they were – and that's what wrong with democracy. Every fucking lunatic and hypochondriac is allowed to join in!

"Here, give him three Mepaquin tables a day and don't let him come near me again."

I promised, faithfully, and never saw him again.

A few days later Corporal Whyles said the MO had left his tent and was out wandering in the desert.

"Depressed?"

"Suicidal, mate."

So much for the medical profession.

Windmill lay in bed for two weeks, and there wasn't a day when he didn't moan, or a night when he didn't wake up, at least once, and say he was dying, or turning yellow or had a pain in his chest. The Corporal and I stuffed every Mepaquin tablet in sight into him and almost drowned him with water, but it made little difference. Windmill was going to suffer and he wanted us to know he was suffering. When he was told that he was the only man in the camp to contract malaria, he became convinced he would receive a medal.

Then, one morning, he woke up and said – "What the hell is all the fuss about? It's only malaria. You'd think I was dying, or something."

Had I got hold of a machine-gun at that moment, I

think I would have killed him.

"You people take life far too seriously. There's people being shot every hour of the day in this war. So what's a dose of malaria?"

I said nothing. Corporal Whyles said nothing. You can't argue with people who have no system.

Corporal Whyles had a system. It wasn't the system the MO was talking about, but it was a system all the same. He said the universe was nothing but chance, life was a joke, most people were insane, religion should be abolished, marriage outlawed, banks blown up, Tories lynched, Members of Parliament shot and wars permitted only between Generals and upper-class twits. Windmill agreed and I said I'd met two Polish anarchists in London who felt the same way.

"Lucky you! If you know their address, give it to me."

I didn't know their address and Corporal Whyles said: "That's war. You meet the only two sensible people in London and they turn out to be Poles passing through."

"Drunk."

"Of course they were drunk. What else would they be, surrounded by lunatics!"

I was beginning to like Corporal Whyles. He wore his uniform as if by accident, he was always fully armed, but the only thing I ever saw him shoot at was a hyena – and he missed.

"Stick to it," I said. "You'll get one yet."

Corporal Whyles stuck to it – but he never managed to kill a hyena.

He was an easy-going Corporal, he did not give orders and he never pulled rank. He said we were trained airmen, knew what was expected of us, no bullshit and just get on with it. What we were doing here – he hadn't a clue – but neither did anyone else. But fuck it! When this war was over, he was going back home to join the Anarchists. I wished him luck.

During the months that followed, Windmill and I passed our time cleaning guns that were never used, sorting ammunition that was seldom fired, burning locusts with petrol and pretending we were fighting a war. Corporal Whyles came to see us every day, Captain Monet inspected us once a week, and every evening we sat in our tents, listening to the announcer on the radio telling us about the war, and Vera Lynn telling us we'd meet again.

On Mondays, the Sunderland flew in with the weekly supply of petrol and food, the occasional book, the mail, and the latest première from Hollywood, donated courtesy of the Yanks. We saw Humphrey Bogart lose himself in *Sahara* – Bette Davis breaking into song in *Thank Your Lucky Stars* and everybody who was anybody raising funds for British War Relief in something called *Forever and a Day*. The only good book to be delivered was *Sister Carrie* by Theodore Dreiser – and that had been destined for somewhere else and arrived in Port Etienne only by mistake.

Sometimes, out of sheer boredom, we attended drinking sessions at the fort. The Gorilla sat behind his desk as usual. J Carrol Naish sat grinning beside him, while Jesus continued to pick lice from the seams of his shirt, burning them over a lighted candle. Corporal Whyles joined us, once or twice, but sat as far away from the lice as he possibly could – in case Jesus tired of burning them and produced an axe instead.

Jesus did not produce an axe. But when we reached the sloppy, sentimental 'Danny Boy' stage one evening, I unfortunately said – "Let's toast our darling mothers" – and even The Gorilla stopped drinking. J Carrol said nothing, Windmill slid quietly under the desk again, and Corporal Whyles dropped his glass on the floor and asked: "Does anyone know what's happening in Crete?"

At that moment I didn't care what was happening in Crete. I was praying for a transfer to Mongolia – or the Russian Front – anywhere as long as it was quick.

Jesus, on the other hand, didn't even raise his head, until presently he said, "I believe we are winning the war. Yes. We are winning."

He returned to burning lice then, as the evening descended into a drunken stupor from which I have never recovered.

One morning, just when I was beginning to think Windmill and I had been posted to Port Etienne because we were too enthusiastic about winning the war and wanted it finished sooner than the Air Ministry had planned, Corporal Whyles arrived outside the armoury and said we were wanted in the Orderly Room.

I didn't even know that there was an Orderly Room and the only Officers I'd seen, since our arrival at the camp, had been the MO, now wandering in the desert, and Captain Monet, who couldn't speak a word of English and occasionally went raving mad and beat the sand with his cane.

The Orderly Room turned out to be a small tent, looking like every other small tent in the camp, but situated discreetly behind the fort and camouflaged to look like a sand dune. The only occupants of the tent were Captain Monet and an RAF Sergeant, whom neither of us had seen before.

"Sit down," the Sergeant said, indicating a wooden bench. "Please."

The politeness was ominous, but Windmill and I sat on the bench while Corporal Whyles waited outside and smoked a cigarette.

"Would you care for some tea?"

"No, thanks, Sergeant."

"You may smoke, if you wish."

Pausing, he then said: "My name is Sergeant Wilson. Not that that matters, of course, because you are not here under orders and are not required to do anything which you would prefer not to do. Is that understood?"

"Yes …?"

"However, should you decide not to take part, you are bound, under the Official Secrets Act, not to disclose any information concerning this operation to anyone outside this tent. Is that understood?"

"Yes…"

"Now, let me make one more thing quite clear. This is not a matter directly, or indirectly, related to the RAF. It is strictly a French affair and you will be entirely responsible to Captain Monet. That is why it is up to you. You can either say Yes and carry on, or you can say No and walk out of here. No questions, no record – and no recriminations of any kind. Is that understood?"

"Yes, Sergeant."

"Very well then. As Captain doesn't speak English and I assume that neither of you speak French, I will put you in the picture. Some weeks ago, the French authorities in North Africa picked up what they believed to be two German agents. Upon investigation, however, these agents turned out to be French nationals. They have been tried and convicted of espionage in Dakar and are now awaiting sentence here in Port Etienne. The reasons for this transfer are extremely complex and should not concern you. The sentence for espionage in wartime is death by firing squad – and this sentence will be carried out at six o'clock tomorrow morning."

"So?"

"So – because they are French nationals, there is, shall we say, a certain reluctance on the part of the Legionnaires at the fort to take part in this execution. Captain Monet does not wish to exacerbate the situation by issuing a direct order and has devised a possible solution."

"I don't think I like the sound of this," Windmill said.

"Let me finish. Captain Monet has already managed to secure the services of four volunteers who are not French to take part in the operation, and he is looking for two more, preferably from among our chaps, to join them. A Firing Squad, as you probably know, is normally made up of a group of six. The rifles are loaded with live ammunition and a certain number of blanks. The Officer in charge will hand you the rifles shortly before the execution – and, after the execution, you will return the rifles to the Officer in charge and go about your business in the normal way. No one will know who has fired the fatal shots and no one will know your names, your rank, or anything whatever about you. You will be returned to camp immediately and that will be the end of it."

"Is this for real?" I asked. "It sounds like something out of a movie."

The Sergeant looked at me. "It is not a movie. I can assure you of that."

"But why us?"

The Sergeant didn't answer.

"Do we have to decide now?" Windmill asked.

"I'm afraid so. And it must be a joint decision. However, if you would like Captain Monet and myself to wait outside for a moment, while you discuss the matter, we will gladly do so."

Windmill looked at me. "I don't think that will be necessary, Sergeant," he said. "For my part, I don't think I could do it. I mean, if it was … "

"You do not have to explain, Harrison" the Sergeant interrupted – and turned to me. "Is that your decision too?"

"Yes, Sergeant. I've never killed anyone in my life. Not that I know of, anyway."

The Sergeant smiled. "You're in the Royal Air Force," he said. "We are engaged in a war. Do not be ridiculous."

"May we go now?"

"By all means. The Corporal will escort you back to your tents. Good morning to you."

"And to you, Sergeant."

Windmill and I left the Orderly Room and Corporal Whyles escorted us back to the armoury.

It was a long day and the night dragged endlessly towards the dawn. I thought of two men – or maybe they were women – sitting in their cells waiting for execution. I couldn't sleep and at six o'clock, Windmill and I stood outside the armoury and heard the grieving sound of gunfire. It seemed a long way off and, for the first time in my life, I wept for those I did not know.

Fourteen

Admiral Jean Darlan, commander of the French naval forces at the beginning of the war and vice-premier in the pro-German Vichy regime, under Marshal Pétain, was a saint. A woman in Dakar told me that. She had a portrait of the Admiral in her window, and every day she went to the local Catholic church and prayed for him.

When the Allied Forces landed in Algeria in November 1942 and captured Admiral Darlan, they too recognised his saintly qualities and, after he had negotiated an end to Vichy resistance in the area, appointed him High Commissioner of French North Africa. The Americans were happy, the British were happy and the locals were happy. The only one who was not happy was General Charles de Gaulle. He said, "There is but one saint in this war – *Moi!*" and, a month later, the Admiral was assassinated by the Free French and his place taken by General Giraud.

General Giraud was not a saint, but he did believe in General de Gaulle. Commander of Allied defences in Northern France until the fall of Sedan, he had been captured by the Germans but managed to escape into unoccupied France. Agreeing with General de Gaulle that there was only one saint, he had made his way subsequently to Algeria to join him, after the Allied invasion of North Africa. As far as General de Gaulle was concerned, you couldn't say fairer than that – and as long as nobody called Giraud a saint, he could be High Commissioner of Timbuktu for all he cared.

When Windmill and I arrived in Dakar on three weeks' leave in 1944, it seemed that the only people in charge were the Americans. They had set up their administrative quarters on the outskirts of the city, which had now become the only place in French West Africa where members of the Allied forces were permitted to spend their leave. American 'Snowdrops' patrolled the streets, American Medical Officers inspected the brothels, American music dominated the airwaves, and the only accommodation available for troops was at the American Forces Camp. Windmill and I found no difficulty with that – given that the food was good, and there were no flies, no lice and no sand in your coffee.

We spent our first night at the American Forces Canteen, drinking beer and listening to Jack Benny on the radio. The following morning we were presented with a history of Dakar by Sergeant Martino, who said it should have been blown up.

"Vichy!" he said, through what appeared to be his mouth. "Can you beat that? Shit – goddamn it!"

Windmill and I said nothing, seeing the Sergeant wore a trail of campaign medals down to his boots, and waved his revolver about as if the slightest disagreement would result in instant death.

"Bastards! Call themselves French. Kiss my ass!"

I wasn't prepared to do anything of the kind, but I nodded lest he put a bullet through me.

"Goddamn it!"

"We're only here for three weeks," I said. "Can you give us some advice?"

"Advice? Shit! Keep your eyes open and piss on Vichy water!"

"If you'll forgive me, Sergeant," Windmill said – "I don't think that's very helpful. Perhaps, a leaflet of some sort …?"

"Leaflet?"

"You know. A list of things to do – or not to do in Dakar. Surely, you've got one of those."

"You're goddamn right, we have!"

"May we have one?"

"Sure. But don't you goddamn Limeys ever think of yourselves? Does everything have to be written down?"

"Well, actually, Sergeant," I said, "I'm not a Limey at all. I'm an Irishman and I'm out here studying to be a Missionary."

"Shit!"

"Can we have the leaflet?"

"Sure. I'm an Italian myself – from the Bronx."

He handed us the leaflet, we thanked him – and managed to hitch a ride into the city.

ATTENTION ALL RANKS

The city of Dakar has been under the control of the French Vichy government since the beginning of the war. This government no longer exists and the city is now under the control of the US and Allied Forces. In your own interests, and in order that your stay here may be a pleasant one, it is essential that you take note of the following rules and regulations:

1: The inhabitants of this city are French citizens. Many of them are Free French and many more are strong supporters of the Vichy regime. You may, therefore, be subject to hostility in certain areas. You are advised to avoid these areas.

2: If you are subject to hostility – do not respond and do not provoke. It is not the policy of the US and its Allies to provoke incidents.

3: A number of bars, restaurants and brothels are barred to Allied Forces. These premises are clearly marked. Any

*member of the Allied Forces found on these premises will be
subject to arrest by the Military Police.*
*4: The wearing of side arms is not permitted in bars,
restaurants or brothels.*
*5: The singing of anti-Vichy or anti-Fascist songs is not
permitted in bars, restaurants or brothels.*
*6: Do not refer to supporters of the former Vichy regime in
Dakar as 'Froggies', 'Fascist Collaborators', 'Brothel Keepers'
or 'Vichy Bastards'.*
*7: In the interest of harmony and stability, it is essential that
we maintain a friendly and working relationship with the
people of Dakar. We are here to liberate, not to conquer.
Should you have any difficulties, contact the Military Police
or the Free French authorities.*
8: Enjoy your stay.

The Free French along the pavements in Dakar saluted
you and wished you well, while those who still supported
Vichy looked at you as if you had kicked their grandmother
in the teeth and were now stealing their children's lollipops.
They crossed the street, ignored you when you asked for
something in the shops, and kept to themselves in bars and
restaurants. In areas where Allied Forces were advised not to
frequent, portraits of Marshal Pétain and Admiral Darlan
hung from the walls and were sold openly, as postcards, in
the streets.

In 'Madame Fi-Fi's' however – a brothel open to all
nations and catering to all tastes – tolerance was a virtue and
politics bad for business. The girls sat naked in the windows
or stood at the doorway, whistling at everyone and anyone,
and promising to give lessons in French, German, Swedish
and Russian acrobatics. They promised courses in
correction, nursing, bonding, animal training, dressage and
missionary work – and offered, to those of a literary

persuasion, a range of artistic masterpieces, fully illustrated and in perfect condition.

Windmill bought a copy of *The Humours and Delights of Sodomy* – which worried everyone at the American base and I bought a version of *Maria Monk* – which worried no one because it was all about bishops and nuns playing hopscotch in a convent in Canada.

Inside Madame Fi-Fi's, the girls displayed their attributes along the length of the bar counter, while the voluminous Madame Fi-Fi herself sat on a sofa near the door, fully clothed, and collected the fees.

"Nice girls. Very clean. All virgins. Plenty jiggy-jig. Sing too."

The girls did sing, though their repertoire was somewhat limited. There was 'Soldier, Come and Tie My Garter', for the English and something called 'Juice Me, Honey', for the Americans – which had to be heard not to be believed. Madame Fi-Fi, however, thought they were all brilliant, and clapped her hands together like a pair of dead fish.

"Best music. Best girls. Pay here for best jiggy-jig."

The troops paid, chose their partners, and together they climbed the stairs to the rooms on the first floor. Madame Fi-Fi smiled.

"Time for jiggy-jig," she said as the doors closed behind them. "Time for plenty jiggy-jig."

Madame Fi-Fi never engaged in jiggy-jig, moving from her sofa only when the troops returned to base and the girls retired to their rooms to rest.

On Saturday afternoons however, Madame Fi-Fi closed the bar, moved the sofa into the centre of the room and held court to a selected few. "No jiggy-jig. Plenty music. Much talk." And on my second Saturday in Dakar she invited me – because, she said, I looked very foolish and was probably a virgin. She did not invite my friend Windmill.

"I think he stink," she said. "I no like him."

There was no answer to that. Windmill didn't like her either, saying she was a raddled old bag who should have been put out to grass years ago.

It was late in the afternoon when I arrived, and Madame Fi-Fi lay stretched out on the sofa, smoking a cigar. There was no one else in the room.

"Sit," she said – pointing to the floor. "Sit!"

I sat on the floor and looked up at her. She was dressed in a long white robe, decorated with ostrich feathers, and she wore a flower in her hair. I had never seen anything like it.

When Madame moved, the sofa moved. And when she nodded her head, the enormous earrings pinned to her ears, and the several necklaces hanging from the folds of her neck, all jangled in unison.

"You like?"

"I like!"

Madame Fi-Fi grinned, and the sofa moved, as she reached down to wind up the portable gramophone on the floor beside her.

"You like?"

"I like."

The gramophone was old, the records cracked, and when she leaned forward again to select her favourite record, the groaning sofa almost took flight.

"Are these the only records you've got?" I asked, as she lay back and listened dreamily to Edith Piaf singing '*L'estrange*'.

She nodded her head. "Piaf is beautiful," she said, as if seeing herself in a mirror. "Very beautiful. Come closer."

"I'm happy where I am," I said, holding fast to my virginity.

"Afraid?"

I was petrified, but brought up to be nonchalant. "No," I replied. "Not in the least. Are you expecting anyone else?"

"Anyone else?"

"More people, you know …?"

She paused before answering. "No," she smiled. "No more people. They bore me."

We listened to Edith Piaf and when Edith had finished, Madame Fi-Fi wound up the gramophone again and we had more of Edith Piaf. Then we had Josephine Baker and Maurice Chevalier, before it was back to Edith Piaf again. I was getting very tired of Edith and was about to put my foot through the gramophone when Madame Fi-Fi switched it off and said: "I think we drink now – yes?"

Anything but another record, I thought, and waited for the sofa to collapse as she reached under her pillow and produced a flask of brandy.

"No glasses?"

"Why you want glasses?" she asked. "We drink from flask."

"There's a movie in this," I said. "I can see it coming."

"*Pépé le Moko*," she sighed – "Jean Gabin."

We drank to Jean Gabin. We drank to Pépé le Moko. We drank to every station on the Paris Metro and then we drank to ourselves.

"You'd make a fortune climbing the stairs," I said, between drinks. "Why don't you do it anymore?"

"Too fat," she mumbled. "You want jiggy-jig with me?"

I almost had a stroke at the prospect, but – "No," I said. "I'm just curious – but thanks for the offer."

"No offer. No way jiggy-jig. You not Jean Gabin."

I was surprised at that, as my mother always maintained I looked like a film star, but I said nothing.

"I give you nice girl," she continued. "Very clean. She be good to you."

"No, thanks."

"You not like my girls?"

"I like your girls very much."

"Your friend not like my girls."

"He prefers literature."

"No jiggy-jig in literature."

"He has a vivid imagination."

She shook her head. "I have imagination. I have plenty imagination. I think I sleep with Jean Gabin. Plenty jiggy-jig then."

She sighed deeply, drained the flask, and lay back on the sofa. "Pépé le Moko," she dreamed. "Pépé le Moko … "

The room was dark and she snored in her sleep.

Sometimes, in the mirrors of my mind, I can see the young, black-haired girl who entered the room, while Madame Fi-Fi slept, and turned on a single lamp, hanging awkwardly over the counter. Her name was Françoise and she was seventeen years of age. She moved gracefully, making no sound as she crossed the room in her bare feet.

"Would you like a drink?" she asked, holding up a bottle of red wine. "Madame won't mind."

"Will she sleep long?"

"We don't open till late," she replied. "She'll rest till then."

I moved over to the bar counter and sat facing her, as she uncorked the bottle and poured the red wine into two shining glasses.

"Peace," she said and raised her glass. "I drink to peace."

We drank to peace as, in the centre of the room, Madame Fi-Fi continued to snore.

"What's your name?"

"Françoise."

I wanted to talk to Françoise. I wanted to know who she was and what she was doing in a brothel in Dakar? Did she work there? Did she climb the stairs and lie on a bed for anyone who paid? Was she related to Madame Fi-Fi?

"Madame has been very kind to me," she said, without being asked. "I have known her a long time."

"In Dakar?"

"Since Paris."

Françoise told me that she was born in Paris, and when the Germans occupied the city, her parents were arrested and sent to a concentration camp.

"Jews?"

"Communists. There was no one else. Madame helped me and brought me to Dakar. She is a good woman."

"Political?"

"Not political. Just kind. When we arrived here, she did not ask me to be one of her girls. She asked nothing of me. She never has."

"What about your parents? Do you know what happened to them?"

"No."

"Maybe you'll hear from them one day."

"Maybe."

She sipped her drink, then moved round the bar and sat beside me. We drank in silence until presently she said – "Madame will not mind if we sit in her room. It is more comfortable there."

"Are you sure?"

"I am sure."

Madame Fi-Fi's room, at the rear of the bar, was warm and spacious. Françoise sat on the edge of the bed and I sat, awkwardly, on the edge of a chair. On a dressing table near the bed were photographs of Françoise and Madame Fi-Fi, and above the bed, a large movie poster, featuring the charms of Jean Gabin.

"Jean Gabin could give you a complex," I said – as Françoise smiled and refilled our glasses.

"He is Madame's favourite movie star," she said. "For me, he is too old."

"I agree with that. He must be at least fifty."

"Have you a girl?"

"No. Do you have someone?"

She shook her head. "Only Madame," she said.

"Do you think I should go?"

"Do you want to?"

"I don't know."

She moved from the bed and sat at my feet, her head resting on my lap. I stroked her long dark hair.

"I could be very good to you," she said.

And she was.

Fifteen

"So what have you been up to?" Windmill asked, as we sat over lunch in the American Forces canteen. "I haven't seen you for days."

"Movies," I said. "I've been to the movies."

"Anything good?"

"*Pépé le Moko*. Jean Gabin. Have you seen it?"

"Christ, no! I hate French movies. All subtitles and heavy breathing."

"This one wasn't. What have you been doing?"

"Wandering around Dakar. And the most interesting thing I've seen so far – a Free French poodle, wearing an American baseball cap."

"You knew it was Free French of course?"

"Of course. It barked, didn't it? Vichy poodles never bark. They whine."

"How the hell do you know?"

"Sergeant Martino told me. You know, the guy we met the day we arrived here? He's a mine of information – especially about Vichy."

"He's an eegit."

"He told me a lot about that brothel we were in, too. Did you know that Madame Fi-Fi is known as Hitler's secret weapon? She's given the pox to half the British Army – to say nothing of the Yanks."

"They probably deserved it. In any case, she doesn't do it anymore. She's retired."

"I should hope so – after all the damage she's done! The

359

only good thing I heard about her was that she was beautiful once. 'Still gave you the pox, but you enjoyed it more. She didn't try to give it to you, did she?"

"No. I just talked to her, that's all."

"Thank Christ for that! Wouldn't want you going home with your dick in a sling. There used to be a song about her, you know. One of the Yanks gave it to me. Same air as "The Isle of Capri".

> 'Twas at the Rue Rafanel that I met her,
> She was French and her name was Fi-Fi.
> She whispered so softly that no one could hear her –
> Would you like to come upstairs with me?
> I must admit she was very attractive,
> And I was a little drunk, too –
> So I slipped fifty francs in her pocket,
> And took my place at the end of the queue.
> I must have waited twenty minutes,
> And I went to her room above.
> There I proceeded to indulge in
> Fifty francs' worth of legalised love.
> When I woke on the following morning,
> I was as worried as worried could be.
> For the sake of a few minutes' pleasure,
> Something dreadful had happened to me.

I did not tell Windmill that there was another side to Madame Fi-Fi, other things that might be said. And I did not tell him of a young girl who entered the room, while Madame Fi-Fi slept, and turned on a single lamp, hanging awkwardly over the bar counter. I did not tell him about Françoise.

Françoise – who was good to me.

In the days that followed, Windmill and I toured the bars, ate well at the American base, and listened to the news on the American Forces Network. We heard that the Americans were winning the war in the Pacific, the British were winning the war in the air, the invasion of Europe was imminent, and the Free French would enter Paris with flags flying.

In the camp cinema, we were wooed by Lana Turner in *Somewhere I'll Find You* – Rita Hayworth in *You were Never Lovelier* – Betty Grable in *Springtime in the Rockies* – Alice Faye in *Rose of Washington Square* – and everybody who was anybody in *Stage Door Canteen* and *Star-spangled Rhythm*.

It was a musical war. A Glenn Miller war, a Benny Goodman war, a Count Basie war, a Jimmy Dorsey war, and a Harry James war – with Gene Krupa on drums. Al Jolson was there, Bing Crosby was there, Bob Hope was there, the Andrews Sisters were there, Rosemary Clooney was there, and they all sang bravely to the music of Jerome Kern and Johnny Mercer, Rogers and Hart, Cole Porter and Irving Berlin. And you could feel we were winning.

It was 'Fascinating Rhythm' – 'Arthur Murray Taught Me Dancing' – 'Lady Be Good' – 'You'll Never Know' – 'I'll See You In My Dreams' and 'The Last Time I Saw Paris'. You were far from home and your 'Dearly Beloved'. Some tears, a little sadness, but keep your spirits up – 'Rally Round The Flag' – 'This Land Is Your Land' and 'We'll Meet Again'.

The war smelled sweet in the American camp. None of our aircraft were missing, the theatre was air-conditioned and no body bags were permitted to pollute the screen. A musical war – 'Praise the Lord and Pass the Ammunition' and we'll all stay free.

Oh, the sky-pilot said it,
And you've got to give him credit,
For the son-of-a gun of a son-of-a gunner was he:

Shouting – praise the Lord and pass the ammunition
Praise the Lord and swing into position
Praise the Lord and pass the ammunition
And we'll all stay free!

Over breakfast, however, only some of us felt free. The black GIs sat at one end of the canteen and we sat at the other. We had been warned about eating in native cafés, warned of the dangers of loose talk, of boozing in brothels and consorting with black women who were riddled with VD and had no idea what this war was about. It was a relief therefore to know that white women were free of all such diseases and blessed themselves, regularly, before hopping into bed.

One evening, while Windmill was indulging in a feast of pornographic literature he had managed to obtain from a back street bookshop in Dakar, and I was listening to Tommy Handley on the radio shouting – "Food Flash! Have you thought what you could do with a carrot?"– Sergeant Martino came in and asked how we were enjoying our leave.

"The grub is good," Windmill said.

"And the dames?"

"I haven't seen any yet," Windmill replied. "Except in the cinema."

"You've been to the brothels, haven't you?"

"Strictly as a spectator, Sergeant. I prefer something more interesting."

"You won't find it in those goddamn books," Sergeant Martino looked at him. "I can tell you that."

"Have you another suggestion?"

"Maybe. What about your friend?"

"He's religious, Sergeant. Only interested in nuns."

Sergeant Martino paused. "Well," he said, "there's an exhibition going on in a joint I know. Want to see it?"

"What kind of an exhibition?"

"Artistic. Interested?"

Windmill was interested.

"I'm going to church," I said. "I'm not into art."

"OK. We'll drop you on the way. Grab your gear and let's get moving."

We moved – in beside Sergeant Martino in a souped-up jeep as he drove towards the centre of Dakar.

When we arrived at the main gate of the local church, Sergeant Martino pulled up, smiling, and asked: "Is this OK?"

"Sure, Sergeant. This will do fine."

The smile faded. "I didn't think you were serious," he said. "Didn't think it one little bit."

"Oh, I'm always serious, Sergeant. Thanks for the lift."

"One born every minute," I heard him say, as he drove off with Windmill. "Every fucking minute!"

I wished them luck and spent the remainder of the evening with Françoise.

The yellowing lampshade on the bedside table, the sepia photographs of Madame Fi-Fi and Françoise. The troops climbed the stairs, the doors closed behind them, Madame Fi-Fi sighed. Jean Gabin.

The windows open, the light of evening, a falling star.

We could hear the music. Edith Piaf, Maurice Chevalier, Josephine Baker.

Fragrance of Françoise.

We heard the troops leaving, the front door closing, the lights being turned off.

The odour of jasmine filled the air and our loving was silent.

At 'Madame Fi-Fi's', Madame slept on the sofa, while we slept in her bed.

When I returned to base, Windmill was seated on the

edge of his bed, nursing a hangover. He said he was dying. He said he hated Dakar, hated the French and couldn't stand the Americans. When I asked about the exhibition he'd attended with Sergeant Martino, he said it was diabolical.

"I thought it was supposed to be artistic?"

"Shit! There was this woman," he moaned – "and this bloody great hound of the Baskervilles – and what they didn't do together, upside-down, inside out, sideways and back to front … Oh, Jesus!"

"You enjoyed it."

"I did not! There are limits even to my depravity. The only thing I could do was get drunk. Have you an aspirin?"

"Sorry."

"I've never felt so sick in my life."

"Go back to bed."

Windmill lay back on the bed, covering his eyes with his hands, and continued to moan. I was tempted to put a pillow over his face and smother him, but decency prevailed.

"You have no idea what it was like," he said. "There were hundreds of people in the audience. All sitting on the floor, pissed out of their minds, playing with each other and screaming at that monster of a dog and that revolting woman on the platform – urging them on – 'Give it to her, Fido! Plunge it in!' I felt sick. I wanted to vomit all over them."

"Why didn't you leave?"

"I did! I went out and got drunk in this stinking bar. Christ knows what I was drinking and Christ knows how I got back here. That creep Martino disappeared. Don't know where he went. I could have been murdered! Where did you go?"

"Church."

"Bollox! I don't believe that for a minute. Are you sure you haven't got an aspirin?"

"No aspirin."

"I thought you were supposed to be a mate of mine?"

"I am. Go to sleep. You'll feel better."

"I will not. I'll never feel better in Dakar. I'll never feel better until this rotten war is over and I'm back in civvy street. Look at it, for Christ's sake! What the hell are we doing here? Have we met one sane person since we joined? They're all either crazy or drunk or whoring in brothels."

"I've met a few who were decent enough."

"Where? In the graveyard?"

"Cut it out! You've had a bad night. You've got a hangover. Just take it easy and go to sleep."

"What's the matter with you?"

"Nothing."

Windmill looked at me for a moment, then turned away. I was tired listening to him, tired of his endless moans, tired of hearing about the lunacy of war, tired of the radio and the news and the music and those endless, mindless voices talking about victory and death. I didn't want to hear any more. I wanted to lie down on my bed, peacefully, silently, with only one thought in my head – Françoise.

I remember the day. I remember ambling into Madame Fi-Fi's, our last weekend in Dakar, and seeing Madame leaning over the bar counter, drinking heavily. It was the first time I had seen her standing up, and she was taller than I had imagined.

"Drink?"

"Why not?"

"Why not?" she said and handed me the bottle. "She was good for you?"

"Yes, she is good for me."

Madame Fi-Fi nodded. "For me also."

We drank to Françoise.

Madame Fi-Fi told me then how she had brought Françoise from Paris to Dakar, treating her as her own daughter. She did not ask her to work in the brothel, she did not ask her to serve in the bar. She fed her and clothed her and protected her from harm. She was good to Françoise, they were good for each other, and asked for nothing in return.

In Paris, Madame Fi-Fi had seen the Germans march triumphantly through the city. She saw the Tricolour being lowered and the Swastika being raised over monuments to the dead and over public buildings, and she had wept for Paris. In the cinema she sat and watched the newsreels. She saw Marshal Pétain sign the armistice with Germany, she saw Hitler dance and Göring clap his hands and she wept for France.

And then, one night, as she was crossing the street by the apartment building where Françoise lived, she saw Françoise's parents being dragged on to the back of a lorry by soldiers and the Gestapo, while Françoise screamed and pleaded for them. A crowd stood in the street, but no one protested and no one moved to interfere as Françoise's parents were driven off into the darkness.

"They will be all right," Madame Fi-Fi told Françoise. "They will be back soon. I will take care of you."

And Madame Fi-Fi did.

Then, that day in Dakar, she leaned over the bar counter and said, "I want her to have hope. I tell her that she will see them again. Always I tell her that. But I know. For a long time I know."

"And she knows now?"

"The Gendarmes tell her. Last night they come here and they say, 'You have no Father, no Mother, Françoise. They die in concentration camp.' It is not right they should say that."

"Is there anything I can do? Can I talk to her?"

Madame Fi-Fi didn't answer.

She had woken up. She had gone to the bathroom. She had seen Françoise lying dead in the bath.

"It is not right," she repeated. "Not right they should say such things."

I remember the day and I remember the room where we both slept. I remember how graceful she was.

I remember Françoise.

Sixteen

"Under the command of General Eisenhower, Allied armies supported by strong air forces began landing Allied armies this morning on the coast of France … "

The aforementioned invasion of Europe by the Allied Forces of Liberation took place while Windmill and I were still cleaning sand from the rifles and machine guns in the armoury at Port Etienne. We had thought that General Eisenhower might have had the decency to inform us of the date of this enterprise, so that we might have had everything ready on time, but the first we heard of it was when the BBC announced that the invasion was in progress, and Allied troops were already storming the beaches of Normandy.

"He could have given us a hint, at least!" Windmill complained. "We might have been able to do something."

"Like what? Pretend to be sick?"

Windmill wasn't amused.

We had returned from our three weeks' leave in Dakar, hoping to find the armoury in the same pristine condition in which we had left it, but Corporal Whyles said that the camp had almost been destroyed in a sandstorm the day before, and the last thing on anyone's mind had been the armoury.

"It's a wreck," I said. "It'll take us weeks to clean up."

"There's no hurry," Corporal Whyles declared. "You're not going anywhere – are you?"

"Well, we had hoped to play some small part in the invasion of Europe," Windmill smiled. "Not that I have any

368

desire to storm the beaches, or anything like that, but just a tiny contribution?"

Corporal Whyles looked at him. "Just consider yourself lucky, mate. Every yard gained in Normandy today will cost a thousand lives. Maybe it's worth it. Maybe not. I don't know. Just consider yourself lucky."

"I do."

"Then clean up and shut up! It's going to be a cold day."

"What's the matter with him, for Christ's sake?" Windmill said, after he walked away. "He's not his usual sweet self anymore."

"I have no idea. Maybe he doesn't like the thought of all those bodies lying on the beach."

"Who the hell does? It's a nightmare."

"And you want to contribute?"

"Well, let's not go mad altogether! But I do feel a modicum of guilt. – I mean, here we are, stuck in this Godforsaken desert, doing nothing of value, serving no purpose that I can see, while thousands of other unfortunate bastards are being blown to bits on the beaches of Normandy. It is not a pleasant thought."

"Corporal Whyles probably feels the same."

"I'm sure he does, but it's different for him. He's a Regular airman – not a bloody Conscript. I didn't want to join this war. I wanted nothing whatever to do with it. I was perfectly happy, sitting at home, reading a book and listening to music. Now look at me – up to my eyeballs in sand, and surrounded by whores, lunatics and drunken Legionnaires."

"You haven't been exactly sober yourself."

"I never touched more than a glass till I joined this lot. I don't know how you do it. It doesn't seem to worry you."

"It worries me."

"You don't show it. What happened in Dakar? You

haven't said a word about that."

"It wouldn't interest you."

"It might."

"Well, let's say that the war came a little closer, that's all."

"What does that mean?"

"It means that ever since we arrived in Africa, everything about this war has been happening a million miles away. We read it in the newspapers, we listen to it on the radio, we watch it on the movies – but we're not involved. Do we know anyone who has suffered in this war? No. Do we know anyone who has fought in North Africa, or Burma or the Pacific? No. We don't know anything about this war. We don't know what's happening in Europe. We don't know what's happening in Russia. We don't know about the Jews, or the concentration camps, or the millions of people being tortured, imprisoned and bombed every day. It's another man's war, a report in a newspaper, a Hollywood movie or a voice on the radio. It is not us."

"Thank Christ for that!"

"Maybe. And maybe we are lucky, as Corporal Whyles said. But I'm not so sure anymore."

"What are you – a martyr? You want to die on the beaches? Sacrifice yourself in a concentration camp? She must have been some woman you met in Dakar! It was a woman, I take it?"

"Go to hell!"

Windmill looked at me for a moment, then shook his head. "I'm sorry," he said. "That was a stupid remark. I'm sorry."

He turned away and spent the remainder of the morning making noises around the armoury, while I listened to the radio and fought a second-hand war.

The Battle of Normandy was going well, the announcer said. It was going exactly according to plan. For months now, the Allied Air Forces had been bombing bridges and railways in Northern France in a massive effort to sever all German transportation links to Normandy. The area was now "a railway desert" and that was only the beginning.

Two hours before the invasion, units of the British 6th Airborne were dropped on the Orne bridgehead north and east of Caen; the 82nd and 101st Airborne divisions had landed in the marshy areas of the Carentan estuary, and the RAF had dropped another 5,000 tons of bombs on German coastal defences. Meanwhile the British fleet had opened fire along a fifty-mile front, blasting everything in sight, including the people of Normandy who were peacefully asleep in their beds.

By now the Second British Army had landed 30,000 men, 300 guns and 700 armoured vehicles on Gold and Sword beaches, the 3rd Canadian Division were storming Juno beach and the Americans had landed on Utah and Omaha – without waking Adolf Hitler, who was also asleep and daring anyone to disturb him, except Eva Braun – but only if she was wearing his favourite see-through nightdress. Unfortunately, Eva was lying out to the world in another room and no one dared to disturb her either without prior permission from Adolf. It was going to be a cold day for everybody.

In Port Etienne, it blew hot and cold. Captain Monet had begun the morning in a state of ecstasy, but by noon was screaming abuse at the radio, banging his head against the wall of the fort because the BBC had failed to mention General de Gaulle or the Free French Forces, who were also part of the invasion.

"Assassins!" he screamed. "BBC assassins!" He then went into a paroxysm of incomprehensible French before falling on the ground in a dead faint.

"I think he's upset," Windmill said. "Should we send for a priest, or something?"

But the only one who looked anything like a priest in Port Etienne was Legionnaire Jesus, and he was more interested in the extermination of lice than anything to do with Captain Monet.

"God reigns," he intoned, as he raised Captain Monet to his feet and carried him to his bed.

"God reigns. Burn the lice!"

In the Gorilla's office, J Carrol Naish sat on the edge of the desk, shouting something about insane asylums, while the Gorilla tried to paint the Cross of Lorraine on the ceiling with a sweeping brush, only he was so drunk he could barely see the open tins of blue and white paint on the floor.

"Have you considered writing a book?" Windmill asked him when we entered the room. "You'd find it much easier."

But the Gorilla had no intention of writing a book. He had invited us into his office to celebrate the invasion. Captain Monet had condescended to join us, but was now lying in his bed. Jesus meantime had planted himself in a corner and was busy burning lice, while J Carrol Naish, having fallen off the desk, now sat on the floor, pouring brandy into himself as if he'd been lost in the desert for a month and had suddenly discovered a water hole.

"I think I believe in God!" he cried, between gulps. "I think I believe in God."

"In the desert?" Jesus asked, hopefully.

"In Paris, you fool! Montmartre! The Champs-Elysés!" he shook his head. "*Les gens sont des cons*," he muttered. "*Les gens sont des cons.*"

I turned to Windmill. "What did he say?"

"Something about people being bloody apes," he said and poured himself a drink.

I looked at Jesus. He seemed saddened and hurt, but said nothing, only continued picking lice from the seams of his shirt.

"I drink to Paris," Naish said.

"Drink?" echoed the Gorilla. "Drink!"

Naish grinned. "Look at him," he said with disdain, "A Boche with a brush in his hand and he drinks to Paris!"

"He's not doing too bad with the Cross of Lorraine either," I said.

"Drink to liberation, you ape! Drink to the hanging of all Boche apes – their balls swinging from street lamps!"

"You're an obnoxious bastard," Windmill said. "Leave the man alone."

Naish looked at him. "The sensitive English!" he sneered. "Not so sensitive when you abandoned us at Dunkirk. Not so sensitive when you bomb the French fleet in Mers-el-Kebir. Pigs! The English look after themselves. They fight for themselves."

"In Normandy," Jesus said, "the English fight for everybody."

"Everybody?" roared the Gorilla. "We drink to everybody!"

"I should put the brush down first," Windmill said. "Paint doesn't really mix with brandy."

"I paint the Cross of Lorraine!" the Gorilla yelled. "The Cross of Lorraine!"

"I can see that. It's very artistic."

"Good?"

"Stinks!" muttered Naish.

"It is very good," Windmill replied. "Now, put the brush away, like a good man, and we'll drink to everybody."

"Jesus too?"

"Yes, Jesus too."

The Gorilla threw the sweeping brush in a corner and staggered towards the desk. He was covered in blue and white paint, and as he sat down and placed his arms on the desk, the scattered papers and daily reports stuck to him.

Brushing them aside, he poured himself a drink.

"Today," he mumbled, and paused. "Today, I know I will not die in the desert. I die in Paris."

Jesus looked at him. "The road to Paris is very long, my friend. It will cost many lives."

"You drink!"

"Water," Jesus said. "I will drink water."

"There is no water," Naish jeered. "You changed it into wine, remember?"

"Then I will drink wine – and I drink to you, Maroc. May you live in Paris."

"He will not live in Paris," Naish grinned. "They will cut his throat."

We drank to the Gorilla. But Naish, struggling to his feet, declared: "I will not drink to apes! I will drink to the liberation of Paris – free of all apes!"

Leaning against the desk, Naish was about to swallow his drink, when the Gorilla, who had appeared to be glued to his seat, incapable of movement, suddenly reached forward and grabbed him by the throat.

"Maroc!" he bellowed. "No ape! Maroc!"

"I think you had better apologise," Windmill said. "He's about to tear your head off and throw it in the dustbin."

Naish, whose face was turning blue, struggled to apologise. The Gorilla paused for a moment, before spitting in his face and pushing him aside.

"Maroc," he whispered. "Maroc. And I die in Paris."

Naish glared at him, but made no move to retaliate.

"Shall we sing '*La Marseillaise*' now?" Windmill asked. "Or should we wait till later?"

There was no reply. As we nursed our drinks, the only sound in the room was the sizzling of lice, over a lighted candle.

Later in the day, when Windmill and I went to visit

Corporal Whyles in his tent, we found him sitting on the ground, listening to the radio. Reports were coming in from the beaches of Normandy and you could hear the guns and the grinding roar of tanks and lorries moving across the strand. Corporal Whyles looked depressed.

"You two been to the fort?" he asked. "I suppose they're all pissed over there?"

"I'm afraid so," Windmill said.

"Drunken bastards. I'm surprised you're not pissed?"

"It doesn't seem to be the day for it," Windmill replied.

"No. You can sit, if you like."

We sat beside him on the ground and listened to the radio and, presently, he said: "I'm sorry about this morning. I'm not feeling too well today."

"Anything we can do?"

"I've been in the RAF a long time," he confided. "Failed air crew, failed Sparks, failed every damn thing I've ever put my hand to. I'm a professional failure."

"They still made you a Corporal."

"For long service, mate. Nothing more. Do you know how many stations I've been posted to over the years? The number of times I've volunteered for Special Service, Malta, Burma, North Africa? It would take a year to count them and not once was I accepted. Failed the interview, failed the aptitude test and, usually, ended up in some pest-ridden hole in the backyard of nowhere."

"Port Etienne?"

"This is the pinnacle of my success! When this war is over, I'll probably still be here – armed to the teeth and shooting at nothing more lethal than a moth-eaten hyena."

He stared at the radio and we listened, for a moment, to the scream of aircraft strafing the beaches, and the excited voice of the war correspondent, describing the scene.

"Maybe I should be grateful. I keep telling people that

375

when they come here. I tell myself the same thing over and over again: 'You're lucky, mate. Dead lucky.' Am I not? Aren't you? Who the fuck would want to be in Normandy today? And how many of those lads are going to leave those beaches in one piece? Not many – I can tell you that!"

He switched off the radio. "Fuck it," he said. "Fuck it!"

"Take it easy, Corp. It's not your fault," Windmill said.

Corporal Whyles looked at him. "Fault, Harrison? Don't patronise me, you twit! Who the fuck do you think you are?"

"Sorry. It was not meant to be patronising."

"I should hope not! Christ Almighty, that's all I need. I've got years behind me in this mob and you haven't got your knees brown yet!"

"I don't intend to get them brown," Windmill said. "The sooner I'm back in civvy street, the better."

"Sure! The Civvy Street Conscript. No time for the Regulars. But who the hell kept you safe at home, if it wasn't the Regulars? It's easy for you. Cushy jobs, nice families, living in nice cushy little detached houses – while the Regulars are out there fighting to keep the wolves from your door. Maybe I failed to do something of value in this war, mate – but, at least, it wasn't for want of trying."

"Good for you, Corporal. May we go now?"

"You can fuck off – the both of you! I don't need you. Get out of here!"

He turned away and, as we left the tent, he switched on the radio again and the sound of war followed us across the desert, to the armoury and beyond.

Windmill said nothing and, when we reached the armoury, he retired to his tent, closed the flap and lay on his bed. He had nothing to say and neither had I. The war would go on, Corporal Whyles would think himself a failure – and bleed for the dying and the dead on the

376

beaches of Normandy. He would not get drunk, like the men at the fort. He would listen to the radio and bleed some more.

At the end of the day, Corporal Whyles switched off the radio and the camp was silent. I thought Windmill might have joined me then, as he often did, for a drink or a chat before settling down for the night, but he remained in his tent and made no answer when I called to him.

Silence, I thought, and the pity of war. It was cold in Port Etienne and as I sat in my tent, drinking brandy that tasted of oil, I wondered how far the Allied Armies had advanced since dawn, when they had first landed on the beaches of Normandy. I did not know then that the Battle of Normandy would last three months and the casualty list would read:

British/Canadian/Polish: 5,995 killed. 57,996 wounded. 9,054 missing. Total: 83,045. United States: 20,838 killed. 94,881 wounded. 10,128 missing. Total: 25,847. Allied Air Forces/Royal Air Force: 8,178 killed and missing. Total 8,178. US Army Air Force: 8,536 killed and missing. Total 8,536. Germans killed and wounded: 200,000. Prisoners of War: 200,000.

Eisenhower was pleased. Montgomery was pleased and Hitler was depressed. It was a good war and everything was going according to plan.

Seventeen

It was not exactly like *Random Harvest*, but Windmill said he felt he'd been released from a mental home, as the Sunderland that was taking us from Port Etienne to Freetown rose from the water and somehow managed to fly. It was the same Marcella that had brought us to Bathurst and, later, to Port Etienne and her engines now sounded to be on their last scatter of coughs, shudders and groans.

"Keep going, Baby. You can do it," the pilot cooed – and I waited for the crash. But the fuselage rattled, the engines spluttered and the pilot held to the joystick and refused to let her die.

"You can't leave me now, Baby," he implored. "I love you. What will people say? That I let you drop down in the drink like some bint with the pox? No, Baby. Not after all we've been through together. Raise your head. Come on, Baby. That's it. Fly, Baby – fly!"

And the Sunderland responded. She raised her head, dragged herself up, rattled and groaned and aimed for the sky.

"You beauty!" cried the pilot. "You loving beauty! She's made it!"

"Thank Christ for that!" Windmill muttered. "I don't think my nerves could have stood much longer."

"Marcella is fine," the pilot said with pride. "She's my girl, a real lady, and I'm the only one she'll respond to. People don't understand that. They think she's for the boneyard – but look at her!"

"I'm trying not to," Windmill said.

The pilot shook his head. "You don't appreciate, mate. You just don't appreciate. I remember you two guys when she first carried you to Bathurst. You didn't appreciate her then – and you don't appreciate her now. I thought the desert might have done you some good – but some guys never learn. Take no notice of them, Baby. Take no notice."

"My name is Ronald Colman," Windmill intoned to the roof of the Sunderland. "I have never heard of the desert. I know nothing about the RAF. I know nothing about the war. I am suffering from amnesia and the last thing I remember is waking up in a chemist shop in Liverpool. Help me … "

The pilot stared at him. "Desert fever," he said. "I thought as much when he boarded at Port Etienne. The last two guys I picked up from there are still in the nuthouse."

"You hear that, Jesus!" Windmill exclaimed. "You know where I live. Take me there. I want to claim my inheritance."

"Are you nuts, too?" the pilot asked me. "Or have you just been struck dumb?"

"I haven't caught my breath yet," I replied. "I'm still trying to remember what Greer Garson looked like."

"Who?"

"Forget it. Will this kite really make it to Freetown?"

The pilot paused, touched the instrument panel with his hand and said – "If winning this war depended on guys like Ronald Colman here, I should hope not. But Marcella is kind. She pities the fool. She'll make it. 'How do I love thee? Let me count the ways' – can't remember the rest of it, but there was a guy in our squadron one time who used to recite that to his baby every time she took to the air. Marcella deserves a poem like that."

"Why don't you write one?"

"Haven't the gift, Old Boy. Haven't the gift."

Neither had Fredric March when he recited it to Norma Shearer in *The Barretts of Wimpole Street*, I thought – but that's Hollywood.

"Some people have it," he sighed. "And some people don't. My gift is loving Marcella. Nursing her, telling her how beautiful she is. She likes that. I can hear her heart tremble and I can feel her pulse. Crazy? I don't think so. An aircraft is like a bird. Handle her gently and she'll feed from your hand. Fly, baby. Fly."

And Marcella flew. Her broad, ungainly bulk hugging the coastline and shadowing the water, she struggled and grumped her way towards Freetown. Marcella was no beauty, but the pilot truly loved her. He stroked the joystick, beamed at the instrument panel, nursed the controls and spoke to her lovingly before take-off and landing. If he could have slept beside her, he would have done so with pleasure. Kissing her fuselage, cuddling her engines and playing with her props.

"How do I love thee? Let me count the ways."

Had the pilot been an artist, he might have painted her in oils and sprinkled her with jasmine. And had he been a poet of stature, he might have devoted his life to writing poems to her beauty, her courage and endurance. She had braved the skies, battled against the enemy, and survived with honour. She deserved respect, she deserved a painting and she deserved a poem.

"How do I love thee? Let me count the ways."

The pilot couldn't remember the rest of it. Neither could I – and Windmill said he was sick at the thought of it.

There were times when I believed that Windmill was dead, and there were no more stars brightening the Universe. Come back, Norma Shearer and bring Garbo with you. Come lie on my bed.

When the Sunderland landed in the harbour at

Freetown, she looked as if she would never rise from the water again. Her nose dipped, her tail rose awkwardly in the air and the fuselage sank deeper into the water.

"She's had it," Windmill said. "Definitely had it."

"Don't you believe it, mate. Class endures – and Marcella will be flying this coast when you two are dead and buried."

He sat in the cockpit and stroked the instrument panel, then kissed the fuselage as we climbed into the waiting bumboat.

"See you later, Baby," he smiled. "Sleep well."

When we reached the slipway, he stood there for a moment, looking back at the lady of his life.

"Sure – she looks a bit battered now. Who wouldn't, after all she's been through? She's the last of her line. The best there is – and when she goes, I'll be right there with her. Drink to her when you get a chance. Champagne, if you can afford it."

Astonished, Windmill, for once, kept his mouth shut.

"He's a nutter," he said later. "An absolute bloody nutter! We could have been killed in that contraption."

He was undoubtedly right – but the face of that pilot as he guided the Sunderland safely through the turbulent air haunted me. He was deeply in love with a flying boat called Marcella and he would remain so until they both sank, or were shot down off the African coast. I promised champagne and Windmill promised a bomb in the post.

Killing is too good for some people, I thought – but said nothing.

We spent two weeks in the transit camp in Freetown. As usual, we had no idea why we had been posted from Port Etienne, and no idea where we were destined to go in the future. The Sergeant in charge greeted us with suspicion, then asked us if we were sane.

"I beg your pardon?"

"You heard. Nobody comes back from Port Etienne sane. They see things."

"Well, the only thing I saw there was sand," I said. "There's nothing else in Port Etienne."

"That's it. So they invent things. The last two guys invented an elephant. It followed them everywhere. They even tied it to a tree before going to bed. You haven't got an elephant, have you?"

"I don't think so," Windmill said, "but you can look behind me, if you like."

"I don't trust people who come from Port Etienne. I don't trust them one inch. How was your trip?"

"On the Sunderland? Pleasant enough," I said – before Windmill could open his mouth – and the Sergeant looked even more suspicious.

"With Sparky Dankworth?" he asked in amazement.

"Well, we didn't get his name," I replied. "But he can certainly pilot an aircraft."

"Can he? So why hasn't he got a crew then? He was in Port Etienne once. Spent three months hiding in the sand, trying to make paper aircraft without paper."

"Did they fly?" Windmill asked.

"Don't be funny," the Sergeant replied. "He's a basket case. Always was – and that's why he hasn't got a crew. Nobody flies with Dankworth. Nobody! And that pile of crap he calls Marcella is ready to blow up. They won't let him fly anything else."

"He's very fond of that aircraft," I said. "He talks to it."

"There you are! Talks to it. Talks to a heap of scrap. Can you imagine any sane person talking to a heap of scrap?"

"Well, I suppose it is better than an elephant," I said. "At least it stays in one place when you land and won't follow you to the lavatory."

"Another comedian. I'm going to keep a sharp eye on you both. Any deviation from the norm – and you're out!"

"I was going to ask you about that," I said. "Any idea where we're going? Even a hint would be useful."

"None. And I couldn't care less. Some go to Malta, some go to Palestine and some go to the nuthouse. If my guess is right, you two are destined for the nuthouse. That's where the last guys from Port Etienne went."

"With the elephant, I presume?"

The Sergeant looked at us for a moment, then said – "Just remember what I told you. Any deviation from the norm…"

"Thank you, Sergeant. You've been very kind," Windmill said – "And most welcoming. Have you got a name?"

"Garvin!" the Sergeant shouted and turned his back. "And you can shove the sarcasm. I'll have none of it!" He had a very broad back, and the sweat oozed through his bush-jacket and glistened in the sunlight.

"Did you ever feel," Windmill asked after the Sergeant moved off – "that you'd managed to escape from one mental institution only to end up in another?"

I refused to answer that question. My nerves were tormenting me.

During the following days, Windmill toured the back streets of Freetown in search of literary masterpieces, while I lay in the sun in an effort to get my knees brown. He was successful and I failed. One night he returned to camp with something called *The Pleasures of Bestiality*, and a few nights later, with a collection of postcards guaranteed to cause heart failure in anyone with even a tither of imagination.

"You seem to have given up the idea of a plantation," I said. "Or is this part of the process?"

"Not at all," he replied. "But I have always been

383

interested in the darker side of literature. I had a friend once. He owned a plantation in Java – and had the finest collection of exotic literature in the world. The Japs have got it now, I suspect – but they wouldn't appreciate it."

"So what are you trying to do – replace it?"

"I don't know. In any case, I haven't seen anything like a suitable plantation site in Freetown. Bathurst, maybe – if we ever get back to it."

"You never told me about your friend in Java."

"He was my mother's friend, really – but he came to visit us quite often and we talked a lot."

"I see."

"You don't – but it makes no matter. We'll talk about it sometime."

He lay back in the bed and stared at the postcards, while I went to visit the open air cinema and saw John Garfield in *Between Two Worlds*. It was not a pleasant experience, in spite of the cast, and as I made my way back to camp I thought of Windmill and his friend in Java. He had never mentioned him before, and I wondered what the story was. Windmill sometimes mentioned his past, then left it hanging there as if to say – "I could and if I would …. " But maybe that's all there was, an unfinished story without meaning or purpose.

He had looked sad when I left him, lying on the bed and staring at his collection of postcards. It was the first time I had seen him so sad. And he was still staring at the postcards when I returned from the cinema.

"Are you OK?" I asked.

"Why do you ask?"

"I'm concerned, that's all. You don't look well."

"I'm perfectly all right. But thank you for your concern. Was the film any good?"

"Not bad."

"Good night," he said – and turned out the light.

He slept without moving and the only sound was the buzzing of insects outside the lattice-screened door.

A few days later, as I was still struggling to obtain a suntan on my knees, Sergeant Garvin appeared on the beach and shouted – "Time to move out!"

"You mean now?"

"Tomorrow morning. Pack your gear. Give the info to your mate. Be at the slipway by eleven."

"I suppose it's foolish of me to ask, but–"

"Shove it! You'll know when you get there."

"You know, Sergeant – all this mystery about where we're going and what we'll do when we get there doesn't exactly fill me with confidence. What do they think we're going to do – ring up Adolf Hitler and give him the news?"

"You get drunk, don't you?"

"Sometimes."

"You talk to people, don't you?"

"Occasionally."

"You write letters home, don't you?"

"Not very often."

"And you go to brothels?"

"Strictly for the view, Sergeant."

"Shove it! People talk, they blabber, and the more intelligent they are, the worse they are. They think they're clever. They think they can drink and fuck and talk without saying anything. There's only one way you can do that – and that's when you've got nothing to say in the first place. When you don't know, you can't say. What you don't see, you can't reveal. Do I make myself clear?"

"As mud, Sergeant."

"That's enough! Gerry isn't licked yet, you know. And those fucking Japs have a long way to go yet. People forget that side of the war. Just because we've managed to invade

Europe, they think it's all over, bar the shouting. But there'll be a lot more dead bodies on the road before this lot is finished, I can tell you that!"

"OK, Sergeant. You've made your point."

"Then, get on with it – and don't ask more stupid questions."

He turned his back. It was still broad and the sweat still oozed, slowly, though his bush jacket.

When I told Windmill, who was engrossed in *The Pleasures of Bestiality* back at the camp, about our impending departure for pastures new, he shrugged and said he didn't care where we were going.

"We could be going back to England," I said.

"I doubt that. It'll probably be some other Godforsaken hole in the back end of beyond. This war is supposed to be about Freedom and Democracy. All I've seen so far is a bunch of lunatics pretending to be Freedom Fighters. The real Freedom Fighters are out there on the ground, being moved down by machine-guns."

"You're depressing me, Windmill. I was hoping that this war would prove something."

"It will. It will prove that those at the top will remain at the top – and those at the bottom will be pushed deeper into the ground."

I tried to remember the good things about Windmill. I tried to remember Betty Grable and how she had inspired me to fly for Democracy and the Freedom of Small Nations. She had million dollar legs. That was good. Ann Sheridan was beautiful and so was Rita Hayworth. And what happened to Carole Lombard? She died. Oh, Christ! And in an air crash, yet!

One day we'll meet once again
Tell me where, Tell me when

One day we'll meet once again
And I'm yours until then.
Each night I wish on a star
That you'll stay as you are ...

I washed my face, packed my kit and sat all night, on the edge of my bed, waiting for the dawn.

Eighteen

From Freetown to Cape Town, from Cape Town around the Horn of Africa and up through the Suez Canal to Alexandria –I felt like Bob Hope on *The Road to Nowhere*. The troopship taking us to Alexandria was obviously the inspiration for B Traven's *The Death Ship*, while the train taking us from Alexandria to Cairo had been designed by Muhammad Ahmad as a torture for Christians.

When we arrived at the station, we were unable to locate the lorry organised to meet us. As everything I knew about Cairo could be written on Boris Karloff's fingernails in *The Mummy*, I thought the only thing to do was to surrender to someone who looked like The Sheikh, then lie back and enjoy it.

Windmill however had been reading something called *The Cairo Poets*, and suggested that if we turned up at the Continental Hotel or the Shepherd's Bar, we were bound to meet at least one passable English poet who might direct us to the nearest RAF camp. But at the Continental, an apparition, wearing a fez, ordered us out because we were improperly dressed, while at the Shepherd's Bar we were commanded to wait in the street because it was "Officers Only and No Bloody Wogs".

The heat was killing us, we were beginning to suffer from dehydration, and democracy was having its worst day since Hitler was elected Chancellor of Germany.

"I suppose we could always sleep in a pyramid," I said. "We'd be kipping with royalty there."

"I don't think so," Windmill replied and kicked his kitbag. "We'd need to be properly dressed for that, too!"

"No point blaming the kitbag, Matey. We'll just have to sit and wait."

"In this heat?"

"Think of the pyramids," I said. "Did you ever imagine you'd be this close to a pyramid? Some people would pay a fortune to be sitting here."

"There're welcome to it. The only thing I want to do is to get this stinking uniform off and wash myself."

We sat on our kitbags on the pavement outside the bar where, within minutes, we were surrounded by legions of clamouring young boys, selling bananas, oranges, melting chocolate and postcards designed to give mothers at home instant heart failure.

"Soldier like chocolate?"

"No!"

"Soldiers like sister?"

"Soldier not like sister. Piss off!"

"Brother?"

"Piss off!"

"Officers not say piss off. Officers like brother. Officers pay plenty piastres for brother."

"Clear off, you little werp! Go home to your mother."

The young boy stared at Windmill, then spat directly into his face.

"English pig!" he jeered before he ran away laughing. The others followed, laughing and screaming "English pig! English pig!" all the way down the street.

Windmill watched them for a moment, then wiped the spittle from his face. "Egypt," he said. "The glories of Empire. What a legacy!"

"There was nothing like that in *The Mummy*, I said – but Windmill didn't answer. He just sat there, looking at the spittle staining his handkerchief, and shook his head.

"Fuck it!" he said. "Fuck everything."

He lapsed into silence and we sat there, waiting for someone to come to collect us.

"Are you two shagging do-lally?" Sergeant Wilson yelled when an hour later he finally arrived in what he described as his piss-shagging-bus – in fact a falling-to-bits lorry. "I've been looking all over shagging Cairo for you!"

"You weren't at the station," I said.

"I was at the shagging station in this piss-flaming-bus surrounded by shagging wogs!"

"Well, we couldn't find you," Windmill said. "So we came here."

"For shagging cocktails, I presume?"

"I'm afraid not. They wouldn't let us in."

"I'm not shagging surprised! You look like two shagged-out flipping wogs. Get into the shagging bus, for Christ sakes."

"It'll be a pleasure, Sergeant. Thank you very much."

"Don't give me that! I've been up to my shagging eyeballs all day picking up shag-artists like you. You shouldn't be let loose – you know that? Shouldn't be let loose!"

Piling our kitbags into the back of the lorry, we sat in the front with Sergeant Wilson as he drove through Cairo, cursing shagging wog drivers who couldn't drive a shagging pram, let alone a shagging bus.

"Get out of the shagging way, you stupid git!" he yelled. "Move, for Christ's sake!"

"I don't think that's very polite, Sergeant," Windmill said. "It is, after all, their country."

Sergeant Wilson almost drove straight into a pyramid. "Jesus Christ! Don't tell me they've saddled me with another one of the 'Free the Wogs Brigade'! My nerves couldn't stand it, mate."

"Well. I was under the impression that's what this war was all about."

"You've been reading too many shagging books! I had a guy here last month dressed as a Muslim who went around giving away free copies of that Left Book Club crap to the shagging wogs. They got rid of him quick. Shipped him off to bleeding Burma."

"You're a true son of the Empire," Windmill said.

"And glad to be so, mate. Shagging wogs!"

He drove through the shagging wogs until presently we arrived at a sprawling collection of tents and Nissen huts on the outskirts of Cairo. Sergeant Wilson pulled up outside one of the Nissen huts and cried – "Out! This is it!"

And it was. A large Nissen hut, containing thirty-two empty beds, all made up and ready for occupation. The beds were comfortable, the floor swept, the windows open and at the foot of each bed there was a small wooden cupboard, polished and glistening in the afternoon sun.

"You'll find a shower at the far end, clean towels and anything else you need. Grab yourself a shower, brush up and make your way to the cookhouse. Any dirty clothes – leave them in the shagging basket outside the back door. The wogs will take care of it. They'll wash them and press them and they'll be ready for you to wear first thing tomorrow morning."

"You wouldn't think they'd be capable of anything like that," Windmill quipped.

"Don't try to be funny with me, mate! They're wogs. It's the only thing they're good at – cleaning and polishing and fucking their sisters. Just keep an eye on them, that's all."

"Yes, Sergeant."

"One more thing – you've got the evening free. You'll find booze in the NAFFI, there's a cinema around the corner, and if you need crumpet there's a couple of brothels in Cairo. One for officers and one for kerb-crawlers. Just follow the stink – and be back here at 11:59 – otherwise you're on a fizzer. OK?"

"I think we'll forgo the pleasures of the brothels, Sarge."

"You can do what the fuck you like. But you'll be leaving here tomorrow at noon and Christ knows when you'll get another chance for crumpet."

"Don't tell me we've got to move again!" I said. "I thought we were staying here?"

"Who the fuck told you that? This is a shagging transit-camp."

Windmill blanched. "I hesitate to ask," he pleaded – "but could you please tell us where we're going?"

"You mean you don't know?"

"Sergeant – we haven't known where we were going since the first day we joined this band of fly boys."

"Palestine, mate. Shagging Palestine. Full of shagging Yids and bleeding Ay-rabs. All over the shagging place!"

"Well, I suppose it is better than Burma," I said.

"Bollox! I wouldn't trust those shagging Yids as far as I could throw them – or the bleeding Ay-rabs. They stink."

"Yes, Sergeant. I think we've got the message."

The Sergeant looked at us, shook his head as if he couldn't believe what he was seeing, and made his way towards the door.

"Shouldn't be let loose," he muttered as he left the room. "Shouldn't be shagging let loose!"

"That," said Windmill, after the door closed behind him, "is the most obnoxious bastard I have ever met – don't you agree?"

I agreed, after which we both stripped to the skin and washed the grime and the dirt from our bodies and our minds.

"I don't think I'll go to the movies tonight," Windmill

said, as we sat in the cookhouse, eating the first decent meal we'd had for weeks. "I'm not in the humour."

"Me neither."

"You want to wander into Cairo?"

"No, thanks."

"Let's get pissed."

We drank ourselves sober in the NAFFI canteen and ended up at the camp cinema where they were showing *Alexander's Ragtime Band*. I never liked Tyrone Power.

The following morning, at eleven-thirty sharp, we paraded before Pilot Officer Swaine, a rake of a man who had never seen action, never piloted an aircraft, and who was perfectly happy to sit behind a desk and paint nude pictures of the Queen Mother and Winston Churchill.

"When this war is over," he exclaimed, "these paintings will be worth a fortune."

Windmill said he was probably right – then asked if he'd ever been to art college.

"No, dear boy – I have not. I did try once, but they said that my imagination was limited – to say nothing of my subject matter – and they were probably right. I have but two subjects – the Queen Mother and Winston Churchill. It is limited, of course, but I firmly believe that an artist should stick to what he does best and forget all this experimental nonsense."

"Oh, I agree, Sir – but why paint them in the nude?"

"I should have thought that was obvious. Because it shows them to be perfectly normal human beings – and not like us. I will admit that it's stretching it a point to describe Mr Churchill as normal in any circumstances – but one does one's best. Do you paint yourself, Harrison?"

"I'm afraid not."

"A pity. I thought we might have had some interesting conversations together on the art of nudity and bodily functions. You are going to Palestine?"

"I believe so."

"A place of infinite contrasts. I will be coming with you and you will be working with me in the armoury near Jerusalem. Has Sergeant Wilson informed you about the situation in Palestine?"

"No."

"I'm sure he has. A regrettable element, not to be tolerated. You'll be relieved to know that he is not coming with us. We shall be accompanied instead by LAC Thomas – a charming young man and mechanical genius, but with no interest whatever in Art. But then, of course, he doesn't have to show an interest, he's a work of Art in himself. Astonishing blue eyes, the most delicate skin and the body of an Adonis. Quite remarkable."

Pausing for a moment, he coughed twice, his whole body trembling at the thought.

"Yes," he sighed. "Yes, indeed. You have your kit packed?"

"Yes, Sir."

"Then meet me in fifteen minutes outside the main gate. We'll leave at noon. Dismiss."

We returned to the Nissen hut, collected our kitbags and were standing at the main gate precisely at noon.

"This could be an interesting trip," Windmill said. "Don't you think?"

"I prefer not to."

When the Adonis arrived in his beautifully waxed and highly polished lorry, his brilliant looks almost gave me a complex.

"Good morning, gentlemen," he said – through a set of dazzling white teeth – "I believe you are to accompany us back to Palestine?"

"If you don't mind," I replied.

394

"A pleasure," he smiled. "Pop your kitbags in the rear and make yourselves comfortable. One of you may sit in the front with me, if you wish? There's plenty of room."

"No, thanks. How long is this trip going to take?"

"A couple of days."

"We're *driving* to Palestine?"

"Of course. We'll be crossing the Sinai Desert late this afternoon and should reach Jerusalem sometime on Friday. We make the trip once a month, you know. Usually to deliver ammo and explosives to Cairo and Alexandria."

"That's comforting."

"Oh, it's quite safe, I assure you – unless, of course, the Arabs are feeling a little restless – but there's no sign of that at the moment."

I looked at Windmill, who was fading rapidly. And by the time Pilot Officer Swaine arrived, carrying his portfolio of nude paintings under his arm, I was wondering why I hadn't joined the Franciscans.

"Good afternoon, Jonathan," he beamed. "And how are we today?"

"Jolly good, Sir. And you?"

"Excellent, Jonathan. Excellent."

"Let me take those paintings from you, Sir."

"Thank you, Jonathan. Are you gentlemen happy in the rear?"

"Delirious!"

"Then off we go, Jonathan. Push-push!"

He climbed into the front seat beside Adonis and we moved off through Cairo on to Ismailia, where we would cross the Suez Canal and enter the Sinai Peninsula.

Nineteen

"There is an old Bedouin proverb," Pilot Officer Swaine declared – as we drove across the most desolate wasteland of sand and rock imaginable – "for when the shooting starts. Climb on your camel and head for the mountaintops."

"There is a similar Irish proverb," I said. "When the rain falls, grab your bike and head for the nearest pub."

The Bedouins obviously had much in common with the Irish and I was looking forward to meeting them. But though we travelled for hours along a bumpy road, covered with drifting sand and scattered rocks, the only Bedouin we saw was a middle-aged man seated beside the road, staring at nothing, while behind him a veiled woman, wearing a black gown, wandered aimlessly across the desert, nodding her head whenever she passed a sand dune.

Jonathan pulled up beside the man and crooned – "Salamat! Salamat!", as Pilot Officer Swaine alighted from the cab and began an elaborate ritual of greetings and blessings – a ritual that seemed to last for hours, as everything had to be said twice regarding the day's news, the size of the man's tent, the health of his family, the ages of his children, the number of his goats, the quality of the cheese, the philosophy of the Bedouin – 'No Government /No Fences' – and finally the uses and abuses of elephant grass and camel dung.

When Pilot Officer Swaine asked what he was doing on the side of the road in this isolated spot, the Bedouin said he was waiting for his wife who had disappeared behind his back while he was kneeling on the ground praying to Allah.

"Allah is great – and there is no God but Allah, you understand – but He did not endow women with the gift of wisdom. Nara is my second wife and, as you can see, she wanders."

"And your first wife?"

"She wanders also, but not so much because she is old."

"And your children?"

"Only the girls wander. The boys do not. Allah is merciful in that respect."

He lowered his head and was grateful to Allah – even for the least of his mercies.

Pilot Officer Swaine also expressed his gratitude to Allah and, after a few more handshakes and promises to visit his tent next time we were in the vicinity, Jonathan started the engine again and we moved on towards Aweigilla, where I hoped to spend my first night in the Sinai, sleeping in a comfortable bed.

"I'm sorry that it took so long to get away from our Bedouin friend," Pilot Officer Swaine said as we drove, "but it is very important that we observe the rules of desert politeness and show peaceful intent. The Bedouins are a proud people, extremely polite, hospitable and, on no account, to be patronised. The Eighth Army refers to them as 'ten minute combat merchants' – but they miss the point. The Bedouin fights only when he has to and sees no sense in taking sides between two opposing invaders. Why should he? The Sinai has been invaded before. Wounds bleed, men die, the sun burns, yet the desert remains the same, and it's a foolish man who pitches his tent near a wadi during the rainy season.

"Sometimes," he continued, "I feel that the Bedouins are the only intelligent people I've ever met. They live their own lives, have few illusions, and can recognise a mirage. And if opposing armies want to commit collective suicide over a few grains of sand, then the wise thing to do is to move to higher ground and let them get on with it. One can always come back later and round up the goats."

I was beginning to like Pilot Officer Swaine, and my admiration for the Bedouins had also moved up a notch. Windmill, however, was suffering from diarrhoea and in no humour to appreciate anyone. We stopped several times to allow him to evacuate his bowels, as he cursed the heat, the desert, the war and the Bedouins and anyone who came near him. He was getting on my nerves, but Swaine was more than sympathetic and Jonathan a model of solicitude, attending to his every whim, washing his hands and his face and tucking him up nicely in the rear of the lorry.

"You'll be all right, Sweetie," he crooned. "Just check your urine and tell me if it turns yellow or dark brown. That's dehydration, you know, and you'll have to drink plenty of water – but only in tiny sips."

"You're very kind," Windmill managed to croak.

"Not at all. I've had lots of tummy trouble myself and I know what it's like. Just relax and I'll drive slowly and try to avoid the potholes. But cry out if you need me, won't you now?"

"Thank you, Jonathan."

I was beginning to feel sick myself, but the thought of Jonathan hovering over me like an Angel of Mercy was enough to effect an instant cure.

"I'll bet Lawrence of Arabia never suffered from diarrhoea," I said.

"I doubt if Mr Lawrence ever suffered from anything," Pilot Officer Swaine smiled, "apart from an inflated ego."

"Now, now, Sir!" Jonathan chided. "The gentleman did do his bit for the Empire."

"So he did. And he also claimed to have walked from

here to Akaba and then floated on a raft of ten-gallon petrol drums, all the way to Gezirat Fara'un though shark-infested waters. It's a good trick, if you can do it."

"You don't believe him?"

"Well, one could hardly accuse Mr Lawrence of telling an untruth – but as Mr Churchill once said, when accused of lying through his teeth in the House of Commons, 'It was not a lie! It was a terminological inexactitude.' I suspect that Mr Lawrence was guilty of many a terminological inexactitude."

"I'm afraid Sir doesn't approve of Mr Lawrence," said Jonathan.

"Shall we move on?"

"Of course, Sir."

We moved on. Jonathan drove carefully, avoiding potholes, manoeuvring through drifting sand and rocks, and occasionally calling out to Windmill – "How are we feeling now, Sweetie? We can stop whenever you want to."

But there was no need to stop. Windmill had fallen asleep and slept soundly, until we reached a dilapidated-looking Army barracks on the outskirts of Aweigilla.

The barracks, which was in darkness, looked as if it had been abandoned by Moses and unoccupied since the Crucifixion. Jonathan pulled up a few yards from the front gates as Pilot Officer Swaine jumped from the cab, firing two shots in the air from a .45 revolver, and waking Windmill, who almost died of shock.

"Frightfully sorry!" the Pilot Officer exclaimed – "but it's the only way to wake them up."

"Are you sure there's anyone in there?" I asked – "Apart from scorpions."

"Oh, yes. There's always someone there. They're probably lying pissed in the basement. In any event, we need water and petrol."

We waited in the darkness, until presently a light was switched on from somewhere inside the barracks, and the gates creaked open. I was expecting Bela Lugosi to appear, but we were greeted instead by a Corporal Sinclair, who looked more like a decaying mouth-organ than a soldier in His Majesty's Army.

"Yis?" he squeaked.

"It's me, Lofty. Everything OK?"

"Yis!"

"We need water and petrol. The usual thing – then we'll camp for the night."

Lofty opened the gates further and Jonathan drove into the courtyard and pulled up beside two uneasy-looking petrol pumps.

"It's OK, Lofty. I'll fill her up. Can you pop a few canteens of water in the cab?"

"Are you sure this is the Sinai?" I asked Jonathan, when Lofty crept off to collect the canteens of water. "It looks remarkably like Transylvania."

"You mean Lofty? He's a darling. He's been out here too long, that's all – and he's terrified of the Bedouins. That's why he locks the place up every night and hides in the basement."

"Where are the others – hiding in coffins?"

"There's only two – and they're probably sleeping it off somewhere. It's not an RAF base, you know. It's run by the Army and only used for storing petrol and water."

"That explains it," Windmill moaned from the back of the lorry. "Are we leaving soon?"

"In a few minutes, Sweetie. We're just waiting for the water."

"It'll probably be blood," I shouted "Don't drink it!"

But Windmill ignored me. He was still feeling sick and was taking no notice of anyone.

When Pilot Officer Swaine reappeared, he said he had found a suitable place to camp for the night close by.

"There's a family of Bedouins camped on the other side of the road, and we've been invited to join them for a meal later."

"You mean we're not staying in Castle Dracula?"

"Good Heavens – no! We'll be much more comfortable outside. Are we all set, Jonathan?"

"Just waiting for Lofty, Sir."

"He's probably fallen down a well somewhere. Come on, Lofty! We haven't got all night."

But Lofty looked as if he had centuries stretching before him, as he approached slowly from a dark corner, carrying two canteens of water.

"Are you all right, Lofty?" Swaine asked him.

"Yis."

"Well, thank you for your assistance. We'll be going now and setting up camp outside. OK?"

"Yis."

Pilot Officer Swaine relieved him of the two canteens of water and climbed into the cab beside Jonathan. "Push! Push! Old Boy," he cried. "Off we go." As we drove out into the silence of the desert, I looked back and saw the gates closing behind us, and then the lights going out.

We set up camp near the edge of the road under more stars than I had ever seen. I had hoped to have been sleeping in a bed, but this was even better. The night was clear, the air crisp and sparkling and the sky such an extraordinary sight that I could well understand why the Sinai at night was considered blessed by many, and regarded as 'Holy Ground'.

"You could sleep on this sand," I said aloud, "and wake up canonised."

"Not unless you prepare your bed properly," Pilot

Officer Swaine advised. "Scoop out a space in the sand, the length of your body, while the sand is still warm. Then lay your ground-sheet and kitbag over it, to retain the heat until it's time to retire. Otherwise you'll freeze to death during the night."

"Are there snakes about?"

"I don't think so – but check anyway before turning in."

I could hear Windmill groaning in the back of the lorry. "Do you mind if I sleep in the lorry?" he pleaded.

"By all means. Jonathan will look after you. I take it that you are not fit enough to join us for a meal?"

"I don't think so, Sir."

"That's OK. You'll be safe enough here, and Jonathan can come back to check on you from time to time."

Jonathan smiled as he hung a kerosene lamp from the side of the lorry. "A night-light," he said. "Very useful and it'll keep you company."

"Does it repel Muslims?" I asked. "I hear there's a lot of them about, and they eat Christians for their breakfast."

Windmill wasn't amused and Jonathan said I was being extremely naughty.

After we had prepared our beds and washed ourselves as best we could with water from the canteens, Pilot Officer Swaine and I started towards the Bedouin camp, while Jonathan saw to it that Windmill, neatly tucked up in bed, had everything he required. I was about to suggest a bedtime story by Enid Blyton might further ease his complaint, but concealed my concern with masterly self-control.

"You don't seem to be very sympathetic towards your friend," Pilot Officer Swaine said, as we approached the Bedouin camp. "You should try to be more understanding."

"I try – but Windmill is one of those people who, if there's a plague in the Congo, would be the first to show

402

signs of it here. He caught malaria in Port Etienne where the only mosquitoes in sight were dead ones. The MO said he had no system. I'm not sure what he meant by 'system', but whatever it is – Windmill hasn't got it."

"Then you must be very kind to him. He is, after all, your friend – and friendship is very important in the desert. The Bedouins value it more than their camels."

"Do you?"

"Jonathan and I have been friends for a long time," he said. "He is kind, generous, even-tempered and closer than a brother. Not very easy to maintain a relationship like that in the Air Force – especially with the difference in rank. But we manage."

"I see."

He looked at me for a moment and said – "I am very fond of Jonathan." I said I was glad and we stood there in silence, waiting for Jonathan, who caught up with us.

"Your friend has settled down nicely," he smiled. "He'll be much better in the morning."

Pilot Officer Swaine patted him on the shoulder, and we moved on towards the camp.

An elderly man welcomed us at the entrance to a very large tent with the usual ritual of handshakes, *Salamats* and "the blessings of Allah". His name was Achmid, he said, adding that he was blessed with two wives, three sons, four daughters, twelve goats and two camels. There was no sign of the sons and daughters, but the goats were wandering about outside and the camels could be heard, puffing and blowing, close by the tent. Achmid said one of the camels had belonged to his brother, who had died recently and, sad though it was, his spirit was now a star in the sky, his body having been washed to perfection by the elders of his tribe, and buried in a grave as deep as he was tall.

Achmid next introduced his two wives, praising their

virtue. He had been tempted to marry a third wife, he said, but decided against it on the grounds that two wives were enough for any man, and besides, he no longer had the strength of twenty years before when he had married his second wife. His present wives nodded in agreement and directed us to sit on a carpet, in the centre of the floor, where they served us with glasses of very sweet tea and a dish laden with pitta bread.

They then went outside to bake more bread over a camp fire, and prepare what Achmid described as Stew of the Pot. He gave no indication of what might be in this Stew of the Pot, but I was hungry enough by now to eat a camel.

Jonathan said the pitta bread was beautiful, Swaine said the tea was nectar from the Gods, but I kept my mouth shut as Achmid stared me in the face, daring me to be poetic.

"You like sweet tea?"

"Yes."

"You like pitta bread?"

"Yes."

"You will like Stew of the Pot."

I'd have been happier with a bottle of stout, but Achmid didn't approve of alcohol and was wedded instead to sweet tea. Every time he saw an empty glass, he filled it up. Every pause in the conversation, he reached for the brass teapot and held it in the air, as if about to pour it over somebody's head.

"My wives make perfect sweet tea," he said.

The Pilot Officer agreed and Achmid refilled his glass.

"They also make perfect Stew of the Pot."

"I'm sure they do," I said.

"The elders like it. My children like it. My brother liked it."

I remembered that his brother had died recently and wondered what from.

Achmid began to recite a poem to his brother and was still reciting it half-an-hour later when his two wives appeared, carrying an enormous blackened pot and another dish laden with pitta bread. They placed the pot in the centre of the floor, laid the bread down within easy reach, then sat close beside us and praised Allah for his goodness and mercy.

There was a pause.

Achmid looked at us. The two wives looked at us. And I looked at Pilot Officer Swaine, who reached for a piece of pitta bread, broke it in two, dipped one half into the pot and tasted the stew. We waited for his reaction.

"You were right, Achmid," he said, with obvious appreciation. "Your wives do make perfect Stew of the Pot."

Achmid smiled. The two wives dropped their veils and smiled. Jonathan beamed, and I decided to beam as well just to keep him company.

It was a meal fit for the Gods. It tasted of sunshine and soft rain. It tasted of rippling streams and romantic movies. It whispered I was a perfect human being, made in the image of God, and I should marry a Bedouin and live naked in the desert. I thought that was carrying things a bit too far, however, and when Achmid asked me whether I liked the Stew of the Pot, I merely said it was very nice and congratulated his wives. He looked disappointed at my apparent lack of enthusiasm, but smiled graciously and poured more sweetened tea into my glass.

When we had finished our meal, Achmid produced a leather pouch of tobacco, rolled himself a cigarette, then passed the pouch around.

"Smoke?"

Pilot Officer Swaine said the tobacco, which smelled of incense, was 'Sinai Sheikh' and contained the secret of life. I hadn't heard of it, but after two or three puffs I wondered

405

what the hell I was doing sitting in a tent, when I might be out making love to a camel, or walking backwards to Australia.

"You like?"

"I like!"

And he liked. And we all liked. Seated there, we listened to Achmid reciting Bedouin poetry to his two enraptured wives and his three, by now, mesmerised guests. I had no idea what the poetry was about, but Pilot Officer Swaine said it was both love poetry and folk poetry of Bedouin battles, Bedouin heroes and their last great fight against the Egyptians more than a hundred years ago.

I had never heard of the last great fight between the Bedouins and the Egyptians, but suddenly I found myself standing bolt-upright in the centre of the tent, shouting – "Fuck the Egyptians! Viva the Bedouins!"

The two wives looked at me in amazement, and Achmid who was about to take another puff of 'Sinai Sheikh' almost choked. For his part, Pilot Officer Swaine said it was time we turned out the lights and headed for home.

"He is young," I heard Achmid say as I stood there ready to face the Egyptians "and he has his dreams."

Achmid didn't know the half of it. Neither did I – that 'Sinai Sheikh' was a mixture of hashish and elephant grass.

I excused myself as best I could, and wandered out into the fresh air. I could see the kerosene lamp hanging from the side of the lorry across the road, and I wondered how Windmill was. He was likely asleep and maybe he, too, was having his dreams.

I was feeling depressed and lonely when, presently, Achmid emerged from his tent and we stood there in the darkness, looking up at the stars.

"You have a woman?" he asked.

"No."

"You have a brother then?"

"No, I do not have a brother."

"Then you must find one," he said, indicating the sky.

"There must be a hundred million stars up there," I said. "Which one do you suggest?"

He paused for the moment. "The brightest," he said. "There is little wisdom in choosing less."

I said I'd have to think about it.

I thought about if for a long time – until Pilot Officer Swaine appeared with Jonathan and said it was time for beddy-byes. I said goodbye to Achmid while Swaine thanked him for the pleasure of his company and the hospitality of his tent. It was an honour to have sat under his roof, he said. He said the Stew of the Pot had been blessed by the Gods and the pitta bread was holy and divine beyond measure. He then thanked Achmid's wives, praising their beauty, their culinary expertise, their kindness and the excellence of their tea. They were a noble and gentle people, he said, and beloved of Allah. I thought that was the end of it, but it was only Achmid's turn.

He had been honoured by our visit, Achmid began. He said we were noble and heroic and a terror to our enemies. He asked Allah to give us strength and his own ancestors to watch over us, and the spirit of his brother to guide us on our travels. He then kissed Pilot Officer Swaine's hand, my hand, Jonathan's hand, and finally as a sign of humility, his own hand. Allah had been good to him, he said. Allah had always been good to him. All praise to Allah.

Windmill was still asleep when we arrived back at the lorry, but he looked better and we did not disturb him. I checked for snakes and other things that crawl and bite – then climbed into my sleeping-bag and tried to sleep.

Sleep didn't come, however, and I lay there thinking of Achmid, the beauty and gentleness of his wives, and the spirit of his brother shining brightly in the firmament above me. I also thought of Françoise. And as I looked out across the vast expanse of desert, silent and empty, I saw Pilot Officer Swaine and Jonathan, standing together, with their arms around each other. They, too, were a gentle people.

Twenty

At the border crossing near Raphia we were stopped by an Army Corporal who ordered us down from the lorry and checked our ID Cards with the aid of a kerosene lamp.

Windmill didn't like him.

"Who the hell does he think we are – enemy parachutists?"

"You'll have to get used to that in Palestine, Sweetie," Jonathan replied. "The 'terrorists' can be very naughty with lorries."

"Like what?"

"Oh, bombs under the bonnet. Brakes cut. Grease on the roads. Very naughty indeed."

The Corporal grunted. "Fucking Yids! Blow your fucking head off quick as look at you."

"That's enough, Corporal!" Pilot Officer Swaine glared at him. "Finish your inspection and we'll be moving on."

The Corporal checked under the lorry, raised the bonnet, examined the wiring, muttered something under his breath and slammed the bonnet down.

"She's OK, Sir."

"Thank you. Come along, Jonathan. Off we go."

We climbed back on and Jonathan drove slowly between the lines of barbed wire fences and further road blocks guarded by soldiers, Bren-gun carriers and armoured cars.

"Another bloody war zone!" Windmill moaned. "If there wasn't one, the Army would create it."

"We'll stop along the road for breakfast," the Pilot

Officer said "and then we'll head for Jerusalem. OK, Jonathan?"

"Yes, Sir. I could do with a bite to eat."

I could have eaten a horse myself, but I said nothing. We had crossed the border early in the morning when it was still dark and we were by now driving slowly along the main road towards the Holy City.

"You see all those orange groves over there?" the Pilot Officer said. "That was once a wasteland. Nothing but sand dunes, until the Jews transformed it. They've built hospitals, schools and community farms where everyone is equal and everything is shared – and it works. There's nothing wrong with these people. They know how to live."

"They can be very pleasant," said Jonathan, "but the Arabs don't like them."

"Do you?" I asked.

"Oh, yes. I love everybody! And I've never been happier in my life than I am here. It's only the so-called freedom fighters that worry me. I'm not sure what it's all about, but I was leaving camp one morning, driving downhill, when the brakes wouldn't work. Someone had drained the brake fluid, cut the connections and poured sand into the petrol tank. Very nasty. I was lucky to escape with my life."

"But you did, Jonathan – didn't you?" the Pilot Officer said.

"Yes, Sir."

"He's the best driver in the world," the Pilot Officer said – patting Jonathan on the knee as we pulled into a small roadside café.

The place was empty, apart from a tall middle-aged Jew who stood behind the counter reading a newspaper. He looked up as we entered and nodded to Pilot Officer Swaine.

"Breakfast?"

"The usual, my friend."

410

We sat at a table near the window and looked out at the surrounding countryside. It was radiant with colour. The sun shining on the orange groves. The sienna of the earth. A paradise of the heart.

"Is this where you usually stop?" I asked Swaine.

"Yes," he replied. "Fresh orange juice, fish and cheese, plenty of coffee and as much bread as you can eat. The guy behind the counter is called Jacob. I don't know whether that's his real name or not. I doubt it, but it doesn't matter. He's been here for years and he's part of the landscape."

When Jacob arrived at the table with our first 'Israeli Breakfast', Swaine thanked him profusely, then introduced what he called "My two gentlemen friends from Blighty". I said I wasn't from Blighty at all. I was Irish and Jacob nodded his head.

"The Irish are everywhere," he said "and so are the English."

I wasn't sure what that meant, but I decided to let it pass. Jacob smiled and returned to his newspaper.

"A dear man," said Swaine. "He owned a restaurant near Tel Aviv before the war. And a very good one, I hear – but a gang of Arab extremists burned him out and killed his wife. That's the story I heard anyway. I don't know whether it's true or not and Jacob never talks about it."

"Have you asked him?"

"No. The situation is complicated enough here and I just take people as I find them. I don't ask questions if I can possibly avoid it. I'd advise you to do the same."

"But it would be interesting to know, wouldn't it?"

"Possibly – but if Jacob wanted you to know, he'd tell you. You can be quite sure of that."

"Maybe he doesn't trust the British?" said Windmill.

"Nobody trusts the British," Swaine smiled. "Not anymore, Harrison. Finish your breakfast and let's move on."

We finished our breakfast and moved towards the door. Jacob thanked us for our custom. We thanked him for an excellent breakfast. He shook hands with Swaine and stood at the door, waving at us as we drove off.

It was late in the afternoon when we reached the RAF camp, just north of Jerusalem. The camp stood on a hill overlooking the city, surrounded by barbed wire fences borrowed from a concentration-camp movie. Armed guards with Alsatians stood sentry at the gate, but the sentries merely nodded, letting us through without checking our ID cards, while the dogs barked.

Windmill looked pale.

"Are you sure this is the right place?" he asked. "I think I've seen this movie before."

"You have," I said. "Only it starred Warrant Officer Payne with his Alsatians back in Padgate."

"You'll get used to it," Swaine replied. "There's been one or two attempted raids recently, but nothing to worry about."

"Do the dogs know that?"

At the armoury gates there was more barbed wire, and after Swaine opened the door to let us in, we were presented with enough rifles, machine guns and explosives to subdue a continent. Thankfully there were no Alsatians to keep us in, but I could still hear them barking in the distance, and they did not sound happy.

"Is there a cinema in the camp?" I asked, and Jonathan smiled.

"Sonja Hennie on ice!" he said. "It's bound to be something like that!"

It wasn't. Rather, Windmill and I sat in a crowded cinema watching *Birth of a Nation*. The movie was silent. The audience were silent. The dogs barked.

Welcome to Palestine.

Twenty-one

During our first few weeks in Palestine, Jonathan combed his hair in the mirror, Pilot Officer Swaine continued painting nude pictures of the Queen Mother and Winston Churchill, and Windmill and I stood guard in the armoury. There we were forced to endure lectures given by Flight Sergeant Warbeck, who claimed to be an Education Officer, yet was convinced that he would be the real King of England and living in Buckingham Palace, if the place wasn't already occupied by Jews.

Warbeck knew nothing about education. Rather he was obsessed with what he described as "the Jewish Problem", and knew, for a fact, that the only reason he had been posted to Palestine was because the Air Ministry was riddled with Jews who had sent him here, hoping he would be shot while trying to escape. But the Flight Sergeant had no intention of escaping and would sweat it out in Palestine, just to spite the bastards.

As it was, he had an ancestor who had been executed at Tyburn because the Jews were determined to prevent him from taking his rightful place as King of Great Britain and Ireland, and there was no way that anything like that was going to happen to him. Instead he would sit quietly in the Orderly Room, concentrate on the deplorable history of the Middle East, and the total lack of security within and without the Mandate.

Flight Sergeant Warbeck believed in security. At our first meeting, he shouted the word three times, banging the table

413

with his fist. "Security!" he cried. "Security! Security!" before proceeding to tell us that in Palestine no such thing existed.

For example, three soldiers had been shot recently in a botched robbery attempt by the Jewish group Irgun, a bomb had exploded in the Station Master's Office in Jerusalem, railway lines had been blown up, three police stations destroyed, six policemen killed and a man shot pasting posters of the underground magazine *Herut* on a wall. He later died in Acre Prison.

The Flight Sergeant wasn't surprised that this kind of thing was happening here. The Jews were employed in all military camps, where they had access to munitions and bomb-making equipment. They worked as clerks in the Ration Stores and knew the strength and location of every British unit. The shops were Jewish. The canteens were Jewish. In fact the whole thing was a disaster and strictly the fault of the British Government, which couldn't make a move without consulting the Americans, most of whom were Zionists and only interested in bagging Jewish-American votes.

The British Sixth Airborne Division, which had arrived in Palestine, was now wasting its time raiding houses and looking for illegal emigrants and printing presses, when everyone knew they were coming and moved house minutes before they arrived. Searching for radio transmitters was another waste of time, as the underground radio station 'Kol Israel' went on air for only six minutes at a time, to avoid tracking devices by the British, tracking devices which were manned by civilian Jews who would pass information on to their mates in the radio station.

If Warbeck had been in charge, he would have sacked all Jews employed in British establishments. He would execute anyone caught reading or distributing subversive newspapers like *Hachazit* and *Hamas' ass* which appeared mysteriously under tables and on lavatory walls, and sometimes were found hidden in kitbags left by incompetent British soldiers, who had no idea what this war was all about.

"Security!" he shouted again, handing us a selection of leaflets and brochures advertising the latest vacancies in the Palestine Police Force.

"Twenty pound a month all found" – provided you were five-foot-six in height, had good eyesight and were reasonably intelligent. As a bonus, they promised a two-month leave in Egypt or Cyprus with a camel or speedboat thrown in – if you managed to survive for two years.

There was no answer to that one and the Warrant Officer left the room muttering – "Security? Security me arse!"

Some days later, however, Windmill and I managed to wangle a twenty-four-hour pass and decided to visit Jerusalem. We were sitting in a bar, near the King David Hotel, when a middle-aged Jew, carrying a satchel filled with posters and broadsheets, approached us, demanding to know what we were doing there.

I said I was there by mistake but Windmill told him to mind his own business.

It was not the right answer.

The man glared at him for a moment and then struck him hard across the face.

He then turned to me. "The British are not welcome here," he said. "Get out!"

"I'm not British," I declared. "I'm Irish, for Christ's sake!"

"Then you should know better. There's a war going on here. Don't you know that?"

"We do now. What's in the bag?"

"Your marching orders."

"Let's have a few."

"Why?"

"If it's in print, I want to read it. OK?"

He handed me several wall posters and broadsheets, then looked at Windmill, who was still sitting with his hand pressed to his face.

"I'm sorry about that," he said. "But you really shouldn't be here. The British are no longer welcome."

"Were they ever?" I asked.

Windmill said nothing.

The man paused, then turned to Windmill. "Mind if I join you?"

"Why not? It's your country."

The man smiled. "I'm glad you think so," he said. "There are many who would dispute it."

Sitting down beside us, he waved his hand at the bar and ordered a round of drinks. A moment later the barman arrived at the table, carrying three drinks on a tray.

"Poisoned?" Windmill smiled.

"No. We haven't reached that stage yet, my friend."

He paused, then swallowed his drink.

I looked at one of the broadsheets while Windmill glanced furtively at the posters. "You know," said Windmill, "you could be arrested for distributing this kind of thing."

"Are you going to do it?"

Windmill shook his head and the man stared at both of us. "I spent two years in the British Army," he said, "fighting Fascism. Many of us Jews did and I would still be doing it if I hadn't been discharged on medical grounds. So, will you arrest me or shoot me? That seems to be the usual choice."

"Not in my book," Windmill said.

"Are you Jewish?"

416

"No. And I'm not anti-Semitic either, if that's what you mean."

"What about you?"

"Some of my best friends are Jews," I said.

"Is that what they call Irish humour?"

"No. You asked me a question and I've answered it. The man who taught me everything worth knowing was Jewish. OK?

He stared at me. "I don't hate the British," he said, "but they made so many promises and never kept one of them."

"Surprise me!" Windmill grinned.

"I'm a Palestinian Jew. Have you ever met one?"

"No."

"'We are accounted as sheep for the slaughter,'" he quoted.

"Not anymore, I gather."

"Not anymore."

He rose from his chair and moved towards the door. "Do you ever read poetry?" he asked me.

"Yes."

"'Let them raise a fist against Me and demand revenge for their humiliation,'" he began quoting again. "'The humiliation of all generations from their first to last. And let them break asunder with their fist the heavens and My throne.'

"Chaim Nachman Bialik," he said. "You should read him."

I said I would as he left the bar, carrying the satchel of posters under his arm, and limping his way across the broad sunlit street.

The poem, which I looked up later, was called 'Be'ir ha-hreygah' (The City of Slaughter), and had been written after the Kishenev pogrom of 1903.

Every day, we learn a little more.

My old friend Mannie Goldman, back in Cork, had never mentioned Palestine or raised his glass 'To Next Year in Jerusalem'. And when I asked him one time about his family and relations, he had replied "Apart from my cousin in America, there are none."

"It's a bloody war zone," Windmill said the following day. "I told you that!"

"So you did."

"We could be bloody killed here, you know! And we could have been shot in that bar yesterday."

"You think so?"

"Don't bloody kid yourself! You heard what that guy said. There's a war going on here."

"I heard – and the only thing he did was slap your face. It's hardly a war crime."

"Read the posters, mate."

"I have," I said, and I began to read aloud from one:

Hadar –
A Jew even in poverty is a prince
Though a slave or a tramp.
You were created the son of a king,
Crowned with David's crown,
The crown of pride and strife.
Tagar –
Despite every besieger and enemy
Whether you rise or fall
With the torch of revolt
Carry a fire to kindle: "No matter."
Because silence is filth
Give up blood and soul
Take the sake of the hidden beauty
To die or to conquer the mount.
Yodefet, Masada, Betar.

"Who wrote it?" Windmill asked.

"Vladimir Jabotinsky."

"I seem to have read about Jabotinsky," Windmill said. "He was a Zionist, wasn't he?"

"He was a poet anyway."

"Died in America, if I remember rightly."

"I have no idea."

"You haven't read enough."

"Maybe. But I'm still young."

"So you are. But I should avoid that blood sacrifice stuff, if I were you."

I promised I would, and continued to read Jabotinsky's poem aloud.

Twenty-two

Hatikvah
As long as within the heart
A Jewish Soul yearns,
And forward, towards the east,
An eye turns to Zion,
Our hope is not yet lost,
Our hope of two thousand years
To be a free people in our land,
The land of Zion and Jerusalem.

One morning, staring at the rain falling outside the armoury, Windmill declared that the only thing he wanted to do now was return to England, sit in his back garden, and watch the roses bloom. He didn't like Palestine, was fed up with barbed wire fences, was sick to death of the Air Force, the war was killing him, and he had given up the whole idea of wanting to live on a plantation.

Swaine, who was lost in the creation of his latest masterpiece, ignored him. By his side stood Jonathan, stunned with admiration by every stroke of the brush.

"It's beautiful" he said. "Quite beautiful, Sir. Is it the Queen Mother?"

"It's Winston Churchill," I said. "I can see the cigar."

Swaine was not amused. "Some people have no appreciation of art," he said. "Look carefully and you'll see quite clearly that it's a portrait of the Queen Mother."

"I'm sorry, Sir. I was never very good at art appreciation."

"Use your imagination, man. That's what it's there for."

"Yes, Sir."

I tried to use my imagination, but the light was dim and I couldn't see through the mist.

"You've changed your style, Sir," I mused. "It's very advanced, isn't it ?"

"Of course it is. One cannot stay in the same place forever, you know. But it's the same subject, don't you agree?"

"I think so … "

"Well, look carefully. Each brush stroke has its own individual message. It reveals her true nature."

"Nude?"

"Certainly. I never paint anything else. You should know that by now."

I stared at the painting and still couldn't see the Queen Mother – nude or otherwise.

"Oh, yes," I said. "It's the Queen Mother all right. I can see it clearly now."

"There you are then. Keep looking and everything will be revealed."

It wasn't. The Queen Mother still looked like Winston Churchill, and the cigar was growing longer.

I hadn't the courage to say that the painting looked more like an advanced rubbish bin than any Queen Mother. So I turned to Windmill, who was beginning to turn green now.

"A kibbutz!" I said – for no particular reason other than to change the subject. "Have you thought about that, Windmill?"

"What! Are you serious?"

"I was just thinking, that's all. If you've given up the idea of a plantation you could always try a kibbutz."

"Go back to sleep for Christ's sake! I wouldn't be found dead living in a kibbutz!"

"Why not?"

"Have you read about them? I have – and it's a crazy idea. Filled with idealists all struggling for a way out."

"You think so?"

"I know so. I've known people like that. Socialists in their youth and reactionaries in middle age – they end up writing books with titles like *I Was Once A Revolutionary* or *The God That Failed.*"

"*The Light That Failed,*" muttered Swaine, between brush strokes.

"Well, whatever. The point is – I have no intention of living on a kibbutz. Would you?"

"I might. It's an interesting idea anyway. I could continue painting and Jonathan could plant oranges."

"Oh!" Jonathan crooned. "I'd like that, Sir."

"I'm sure you would, Jonathan."

"Jesus!" Windmill exclaimed from the window. "Are there anymore at home like you?"

"Now, Harrison! Cheer up and don't let the rain get you down."

"I never thought it rained in Palestine."

"Well, it does. Now, shut up! I'm trying to concentrate."

Windmill lapsed into silence and Swaine carried on painting the Queen Mother while Jonathan cooed.

Suddenly, the armoury door burst open and an RAF officer came in with a gun in his hand. "Raymond Chandler? How are you?" I was tempted to say – but thought better of it when I saw that the Thompson machine-gun he was holding was pointed directly at my vital organs.

"Get your hands up!" he yelled. "Down on the floor – all of you!"

"Is this a joke?" Swaine asked.

"No joke. Down on the floor and be quick about it. All of you!"

Swaine dropped the brush he was holding as we all sat on the floor. Meanwhile the Officer waved to his companions outside. As he stepped aside, four Other Ranks and what looked like three Arabs entered the armoury.

"Tie them up!" the officer ordered. "Gag them and grab what you can."

All of which they did. We were tied up, hands behind our backs, and gagged. It was done swiftly and with ease. A silent movie. The rain falling on the tin roof of the Armoury the only sound.

The Officer stood over us.

"Stay as you are," he said. "Don't move and no one will get hurt."

I don't know whether he expected an answer, but I had an oily rag stuffed in my mouth and couldn't even breathe.

Through a gap in the door I could see a lorry and jeep parked outside. By now the Arabs had begun loading the lorry with everything they could find in the armoury, while the Other Ranks loaded the jeep with small arms and hand grenades.

"Leave those Brownings behind!" the Officer said. "They're useless on the ground. Just grab the others."

Within minutes the armoury was cleared of everything serviceable, and the Officer and his companions had disappeared into the rain. As the lorry and the jeep moved off, I could hear them heading towards the runway at the far end of the camp. We sat there for a minute until Swaine managed to undo the rope from behind his back and released the rest of us. In one bound he was free, I thought, but this beats all.

In the distance we heard shots being fired and the sound of a lorry screaming to a halt.

There was silence for a moment as we waited for more gunfire, but nothing happened. The movie was over.

We discovered later that the lorry had skidded off the runway and ploughed into a nearby ditch where it got stuck in the mud. However the raiders had jumped out, and, piling into the jeep with all the small arms they could carry, managed to escape through the rear gate of the camp – wide open and unguarded.

The following day, all Jewish drivers of RAF lorries were instantly dismissed. Warbeck would be pleased. But he wasn't. He was ready to explode.

"Security!" he yelled as Windmill and I stood before him in the Orderly Room later. "You couldn't guard a fucking nursery – either of you."

"It wasn't our fault," Windmill said.

"Are you dense? A guy breaks into the armoury, dressed in an RAF uniform, and you couldn't tell he was Jewish?"

"How the hell were we to know?" Windmill asked. "He had a Scottish accent for one thing – and it could have been an exercise for all we knew."

"An exercise! What's the matter with you, Harrison? I can spot a Jew a mile off. As for those bloody Arabs – anyone could see that they were Jews. You've only to look at them for Christ's sake. Terrorists and gangsters!"

He paused for a moment, then rose from his desk.

"And these – where did you get them?" he screamed, glaring at a number of posters laid out on the desk.

"No idea," Windmill replied innocently. "They just appeared."

"They just appeared!" he sneered. "And you've read them of course?"

"Of course. How else are we to know what's going on in this place?"

"You ask me, you twit! Well I'll tell you. Lack of security, that's what's going on! Jewish drivers. Jews in the shops, Jews wandering all over the fucking place!"

"Yes, Sir."

He turned to me. "I take it you've read them, too?"

"Yes, Sir, I'm trying to educate myself," I said. "And I like poetry."

"Poetry? You know what I think of poetry? Shit! Subversive shit."

Grabbing the posters from his desk, he tore them up and threw them into the wastepaper basket.

"Shit – and more shit! Fucking Yids!"

"Will that be all, Sir?"

"It will not! I am recommending an immediate posting for both of you."

"May we ask why, Sir?"

"Why? If I had my way you'd both be shot! But you'll be kicked out of the armoury and posted at once to a less sensitive area. Now get out!"

Windmill and I left the Orderly Room and returned to our billet.

The armoury was secured. Search lights were installed and the barbed wire fences grew higher. Watch towers blossomed and the entire camp was placed under guard by armed units of the Arab Legion.

It was also the end of our stay in Palestine.

A week later we were posted back to England. The war in Europe was over. The battle for Israel was just beginning.

425